Destination Hell

Destination Hell

by Sylvia Bambola

Heritage Publishing House

Copyright © 2022 by Sylvia Bambola. All rights reserved. No part of this book may be used or reproduced in any manner whatsoever without written permission of the publisher.

For information contact:
Heritage Publishing House
heritagepubhouse@gmail.com

ISBN: 978-0-9657389-6-5

Unless otherwise indicated, all Scriptures taken from Holy Bible, King James version, Cambridge, 1769

Also by Sylvia Bambola

Non-Fiction
Biblical Gardens of God and Valleys of Man
Encountering Jesus Throughout the Bible
The Coming Deception
12 Questions New Christians Frequently Ask
Following the Blood Trail from Genesis to Revelation

Fiction:
Mercy at Midnight
The Babel Conspiracy
The Daughters of Jim Farrell
The Salt Covenants
Rebekah's Treasure
Return to Appleton
Waters of Marah
Tears in a Bottle
Refiner's Fire

To
My Children and Grandchildren
With Love

Table of Contents

Introduction 1
The Narrow Road 3
The Counterfeit Narrow Road 35
The Broad Way 113
Hell on Earth—the Seven Year Tribulation 205
Hell of the Underworld 301
Hell in the Lake of Fire 325
Notes: 345

Introduction

People rarely talk about hell anymore, even in churches. It seems it has faded from the mind and theology of many Christians while at the same time completely erased from the secular conscience. A myth, a joke, a manipulation tactic is how many would describe this region once feared and warned against. But here's the hard reality: just because few believe in hell anymore doesn't mean it no longer exists.

Though hell is a subject not adequately covered, writing this book was totally unexpected and couldn't have been further from my mind. I planned on going in an entirely different direction when I found myself drawn again and again to this subject. Then I began waking up in the middle of the night, my mind full of Scriptures and ideas, which I jotted down. Before long, these scribblings became an outline for *Destination Hell*.

This book explores how and why the road to hell is becoming more clogged daily; why it seems America is now racing toward it; the soon coming hell on earth which the Bible describes as the

Sylvia Bambola

seven-year Tribulation; the hell of the underworld; and the final hell in the great lake of fire.

Because it is a difficult subject, I ask the readers to please remember we have a wonderful and merciful God Who loves us and desires to lead us in the right direction. His heart is to spare everyone from this horrific destination.

The Narrow Road

Are we inherently good? Some think so. But thanks to Adam and Eve, our original parents who blew it in the garden, we received a sin nature, making us inherently sinful. Romans 3:23 says, *"For **all** have sinned, and come short of the glory of God."* All means all. No matter how exemplary a life, it is still marred by sin, though there are some who would argue the point. But here's what 1 John 1:8 says to them. *"If we say that we have no sin, we deceive ourselves, and the truth is not in us."*

Man instinctively knows this. That's why for thousands of years he has tried to come up with ways to appease God Whom he knows he continually offends. As a result, various vain and idolatrous religions sprang up, each claiming to be enlightened and to know the road back into God's good graces. Before long, man concocted a smorgasbord of beliefs consisting of a battery of works. Others cut God out of the equation completely, believing they could become gods themselves.

Many of these beliefs are still with us. Solomon, in Ecclesiastes 1:9, said there is nothing new under the sun. And he was right. Satan is still using the same lies he used in the garden, trying to convince us we can do things our way and even become "gods."

Worldwide, hundreds of cults attest to this, each with their own brand of truth, and usually headed by an autocrat—a man or woman calling all the shots. These cults frequently twist Scripture in order to apply them to their teachings. Brainwashing techniques are often employed, along with promises of a better life here and now, and eternal life, hereafter, *if* the initiates follow the cult's guidance and rules.

But these lifestyles are anything but Scriptural. Those who have come out of a cult often testify to a life of mental, sexual, and physical abuse at the hands of their leaders and fellow cult members.[1]

It's a tragic scenario. But even during the days of the apostles, Jude 4 warned against such unscrupulous people. *"For there are certain men crept in unawares, who were before of old ordained to this condemnation, ungodly men, turning the grace of our God into lasciviousness, and denying the only Lord God, and our Lord Jesus Christ."* Notice, these men are carnal, looking to indulge their vices and

Destination Hell

wantonness at the expense of others. And though they may achieve their evil goals, it will not end well for them. Jesus said in Matthew 18:6, *"But whoso shall offend one of these little ones which believe in me, it were better for him that a millstone were hanged about his neck, and that he were drowned in the depth of the sea."* Mark 9:42 and Luke 17:1-2 repeat this.

Webster defines millstone as, "a large, flat, round stone used for grinding grain or other substances." These massive stones are dragged by a donkey or other strong animal. Imagine such a thing around your neck! And to those who corrupt or lead little ones, the young and vulnerable believers, astray through a cult or other means, Jesus said it would be better for them to have this stone anchored around their neck and drown!

Cults are dangerous. They are deceptive and have damaged many lives. That's why everything so-called "religious" leaders teach should be judged by the pure Word of God. And that's why it's so important for Christians to know God's Word.

When religious deception occurred in ancient Israel, Judges 21:25 referred to it as a time when everyone did what was right in their own eyes or whatever they wanted rather than obeying the commandments of God.

There has always been deception and darkness in the world. But because God is merciful and deeply desires a relationship with man, He established a connection with Abraham, whom He called His "friend." Abraham's descendants became God's chosen people. Through them came the Ten Commandments, the Holy Scriptures, the prophets, and finally the Messiah and Savior, Jesus, Himself. This legacy is rich and deep and full of promise.

It also exposes the fallacies of other religions, for why would Jesus have to come and die if any of them were correct? The answer is obvious. He wouldn't. While other belief systems focus on what we need to do, Jesus focused on what God needed, and that was to reconcile man back to Himself. And because God is holy, nothing but Jesus' blood could do it.

After Adam and Eve's folly, God killed an innocent animal to cover the rebellious couple (Genesis 3:21), thus indicating this would be the way forward. It established that the only acceptable payment for sin was through the shedding of innocent blood. This truth was restated throughout the ages via Abel, Noah, the Jewish Temple, and the ritual animal sacrifices performed by Levitical priests. God also spelled it out clearly in Leviticus 17:11 when He said, *"For the life of the flesh is in the blood: and I have given it to you upon the altar*

Destination Hell

to *make an atonement for your souls: for it is the blood that maketh an atonement for the soul."* In the New Testament, Hebrews 9:22 adds, *"almost all things are by the law purged with blood; and without shedding of blood is no remission* (of sins)."

But the Old Testament was only a shadow of what was to come. Saint Augustine concluded that the Old Testament is the New Testament concealed, the New Testament is the Old Testament revealed. How true! There are countless types and foreshadows in the Old Testament that come to light in the New. My book, *Following the Blood Trail from Genesis to Revelation*, details the importance of innocent blood as a sin covering. Starting in the Old Testament and culminating in the New, we see the wages of sin finally paid in full by Jesus. And just before Jesus died on the cross, He said, *"It is Finished."* There was nothing left to be done. Jesus fully satisfied the Father's sense of justice and holiness. And He did this while we were yet sinners. Before we even knew Him, cared about Him, or loved Him, He died for us, (Romans 5:8).

Because of what Jesus did, Romans 8:1 tells us, *"There is therefore now no condemnation to them which are in Christ Jesus, who walk not after the flesh, but after the Spirit."* We are no longer condemned but are accepted by God. How wonderful is that?

Sylvia Bambola

Below is a glimpse into the magnitude of Jesus' sacrifice:

Jesus becomes the Passover lamb.

The Temple priests offered two lambs daily: one in the morning, accompanied by trumpets to announce the first sacrifice as well as the opening of the doors of the Temple; and one in the afternoon, indicating the last sacrifice of the day. During the six hours in between, priests oversaw the sacrifices made by the people for their individual sins.

Exactly at the third hour or 9 a.m., when the priests offered the first lamb of the day, Jesus was crucified. And He hung on the cross for six hours, the very six hours when people brought their personal sacrifices to the temple. During this time, He became sin for us, taking on all our shame, guilt, and emotional anguish. Then, at the ninth hour or 3 p.m., as the priests offered their second and last lamb of the day, Jesus died.

And just as the high priest, according to Leviticus 16:15-19, went into the Holy of Holies once a year and sprinkled the blood of the sacrifice on the altar and mercy seat seven times, so Jesus also shed His blood seven times. In the Bible, seven symbolizes God's perfection or completion.

Destination Hell

(Note: the section below was taken from my book, *Following the Blood Trail from Genesis to Revelation*.)

The first time Jesus shed His blood was during the agony in the garden where He sweated *"great drops of blood,"* (Luke 22:44). Second: when they tore off His beard and struck Him in the face (Isaiah 50:6; Luke 22:63-65). Third: at the whipping post when He received thirty-nine lashes that split open his back. Fourth: when Jesus was crowned with thorns and the soldiers beat Him over the head with a reed, driving the thorns deeper (Matthew 27:29-30). Fifth: when they nailed His hands to the cross; hands that had healed so many. Sixth: when they nailed His feet to the cross; feet that had walked the dust of the earth as He went about showing us how to live. And seventh: when the soldier pierced His side, and blood and water came out (John 19:33-34).

If there was any other way to restore man to God, Jesus would not have had to come, endure scorn and abuse, be nearly flogged to death, mocked, then nailed to a wooden cross to die an agonizing death.

But because He did, Jesus has the right to say, *"I am **the** way, **the** truth, and **the** life: no man cometh unto the Father, but by me,"* (John 14:6), making Jesus the only way, the narrow path. In contrast, the road to perdition is wide, a veritable superhighway clogged with those who believe there are many ways to God. But saying there is another way is like taking Jesus' blood and pouring it down the drain. It would also be calling Him a liar.

Additionally, those who would like to say that Jesus was just a "good man" or "good teacher" have not read the many claims He made about Himself. Aside from claiming to be the only way to heaven, some of His other assertions were His claim to be the Son of God (Mark 14:62); to be in the Father (John 14:10-11); to be not of this world (John 8:23); to be the light of the world (John 8:12); to be the door (John 8:28); to be the resurrection and life (John 111:25). Either they are true, or Jesus was a mental case with a god complex. There are no other options. And if true, then our only way out of hell is through accepting Him as Savior. ALL those who don't are on that clogged road heading to the inferno.

Jesus stressed this when He said in Matthew 7:13-14, "*Enter ye in at the* **strait gate**: *for wide is the gate, and broad is the way, that leadeth to destruction, and many there be which go in thereat: Because* **strait is the gate**, *and* **narrow is the way**, *which leadeth unto life, and few there be that find it.*"

Destination Hell

That word "strait" is *stenos* and means narrow. It is mentioned three times, firmly establishing God's Word. I also believe it is a nod to the Trinity. In addition, the word "narrow" here also means covenant. Those who have a covenant with God are the ones on this narrow pathway.

Then there's this in Acts 4:12, *"Neither is there salvation in any other* (than Jesus): *for there is none other name under heaven given among men, whereby we must be saved."* It couldn't be any plainer.

Now, wonder of wonders, those who accept what Jesus did for them are no longer ruled by a sin nature. Rather, they are new creatures in Christ. *"Therefore if any man be in Christ,* **he is a new creature**: *old things are passed away; behold, all things are made new,"* (2 Corinthians 5:17).

Also, 1 Corinthians 15:22 says, *"For as in Adam all die, even so in Christ shall all be made alive."*

Oh, how good is our God! Adam brought sin into the word, destroying our union and fellowship with God, but Jesus restored it, along with the promise of eternal life for all who believe in Him.

Though there is nothing else needed because salvation is complete, it is important that we renew our minds by the Word of God. According to 1

Thessalonians 5:23, we are a three-part man: spirit, soul, and body. Notice they are listed in order of importance.

That word "spirit" is *pneuma* and means, "breath." It is our spirit man that is revived after we accept Jesus which enables us to commune with God. The body is *soma*, which encompasses the body as a whole. It's our fleshly house, the storage unit that holds both spirit and soul.

But the mind is the one needing help. It is *psuche*, from which we get psychology and psyche. Since the mind influences what we do, it needs to be renewed by the Word of God in order for us to successfully live this new, born-again life. If we are spiritually minded, we will follow the promptings of the Holy Spirit. If we are carnally minded, we will follow our fleshly desires. The mind determines who we will serve. That's why Romans 12:2 says, *"Be not conformed to this world: but be ye **transformed** by the renewing of your mind, that ye may prove what is that good, and acceptable, and perfect, will of God."*

Before coming to the Lord, we all lived carnal lives. That's the natural life of man due to our sin nature. That means worldly thinking dictated our actions. These thought patterns must now be replaced. If not, we will continue to cater to the flesh and

Destination Hell

lament as Paul did in Romans 7:19, *"For the good that I would I do not: but the evil which I would not, that I do."* In verse 24 he even called himself "wretched." That's the same word for miserable. And that's just what we'll be. Our spirit will be reborn but our unrenewed mind will make us miserable because it will continually pull against our spirit and the Holy Spirit. Remember, Romans 8:1 tells us that we are no longer condemned BUT we are to walk guided by the Spirit. That's the way to know God's will for our lives. And that's the only way to truly experience His joy and peace. It's the Holy Spirit Who empowers us to live the Christian life. We can't do it without Him.

Also note that the word "transformed" in Romans 12:2 is *metamorphoo* and means, "to change." From it we get "metamorphosis" which describes the transformation of a worm-like caterpillar into a beautiful butterfly. God's lessons and examples are inscribed in the heavenly constellations (which lay out the entire message of salvation) as well as in nature. The caterpillar is a good illustration of our change from a lowly sinner to a beautiful new creature after we come to Jesus. Only then can we live full, valuable lives for Him. This is what the narrow road leads to.

But sadly, the wide road is the one most traveled. People want to "do their own thing." But Jesus left no room for that. He was clear. We cannot invent vain theologies that fit our lifestyle, which make us feel comfortable or good about ourselves or that allow us to do whatever we want, though the temptation is strong. And because we can't, people prefer the broad way. Jesus exposed this mindset when He said, *"This is the condemnation, that light (Jesus) is come into the world, and* **men loved darkness rather than light, because their deeds were evil***,"* (John 3:19).

Because people don't want to change or want their evil lifestyles exposed, they will reject God. Aldous Huxley is one example. Author of the dystopian novel, *Brave New World,* and nearly fifty other novels,[2] he is quoted as saying, "For myself, as no doubt for most of my friends, the philosophy of meaninglessness was essentially an instrument of liberation from a certain system of morality."[3]

Lee Strobel, a former atheist and author who became a Christian, said pretty much the same thing. "I was more than happy to latch onto Darwinism as an excuse to jettison the idea of God so I could unabashedly pursue my own agenda in life without moral constraints."[4]

How many feel this way, though they don't verbalize it? And this must break God's heart because He knows what it means in terms of eternity.

That's all well and good, but why should we believe the Bible is really the Word of God? After all, it's made up of sixty-six books, written by forty-four different people. Isn't it just a collection of stories to convey various lessons? Why should we allow it to govern or control our life?

There are many proofs that the Bible is the infallible Word of God. And as such, you can trust it. Below are a few:

It has incredible integrity. This integrity was attested to by the Dead Sea Scrolls discovered in a Qumran cave in 1946. The Isaiah scroll, as well as others, reveal that their text are neither changed nor corrupted but remain virtually identical to our modern translations.[5]

In addition, the sheer number of ancient Biblical manuscripts far exceed those of any other ancient manuscripts touted as legitimate, including the *Odyssey* and *Iliad* combined. Josh McDowell does an excellent job of laying this out. For example, he cites there are only ten surviving manuscripts of Julius Caesar's, *The Gallic Wars*, which the world recognizes as authentic. Compare that to **thousands** of New Testament manuscript fragments. In addition, most of the manuscripts we deem credible, such as *The Gallic Wars*, were written hundreds, sometimes over a thousand years after the actual event verses some New Testament manuscripts or fragments dating only forty to sixty years from the original.[6]

But that's not the only proof of the Bible's credibility. Hundreds of Old Testament prophecies have come true. One such example concerns the nation of Israel. Hosea 3:4-5, Ezekiel 37:11-12, and Ezekiel 11:17-20 all predicted the regathering of the Jews into their homeland. This happened. Despite all odds, Israel became a nation in 1948, just as the Bible foretold it would over twenty-five hundred years before.

But the Bible contains many other prophecies, some regarding Adam, Abraham, Sarah, Noah, Moses, just to name a few, all of which have come true. Moreover, there are three-hundred fulfilled prophecies concerning Jesus' first coming.

Any mathematician will tell you this is mathematically impossible. Stephen M. Bauer, in his book, *The Math of Christ*, examines just forty prophecies concerning Christ's first coming and concludes that, "the combined probability of all these forty events happening is one times ten to the 136th power. That's a 1 with 136 zeros behind it."

Destination Hell

He further adds, "all the atoms in our entire observable universe is a number considerably smaller than the odds of these forty prophecies coming to pass."[7] In other words, it's absolutely impossible, at least in the natural. But we know that with God, all things are possible!

In addition, prophecies about Jesus' soon return, as well as the rise of the One World Government and One World Religion, are beginning to take shape. These are discussed in a later chapter.

The apostles also validated the Bible with their lives. Matthias replaced Judas after Judas betrayed Jesus and hung himself, returning the original number of apostles to twelve (Acts 1:24-26). Everyone, except John, was martyred for their faith. Who in their right mind would willingly die for something they knew wasn't true? These men had known Jesus personally, had seen His miracles, heard His teachings, and testified that Jesus was the Messiah, the Son of the Living God, the only Savior of the world, and they gave up their lives to preach it.

The Bible also has the power to change lives. It certainly changed mine. I've lived on both sides of the street; one without Jesus and His Word, and one with. I can tell you there is no comparison. Though my lifestyle was not as dramatic or destructive as some, I can say that life without Jesus and His Word is often shallow, unfulfilling, and unsettling. On the other hand, knowing Jesus, which also means knowing His Word because He **IS** the Word made flesh (John 1:14), gives us an anchor, a hope, and a wonderful future.

Incalculable numbers of people have also testified to this; how they were freed from bondage and addiction to drugs, pornography, and other vices; how their lives have turned around from depression to victory, from sickness to health, from divorce to reconciliation, and so on.

Many in the Old Testament understood the power and authority of God's Word. Isaiah 40:8 tells us that, *"The grass withereth, the flower fadeth: but the word of our God shall stand **forever**."* This world is constantly changing, but God's Word never changes. It never becomes obsolete. It will be around for all eternity because forever is forever.

Psalm 119:89 also says, *"**Forever**, O Lord, thy word is settled in heaven."*

Psalm 119:105 is one of my favorites and says, *"Thy word is a lamp unto my feet, and a light unto my path."* God's Word is the lamp that shines light on our walk in this world, keeping us from stumbling and falling. Many people say, "follow your heart." But

Destination Hell

the Bible tells us that the heart is deceitful and desperately wicked (Jeremiah 17:9). Therefore, following our heart will usually lead us astray. Instead, we should follow God's Word. How much misery and sorrow could be avoided by walking only in the light of that Word?

Jesus also validated the Bible when He was tempted in the wilderness by the devil. His response to Satan was, *"Man shall not live by bread alone, but by **every** word that proceedeth out of the mouth of God,"* (Matthew 4:4). Notice, Jesus said **every** Word of God, not just the ones we like or agree with. God will never conform His Word to satisfy us or what we want to believe. We must conform ourselves, our thoughts, our lifestyle, to His Word.

If that weren't enough, Jesus further added this in Matthew 24:35, *"Heaven and earth shall pass away, but **my words shall not pass away**."* Jesus was referring to His Words in the New Testament, which will last even after the old heaven and earth are replaced by the new. He was saying His Word is enduring and important. We need to take it seriously.

He also said in John 5:39, *"Search the scriptures; for in them ye think ye have eternal life; and they are they which testify of me."* What did He mean? He meant the Old Testament spoke about Him. In fact, the entire Bible, both Old and New Testament, is about Jesus, the very Word of God Who fulfilled the law and the prophets.

2 Timothy 2:15 tells us that God's Word is *"the word of truth."* And Titus 1:2 says that God *"cannot lie."*

Then in Matthew 22:29, Jesus said, ***"Ye do err***, *not knowing the scriptures, nor the power of God."* We have already seen that God's Word will endure forever. It is His eternal Word. It will never change. And if we don't know or follow His Word, we will err. That word, "err" in Greek (*planao*) means, "to cause to go astray, be deceived or seduced." If we don't want to be seduced or deceived, we need to be firmly grounded in the Word of God. The last days, especially, will be marked by deception, and the only thing that will keep us from falling into its vortex is knowing God's Word and being led by the Holy Spirit.

Then 2 Timothy 3:16 tells us that, ***"All*** *scripture is given by inspiration of God, and is profitable for doctrine, for reproof, for correction, for instruction in righteousness."* God's Word will instruct us in righteous living. It will correct us and give us a firm foundation.

Destination Hell

But there were other "gospels" written that are not in the Bible. Why shouldn't we believe them, too?

While other so-called gospels were written, including Gnostic gospels such as the Gospel of Judas, Thomas, and Mary Magdalene, they never made it into the canon of sacred text because they did not teach the Gospel of Jesus, the Author of our salvation. Rather, they perverted or watered-down Jesus' message or offered another gospel entirely. In addition, many were forgeries, written by those assuming the identity of a disciple or early church leader.

The reality is that the four gospels, the epistles, and other works currently in our Bible were considered by early believers to be Holy Spirit-authored-and-inspired from the beginning. Because they held authority from the start, forgeries and other erroneous gospels were easy to spot. After the death of the apostles, their works were given credence by the early church fathers. So, at the time of the Council of Nicaean in 325 A.D., those in attendance only approved what already was accepted as sacred Scripture and which eventually became canon in 397 A.D. The fact that the numerous heretical texts didn't make it in our official Bible shows that God is more than able to protect His Word.[8]

So . . . is the Word of God true? Yes. The Dead Sea Scrolls validate it, the apostles validated it, Jesus validated it, the Word even validates itself through fulfilled prophecies. It has the power to radically change lives. It provides a guide out of our darkness, and a firm foundation on which to live. And it is powerful and full of promises for those who believe.

Thus, the validity of the New Testament was established early on. And before Jesus ascended into heaven, He gave his disciples a final instruction in Mark 16:15-16 called the Great Commission, *"Go ye into all the world, and preach the gospel to every creature. He that believeth and is baptized shall be saved; but he that believeth not shall be damned."* This Great Commission was birthed at Pentecost and built on the Word of God.

But knowing how difficult this was going to be, Jesus didn't leave us defenseless. All believers are sealed with the Holy Spirit. His stamp is on us (2 Corinthians 1:22, Ephesians 1:13, 4:30). It's interesting to note that this will be copied by the antichrist who will put his mark or seal on those who follow him (Revelation 13:16).

Jesus, through Paul, also told us that living the Christian life would be a battle, and certainly impossible without the Holy Spirit. We are in a war. That's why Paul wrote in Ephesians 6:10-18 that, *"we wrestle not against flesh and blood but against principalities, against powers, against the rulers of the darkness of this world, against spiritual wickedness in high places."*

Our battle is with evil spirits. Paul was referring to demons, fallen angels, and Satan. He also mentioned the *"wiles of the devil."* That word "wiles" means, "to lie in wait." And that's what Satan does. He waits for an opportunity to ambush and trap us, to bring us down, to defeat or discourage us, and he doesn't play fair. He usually strikes when we are most vulnerable; when we are stressed, tired, or alone. Peter warned about this in 1 Peter 5:8, *"Be sober, be vigilant: because your adversary the devil, as a roaring lion, walketh about, seeking whom he may devour."*

God has given us all the tools we need for victory. He has also given us holy angels who minister and protect us (Hebrews 1:14). We just need to engage in the battle, submit to God, resist the devil, **then** he will flee (James 4:7).

What exactly is this gospel we are to preach?

Gospel means "good news." And oh, what good news it is! It's all about Jesus, the Son of God, the second person of the Trinity, Who was born of a virgin yet remained fully God while being fully man. It's about how He suffered and died for our sins in order to make a way back to God the Father. And no matter what we've done, no matter how evil our lifestyle, God will accept us if we receive Jesus as our Savior. He will not cast us out (John 6:37).

The gospel tells us that salvation comes through Jesus alone. Romans 6:23, *"For the wages of sin is death; but the **gift** of God is eternal life through Jesus Christ our Lord."* After dying on the cross, Jesus was buried, then descended into hell. After three days He rose again. He ascended into heaven where He sits at the right hand of the Father. And He will come again in power and glory to rule and reign over the earth.

A strange message, to be sure. A holy God whose love is so great He came to earth to bleed for His creation so He could renew fellowship with them? Yes, incredible but true. *"For God so loved the world, that he gave his only begotten Son, that whosoever believeth in him should not perish, but have everlasting life,"* (John 3:16). God is so wonderful and good. How could His goodness not lead us to repentance (Romans 2:4)? And remember, Romans 6:23 tells us it's a gift! So does Ephesians 2:8-9, *"For by grace are ye saved through faith; and that not of yourselves: it*

Destination Hell

*is the **gift** of God: **Not of works**, lest any man should boast."*

A gift can't be earned or it's not a gift. And notice it is NOT by works. Isaiah 64:6 imparts this sobering truth, *"But we are all as an unclean thing, and all our righteousnesses are as filthy rags."* No matter how righteous or good our deeds, when compared to the holiness of God they are nothing but filthy rags. And how could filthy rags ever save anyone? We need to be covered by the righteousness of Jesus. Our rags just won't cut it.

And 1 Peter 1:18-19 adds this: *"Forasmuch as ye know that ye were not **redeemed** (ransomed, saved) with corruptible things, as silver and gold, from your **vain conversation** (empty, profitless behavior) received by **tradition** (traditionary law) from your fathers; **But with the precious blood of Christ, as of a lamb without blemish and without spot.**"*

If we lived to be a hundred and worked every day for the Lord, it would never be enough to earn our salvation. It just can't be done. Simple as that. We must receive it by faith.

So, the church had her marching orders: preach the gospel so that man can be saved and spared the pains of an eternal hell, and instead, inherit the Kingdom of God. God desires that none should perish (2 Peter 3:9). He doesn't want anyone going to hell. But He has given us free will, so, the choice is ours.

But the gospel was to be preached with care. No adulterations, only God's pure Word. The warning was severe: *"Though we, or an **angel** from heaven, preach any other gospel unto you than that which we have preached unto you, let him be **accursed**. As we said before, so say I now again, If any man preach any other gospel unto you than that ye have received, let him be **accursed**,"* (Galatians 1:8-9).

Notice, Paul said it twice: anyone who perverted the gospel of Jesus Christ was cursed. This is a serious claim. It means those who do this are cursed by God. And that which is cursed by God is devoted to destruction. Where does that leave Joseph Smith who claimed the angel Moroni gave him another gospel (Mormonism), and Muhammad, who claimed he got gospel add-ons from the counterfeit angel Gabriel (Islam)?

So, the apostles were to handle God's Word with care. But right from the beginning, Satan inserted his agents into the body of Christ for the very purpose of compromising it. The Corinthian church was an example. Paul had to warn them about, *"false apostles, deceitful workers, transforming themselves into the apostles of Christ. And no marvel:*

Destination Hell

*for **Satan himself is transformed into an angel of light**. Therefore it is no great thing if his ministers also be transformed as the ministers of righteousness; whose end shall be according to their works,"* (2 Corinthians 11:13-15).

Then to the church in Ephesus Paul said, *"For I know this, that after my departing shall grievous wolves enter in among you, not sparing the flock. Also of your own selves shall men arise, speaking perverse things, to draw away disciples after them,"* (Acts 20:29-30).

Paul warned believers in Corinth and Ephesus that outsiders would come spreading error and dividing the church. In addition, there would be those internally who would introduce false doctrine to attract followers.

And indeed, that happened. The Gnostics, Nicolaitans, and Judaizers all tried to subvert or dilute the gospel. The Gnostics claimed to have secret knowledge and that their primary religious authority came from one's supernatural or personal religious experiences rather than the Word of God. The Nicolaitans believed in a church hierarchy, with those at the top controlling the lesser ranks. This meant they dictated what those below them believed and how they practiced their faith. And the Judaizers taught that Gentiles must first become Jews before accepting Jesus.

Note, all three groups added something to the gospel. By doing that, they inferred Jesus wasn't enough. His sacrifice was incomplete thus more was needed either in the form of their own supernatural experiences (Gnostics) or through a controlling hierarchy (Nicolaitans) or having to conform to Judaism before salvation can be had through Jesus (Judaizers).

So, the early church had to be wary of false doctrines. She also faced persecution by and hatred from pagan merchants who took a dim view of people converting. When they did, they no longer bought the merchants' idols or their meat offered in temple worship. One such example is in Acts 19:23-28.

"And the same time (that Paul sent Timotheus and Erastus to Macedonia) *there arose no small stir about that way* (Christianity was called The Way). *For a certain man named Demetrius, a silversmith, which made silver shrines for Diana, brought no small gain unto the craftsmen; Whom he called together with the workmen of like occupation, and said, Sirs, ye know that by this craft we have our wealth. Moreover ye see and hear, that not alone at Ephesus, but almost throughout all Asia, this Paul hath persuaded and turned away much people* (converted them to Christ), *saying that they be no gods, which are made with hands: So that not only this our craft is in danger to be set at nought; but*

Destination Hell

also that the temple of the great goddess Diana should be despised, and her magnificence should be destroyed, whom all Asia and the world worshippeth. And when they heard these sayings, they were full of wrath, and cried out, saying, Great is Diana of the Ephesians." This created an uproar in the city. People were losing their livelihoods and were angry. They hated not only Paul for doing this but the converts who followed his teachings.

Paul had already encountered this kind of thing in Acts 16:16-34 when a girl with a spirit of divination followed him and Silas, crying, *"These men are the servants of the most high God, which shew unto us the way of salvation."* Finally, Paul got tired of it and cast out the spirit, causing her to lose her ability to earn money for her master. This made the master angry enough to haul Paul and Silas before a judge, which created a riot, followed by the beating of Paul and Silas and their imprisonment. How did it end? The jailer and his entire family came to the Lord! No matter the hardship or persecution, God will always have the last word.

Pagan priests were also alarmed when their contributions began to diminish as people converted to Christianity.[9] On top of that, the church was fiercely persecuted by the Roman Empire who viewed their Caesars as gods and were offended when Christians did not. Still, the church not only survived, but thrived.

Then in 313 A.D., Emperor Constantine legalized Christianity via the Edict of Milan, giving Christianity a protected status and its adherents the right to practice their faith without injury. Constantine followed this up with his Edict of Toleration in 324 A.D.[10] This created an influx of fake believers because Constantine tried to convert people by offering them perks or benefits. But the real damage to the church came when Emperor Theodosius, in 380 A.D., established Christianity as the state religion of Rome. And between then and the 5th century, Christianity became the dominant religion of the Empire.[11]

Like the fake converts after Constantine's edicts, so again, after Christianity became the state religion, not all converted out of a genuine belief in Jesus. Rather, some joined the church out of a desire to enrich themselves, hoping it would garner them better trade deals, more influential friends, or better jobs. So, when they entered the fold, they brought with them their pagan beliefs and rituals. And many of these beliefs and rituals found their way into the church. Suddenly, people were kneeling before statues lining the sides of their churches. Medallions and medals hung around necks as totems for protection or favor. The office

Destination Hell

of bishop and elder gave way to a formal priesthood. Resurrection Sunday became the pagan Easter, after the goddess of fertility (Eostre or Ishtar).[12]

Slowly, church tradition began carrying the same authority as the Word of God even though Jesus had rebuked the Pharisees for doing this very thing (Matthew 15:3-6). Scriptures were only written in Latin, a language that began to change after the Western half of the Roman Empire fell in 476 A.D., making it less universal.[13]

And finally, God's Word was chained to pulpits, inaccessible to the common man and available only through the interpretation of an ordained priest. Those in the body of Christ were no longer kings and priests as described in 1 Peter 2:5, 9 and Revelation 1:6.

What could go wrong?

As the Word of God was smothered, the world grew darker, culminating in what history calls, The Dark Ages. Historians debate the timeline. Some claim it began around 400 A.D. and ended around 1600 A.D. Others say it was more like 500 A.D. to 1500 A.D. while others say it only lasted about 800 years. Still others say the Dark Ages never existed.[14, 15] Nevertheless, it refers to the period when European culture and economics deteriorated while the state religion of Rome dominated.

Eventually, brave men like Martin Luther (1483-1546)[16] and William Tyndale (1494-1536)[17] faced persecution and danger by translating the Bible from Latin to the language of their people. Once the Word was out, it again began turning the world upside down. America was founded on it. And the Word impacted countless nations through revival. Names like Maria Woodworth-Etter, who moved powerfully in the Holy Spirit; Evan Roberts, the eminent evangelist; Smith Wigglesworth, a man of faith who could raise the dead; Kathryn Kuhlman, who believed in miracles and healings, and saw them; and William Branham, who lead the "Voice of Healing" revival in the 1940s,[18] all became household names and brought many in the church back to its Scriptural roots.

The true church has always survived. God has always kept a remnant to ensure His pure gospel would be preached. Please note that when I talk about the remnant church I am not talking about a building or denomination. I am speaking about people who are faithful to Jesus and His Word. The apostate church also includes people from different denominations who have departed from the truth.

Destination Hell

God will ensure that His gospel is preached until the time of the Rapture, when the Church Age ends. When that time comes, He will tell believers to, *"Come up hither!"* and we will be gone. And that time is fast approaching.

But in the meantime? What should we do? We are to occupy until He comes (Luke 19:13). That word "occupy" means, "to work, to busy oneself." We are not to be complacent. We need to live all out for God wherever He has planted us. Ephesians 5:15-16 tells us to, *"See then that ye walk circumspectly, not as fools, but as wise, Redeeming the time, because the days are evil."*

We are the salt and light of the world. We must stand up and do what is right even when we are called racists, homophobes, Islamophobes, intolerant, or haters. We must declare truth. In addition, we are to share the gospel because until the trumpet sounds and the command to *"come up hither"* is heard, the Holy Spirit will still be bringing people to salvation.

The church I attend has a vibrant street ministry and people are coming to the Lord almost every week. God's Holy Spirit is still moving, still wooing people, and drawing them to the Lord. And certain groups seem to be getting an additional touch. For some time, the Holy Spirit has been moving among Muslims, in nations impossible to reach with the gospel. Jesus has been appearing to them in dreams and visions. As a result, many have accepted Him as Savior. Now, it seems He is moving among young people. And He will keep moving until the very second the Church Age ends. And then will come a time of great horror and suffering.

Oh, may we stay on that narrow road until His appearing!

The Counterfeit Narrow Road

Alongside the church of the narrow way is the apostate church. Satan has used people to come against the church or pervert it for centuries, hoping to destroy its effectiveness in the world. To that end, he has succeeded. Sadly, the apostate church in America is alive and well. Its deterioration is one of the greatest tragedies of our time. It is a church that has become an extension of the world, offering a counterfeit road, a look-alike-almost road. But almost doesn't count.

Webster defines counterfeit as "made in imitation of something genuine with intention to deceive or defraud." And that's what the apostate, counterfeit church does. It deceives and defrauds its members and leads them astray.

Let's begin by looking at Jesus' letters to the seven churches in Asia Minor. A collection of Roman provinces in today's western Turkey, Asia Minor boasted of a rich Hellenistic civilization.[19] The seven churches were: Ephesus, Smyrna, Pergamum, Thyatira, Sardis, Philadelphia, and Loadicea. They are long gone, but at the time Revelation was written they represented seven actual churches. They also represented the entire Church Age, the characteristics of each stage of the Church Age, the spiritual condition of the church as a whole, and finally, the picture of both the remnant and apostate church.

First, a brief look at what these letters say about the seven stages of church history and their timeframe.

Ephesus: It was once the terminal of an important trade route but by the time the church was planted, its glory days of trade were past. Deforestation and overgrazing had silted its great harbor. A stronghold of pagan worship, it boasted of a temple dedicated to Diana, the goddess of fertility, hunting and the moon. Her temple numbered among the seven wonders of the world and brought great wealth to the city. In addition, Ephesus was the seat of Roman governance for the province.[20]

This was the church of the apostles, begun around 30 A.D. and ending around 100 A.D. It was zealous and spread the gospel throughout and beyond the Roman Empire. But by the time of this letter, their zeal had waned.

Destination Hell

Smyrna was prized by Rome as a bridgehead and buffer. Their citizens claimed they were the first to erect a temple honoring Rome, then went on to build a second temple to Rome's gods. It eventually became the center of Caesar worship. This church was fiercely persecuted by Rome until Constantine's Edict of Milan in 313 A.D. which protected Christians and gave them the right to worship freely.[21] It represents the Church Age from 100 A.D. to 312 A.D., a time when believers were often martyred, especially under Emperor Domitian.

Pergamum is near the Aegean Sea, and from which the hills of Smyrna can be seen. It was a place of gross idolatry, especially Caesar worship. But other gods such as Asklepios, Dionysus, Athene and Zeus were worshipped. Indeed, Jesus called Pergamum the "seat of Satan," referring to the altar of Zeus, the very Zeus the citizens called "savior."[22] Extremely worldly, it became the religious foundation of the Holy Roman Empire and encompassed the time from 313 A.D to around 600 A.D.

Thyatira lies between two rivers, Hermus and Caicus, and is twenty miles southeast of Pergamum. Though in the minority, many Jews settled there in search of economic opportunities. It was noted for manufacturing bronze armor, as well as for its leather, wool, and linen industries.[23] Representing the timeline from 600 A.D. to 1517 A.D., it was a worldly and apostate church that compromised for the sake of power and wealth. It oversaw the buying and selling of indulgences. It also saw the Dark Ages, a deterioration of Europe's civilization and economy, while the church itself prospered.

Sardis is located in central Asia Minor. Its highway linked Smyrna, Pergamum, and Ephesus. It boasted of a vibrant Caesar cult. Scottish archaeologist, Sir Mitchell Ramsay, called it, "a city whose name was almost synonymous with pretention unjustified, promises unfulfilled, appearance without reality, confidence which heralded ruin."[24] Jesus called this church, "dead." Historians believe Sardis represents the period from 1517 to the 1700's.

Philadelphia: After the devastating earthquake of 17 A.D., the Roman Senate sent the city aid, bringing Philadelphia under Rome's umbrella. Its Jewish population greatly opposed the Christians and the spreading of the gospel.[25] It represents the revived, missionary church, active from around 1648 until 1900. It saw the rise of men like John and Charles Wesley and George Whitefield who believed the Bible and preached it to countless others.

Destination Hell

Laodicea: Located near central Turkey, it is perched one hundred feet above the River Lycus. It was both renown and wealthy due to it being a layover for Rome's cargo shipments. It was also a banking center where money from various Roman provinces could be exchanged.[26] It was lukewarm, with superficial faith, but didn't know it. It was liberal and loved the world. It represents the final church, and spans from 1900 to the present.

Next, we'll see what Jesus had against them, giving insight into the last-days apostate church.

Ephesus: *"Thou hast left thy first love,"* (Revelation 2:4). Though they were doing many good things, their love for Jesus had cooled, causing them to lose their zeal.

Smyrna: Jesus had nothing negative to say about this church.

Pergamum: *"I have a few things against thee, because thou hast there them that hold the doctrine of Balaam, who taught Balac to cast a stumblingblock before the children of Israel, to eat things sacrificed unto idols, and to commit fornication. So hast thou also them that hold the doctrine of the Nicolaitanes, which thing I hate,"* (Revelation 2:14-15).

This is an extensive list. Not surprising. Remember, Jesus called Pergamum the seat of Satan. It was an evil, idolatrous city. But what is the doctrine of Balaam? He was a prophet who sold his services to Moab's King Balac (Balak). The king hired Balaam to curse Israel and stop them from taking over the Promised Land. So first, Balaam compromised for personal gain. Next, because God wouldn't allow him to curse Israel outright, Balaam concocted a strategy for Israel's downfall. He told King Balac if the pagan Moabite women seduced the Hebrew men, and led them into idolatry, it would offend God, causing the loss of His favor and protection. It worked. The Moabite women became a stumbling block to Israel.

Also, the Pergamum church had Nicolaitans among them. Recall that the Nicolaitans operated in a church hierarchy, controlling those below, their beliefs and how they practiced their religion. Prominent in the Holy Roman Empire, this church, rather than Scripture, dictated everything people did, how they lived, what they ate, etcetera.

Thyatira: *"I have a few things against thee, because thou sufferest that woman Jezebel, which calleth herself a prophetess, to teach and to seduce my servants to commit fornication, and to eat things sacrificed unto idols,"* (Revelation 2:20).

Destination Hell

Jesus said this church harbored Jezebel. The Jezebel spirit is a seducing spirit which manifests in false prophets, false teaching, false doctrine, lying, perversion, and spiritual fornication. It is apostasy and compromise for the sake of power and wealth.

Sardis: *"I know thy works, that thou hast a name that thou livest, and art dead,"* (Revelation 3:1). This church was full of dead works. Though they made a name for themselves, God wasn't impressed.

Philadelphia: Jesus had nothing negative to say about this church.

Laodicea: *"I know thy works, that thou art neither cold nor hot: I would thou wert cold or hot. So then because thou art lukewarm, and neither cold nor hot, I will spue thee out of my mouth. Because thou sayest, I am rich, and increased with goods, and have need of nothing; and knowest not that thou art wretched, and miserable, and poor, and blind, and naked: I counsel thee to buy of me gold tried in the fire, that thou mayest be rich; and white raiment, that thou mayest be clothed, and that the shame of thy nakedness do not appear; and anoint thine eyes with eye salve, that thou mayest see,"* (Revelation 3:15-18).

This truly is a sad church. They are affluent and think they have everything. But because they are lukewarm, God sees them as poor, wretched, blind, and naked. Laodicea also means, "the people judge or decide." This is not a church governed by God's Word, but by what the people attending think and want to have tickling their ears.

If we put it all together, we get a disturbing picture of the end times apostate church. It has lost its zeal and love for Jesus (**Ephesus**). Its prophets have sold themselves for money, power, or fame. It practices spiritual adultery and is tightly connected to the world system. It imposes a hierarchy over the rest of the body which it tries to control (**Pergamum**). It harbors a Jezebel spirit and teaches false doctrine (**Thyatira**). It is full of dead works (**Sardis**). And though it is wretched, poor, blind, and naked, it thinks it is rich (**Laodicea**). It is a church controlled by the spirit of the world rather than the Holy Spirit. These things make the apostate church filthy in God's eyes.

It's interesting that Jesus ended His letter to the Laodicean church by saying: *"Behold, I stand at the door, and knock: if any man hear my voice, and open the door, I will come in to him, and will sup with him, and he with me,"* (Revelation 3:20).

Supping with Jesus indicates fellowship. But we see Him **outside** wanting to get in. This last-day's

Destination Hell

church will not even allow Jesus, via the Holy Spirit, into their assembly, nor do they have any fellowship with Him. It is completely carnal, operating in the flesh. What a miserable picture of the end-time church! This is the church left behind after the rapture to face the horrendous seven-year Tribulation.

And what of the remnant church? Its characteristics are found in both Smyrna and Philadelphia, the only churches Jesus did not criticize.

Though **Smyrna** was poor, He called them *"rich,"* meaning spiritually rich. He also said they would suffer; thus, they are the persecuted church. Then He encouraged them to be faithful unto death, indicating martyrdom, and that He would give them "a crown of life," (Revelation 2:9-10).

Philadelphia was similar. Jesus acknowledged they had only *"a little strength,"* but praised them for keeping His Word, for being faithful to the gospel message. And the word, *"strength,"* is *dunamis* and means, "miraculous power, worker of miracles," It's literally referring to their meager ability to work miracles.

Nevertheless, Jesus made this wonderful and incredible promise: *"Because thou hast kept the word of my patience,* ***I also will keep thee from the hour*** *of temptation, which shall come upon all the world, to try them that dwell upon the earth,"* (Revelation 3:10). Jesus was referring to the seven-year Tribulation and that they would not be part of it.

Thus, we see that the remnant church of the last days will faithfully preach God's pure, uncompromised Word. It will not be a friend of the world but hated and persecuted. It will also be a church with limited ability to perform miracles. But this is the church spared the seven years of hell on earth. This is the raptured church.

Does the remnant church exist today?

All one need do is look around to see the evidence of its existence. Throughout the world, Christians are martyred for their faith. They are butchered, imprisoned, tortured, censored, defamed, and cancelled. And though there are testimonies of miracles, they aren't as common as they should be, and in that sense, it is weak. But this is the church that preaches God's Word without compromise. And it is not a friend of the world. Rather than carnal, it is guided by the Holy Spirit. And it understands its primary mission is to win souls for Jesus, not accumulate worldly power or wealth.

Destination Hell

Is there any indication that the apostate church also exists today?

Yes. And it has been years in the making. And none of it has taken God by surprise. He knows the beginning from the end and everything in between. He knew it would happen and gave us ample warning in Scripture. But let's see for ourselves.

One of the deadliest blows to the church came in the 1940s when Marxism crept into our colleges and schools. This also included Christian colleges and seminaries. Robert Jeffress, Senior Pastor of First Baptist Church in Dallas, and a Baylor University graduate, said this about his alma mater in an interview with Tim Moore of Lamb and Lion Ministries. (I paraphrase) Baylor, a supposedly Christian college, has been sliding into apostacy for almost sixty years. They no longer teach that the Bible is the inerrant Word of God but tear it apart and claim it is only a collection of stories.

What's happening in Christian universities and seminaries could fill a book. One recent example is Methodist Emory University's commissioning of two murals. One features a transgender flag, the other features three politicians, including the radical Stacey Abrams.[27]

And Harvard, once a Christian college founded by Pastor John Harvard, a college where Christian ministers filled the position of president for its first seventy years of existence, has finally hit bottom. Recently, it named atheist Greg Epstein as its head chaplain. To get a feel of his philosophy, here's one of his quotes: "We don't look to a god for answers, we are each other's answers."[28]

What a far cry from the Harvard of 1636 when they advised students to "be plainly instructed and earnestly pressed to consider well the main end of his life and studies is to know God and Jesus Christ which is eternal life and therefore to lay Christ in the bottom as the only foundation of all sound knowledge and learning. And seeing the Lord only giveth wisdom, let everyone seriously set himself by prayer in secret to seek it of Him. Everyone shall exercise himself in reading the Scriptures twice a day that he shall be ready to give such an account of his proficiency therein."[29]

Then there's this. Recently, liberal Pastor John Pavlovitz verbalized the current thinking of many liberal churches that believe the Bible shouldn't be considered the final "Word of God," since God "speaks new things to modern believers."[30] The implication is that new revelations from God can be used to justify whatever liberal stance is wanted.

Destination Hell

The impact Marxism had on education was profound. In seminaries, the true gospel was repackaged into a social gospel. Conspicuously absent was the guidance of the Holy Spirit and sound teaching of Scripture. Instead of seminaries grounding our future religious leaders in unblemished doctrine, these institutions became cemeteries pumping out spiritually dead pastors. Many graduates left with tattered faith, questioning the validity of the Bible and the true role of the church. These liberal pastors then conveyed their apostasy to their parishioners, who in turn began questioning the inerrancy of God's Word, salvation only in Jesus, and His soon return.

Few connected the dots that Karl Marx, the father of Communism, came out of the Illuminati, a Satanic organization. His *Communist Manifesto* was virtually a replica of *The Illuminati Manifesto*, and also formed the basis of the secular *Humanist Manifesto*.

All of them, the Illuminati, communism, and secular humanism, have similar beliefs and goals. They want to create a global society with a social and economic order that facilitates the redistribution of wealth. Rejecting the need for salvation, they believe Christian salvation is "harmful." Instead, they believe man must create his own religion. They also have seventeen common strategies deemed necessary to achieve their goals:

1. Reject traditional religion
2. Reject concept of sin, salvation, and the need for God
3. Promote idea that morals and ethics are situational
4. Push idea that a better world can be achieved through intelligence and reason
5. Encourage personal freedom without moral restrictions
6. Promote abortion, sexual exploration, and divorce
7. Promote euthanasia and suicide
8. Promote democracy (mob rule) rather than a democratic republic
9. Promote concept of "separation of church and state"
10. Promote economic socialism
11. Promote government control over every area of life by using "anti-discrimination" as a tool
12. Destroy nationalism and promote concept of a "world community"
13. Promote the need for an international court
14. Promote environmentalism and population control
15. Provide birth control to developing nations
16. Remove all barriers to scientific research

Destination Hell

17. Promote international cooperation as absolutely essential[31]

The secularization of seminaries and Christian colleges went on to profoundly affect Protestant churches. They are in deep trouble. Fewer and fewer pastors preach about sin and hell, choosing instead to preach God's love. And this is a wonderful teaching. God is love itself and He loves each of us, whether saved or unsaved. And it is His very love that leads us to repentance. But He is also a God of justice, Whose holiness, at times, demands judgment. So, to preach only His love and not His justice, is unbalanced, and has left much of the church, unbalanced.

Alongside this, only 2% of pastors teach Bible prophecy, though it is 27% of the Bible. Jesus was displeased with the religious crowd for not knowing the season of His first coming. He will be equally displeased that so many in the body of Christ don't know the season of His return.

Why don't pastors preach these things? Is it fear of offending; fear of losing attendance? And let's be honest, that could mean loss of revenue. Perhaps they think Bible prophecy is too confusing or difficult to understand. But it's hardly that. If all the prophecies of Jesus' first coming were fulfilled literally, why can't we expect that all prophecies of

Sylvia Bambola

His gathering us up in the rapture, then His return at the end of the seven-year Tribulation, be literal, also?

Because liberal seminaries have pumped out liberal pastors with no sure foundation, they seek to make people "feel good." Not willing to "rock the boat" or offend anyone, they end up offending God. They are also more "tolerant," accepting other religions as equal to their own. Because they are carnal, they compromise with the world. Not wanting to be considered old fashioned or obsolete, they seek relevance in an evil society. Consequently, they have seduced many into believing the Bible is obsolete, and that spiritual relevance can be found elsewhere.

This has allowed a worldly mindset to take hold; a mindset that on the surface sounds enlightened and loving. But is it? Is it loving to let a drowning man drown without offering him a life preserver? Is it loving to let someone drink poison just because it tastes good? Saying all roads lead to God might make people happy, but it will lead to their eternal demise. How can it be loving to preach a false message that will send people to hell?

Willian D. Watkins, a Christian author, talking about how things had changed from the 50s to

Destination Hell

now, said this: "Being tolerant never meant condoning immoral behavior, letting harmful beliefs go unchallenged, or permitting a person's dangerous lifestyle to influence, much less be taught to others. In those days we may have disagreed about what is true, but few challenged the bedrock conviction that 'true' is the opposite of 'false,' and the truth does not tolerate untruth. We believed then that some beliefs and lifestyles promoted the common good while others undermined it."[32]

Doesn't 1 Timothy 4:16 say, *"Take heed unto thyself, and unto the doctrine* (the gospel of Christ); *continue in them: for in doing this thou shalt both save thyself, and them that hear thee"*? And what about Titus 1:13-14? *"This witness is true* (the gospel of Christ) *Wherefore* **rebuke them sharply**, *that they may be sound in the faith; Not giving heed to Jewish fables* (or any other fiction and lies) *and commandments of men, that turn from the truth."*

The absence of sound doctrine will always lead to compromise and error. And this has resulted in our churches becoming anemic, filled with inaccuracy, and totally unprepared for what is coming.

The job of pastoring is difficult, demanding, and often exhausting. If the pastor is not grounded in the truth of Scripture, if his belief is superficial and worldly, full of compromise and wavering, and based on a fleshly commitment rather than a true anointing from God, then I would think that job is impossible. How can a person give what he does not possess? It is God's Word that gives one hope. It is His Holy Spirit that fills us with peace, joy, and love. One's own hope, peace, joy, and love are finite. They can be quickly exhausted and even extinguished, leaving a pastor without anything to impart to others.

The truth is most pastors have failed us. By not teaching the full counsel of God they rob Christians of hope. As the world gets darker, it becomes more confusing and hopeless. If Christians don't understand that these things were predicted in Scripture and are heralding the soon return of Christ and that we will be spared the worst of it in the rapture, then Christians can become despondent, hopeless, and fearful. To deny their congregation this hope is a grave disservice.

This poor shepherding has produced dead, apostate churches filled with members without foundation, who go through superficial motions, accept false doctrine, and commit spiritual adultery with the world. And like Laodicea, they don't even know it.

Destination Hell

The pandemic has only added to the problem. When some former solid Bible-based churches finally reopened, it wasn't the teaching of the gospel that was first and foremost on their agenda. Rather, it was a "woke" message. "Woke" is another name for social justice but in reality it's just a cover for all sorts of evil.

Just what were these "woke" messages? They were sermons on white guilt and privilege, and the Marxist social justice gospel. Others touched on things like the importance of Black Lives Matter (which is also founded on Marxist philosophy), critical race theory, liberation theology, and Kingdom Now, rather than the gospel of Jesus. Some of these pastors even publicly apologized for being white, an absurdity since that's how God made them.[33]

But part of the church has been "woke" long before now. Consider the World Evangelical Alliance. They entered the "green" movement years ago by launching a clean energy campaign entitled Project 2025 with the hope of getting 20% of its members to convert to renewable energy.[34] Yes, we are to be good stewards of the earth, but what does that have to do with the gospel? Instead, why not put this effort into getting 20% of their unsaved community to Christ?

Sylvia Bambola

A further clarification and description of what is going on in these apostate churches:

I have already discussed the grosser aspects of Christianity's decline in my book, *The Coming Deception*, which includes churches doing "Clown Communions" when the pastor and congregants dress up as clowns; churches giving communion to their pets; the porn movie entitled "Missionary Positions" shown under the guise of helping those addicted to porn; and a nude church where no one, including the pastor, wears clothes.[35] And as recently as December 2021, St. Luke's Lutheran church in Chicago, hosted a "drag queen prayer hour" for children! God help us!

Aside from these vile practices, many subtle attitudes have, over time, corrupted the church. These include the social gospel, replacement theology, seeker sensitive churches, purpose-driven churches, the Emerging Church, a Palestinian Jesus, Chrislam, mystical Christianity which includes Christian Wicca, Christian yoga, and Christian psychics.

They are briefly described below:

The social gospel. What is it? As a movement, it began in Protestantism in the early 1900s with an emphasis on helping the poor and downtrodden.

Destination Hell

And though it did good works, it was inherently flawed. Why? Because, at its foundation was the belief that Jesus would not return until the world was free of social evils, and this was to be accomplished by **human effort**. Thus, they believed they would be the instruments God used to bring about the Kingdom of God on earth,[36] that the salvation of the planet would come through the "works" of their hands.

Walter Rauschenbusch, the movement's leader in the early 1900s, described the Kingdom of God according to the social gospel as: "a prophetic, future-focused ideology and **a revolutionary, social and political force that understands all creation to be sacred; and it can help save the problematic, sinful social order.**"[37]

There is no denying that Christians are to do good. Scripture is full of the admonition to care for the poor, the widows, and orphans. And Galatians 6:10 says, *"As we have therefore opportunity,* **let us do good unto all men***, especially unto them who are of the household of faith."* That's why ministries dig wells in areas where there is only polluted water. That's why they offer free meals to poverty-stricken children at their mission schools. That's why they build orphanages and rescue centers for battered women, etcetera.

But Jesus said the poor would always be with us (Matthew 26:11), meaning as long as we are in a fallen world, we will never eradicate poverty or the social ills that contribute to it. And this fallen and broken world is ruled by Satan. Therefore, the church will NEVER be able to bring God's Utopia to earth. Peace will only come when the Prince of Peace returns. And Jesus never said the Kingdom of God was a revolutionary or political force or that man would be able to save the world's "sinful social order."

Gradually, this social gospel replaced the true gospel. But while the Social Gospel Movement is no longer, its ideology, as well as Liberation Theology, is still prevalent. Some of it has been repackaged into Kingdom Now or Dominion Theology. All of them want to achieve the Kingdom of God on earth through human means.

Kingdom Now and Dominion Theology teach that God has already rid the world of the evils of sickness and death. It states that the church can convert the entire globe to Christ, even if that means using force. But that necessitates controlling social institutions and governments. Only after this, can the world be turned over to Jesus.[38]

This contradicts Scripture that says, *"We know (positively) that we are of God, and **the whole world***

Destination Hell

(around us) is under the power of the evil one," (1 John 5:19 Amplified). John wrote this after Jesus ascended into heaven. He understood that Jesus had paid for the sins of mankind, had conquered both death and hell, yet in spite of this, John clearly indicated that at least for now, and for reasons we may not understand, God allows Satan to retain control until Jesus is ready to return to earth and claim His rightful throne.

Kingdom Now and Dominion Theology reveals the utter arrogance of man and lack of adherence to God's Word. It makes man his own prince of peace.

The Social Gospel, Liberation Theology, Kingdom Now and Dominion Theology are not the Great Commission. The Great Commission is sharing the gospel of Jesus Christ with people. And yes, meeting their needs when possible. But that's a far cry from preaching that we need to bring Utopia to the world. This is a worldly concept devised centuries ago and rooted in demonic secret societies.

Replacement theology teaches that the church has replaced the nation of Israel; that God is finished with Israel because they rejected Jesus; and that all Scriptures mentioning Israel really apply to the church. In order to twist Scripture that way, one would have to be a contortionist. This theology is a form of anti-Semitism and is played out in the BDS movement (**B**oycott, **D**ivest, **S**anction) by churches who now refuse to buy goods from Israel. Spearheading this movement is the World Council of Churches which is clearly anti-Israel, anti-Semitic and pro-Palestinian. It even "compares Israel with the South African apartheid regime."[39]

Others who are divesting themselves from Israel are the Mennonite Church (USA), Presbyterian Church (USA), United Church of Christ, and the pension board of the Methodist Church.[40]

Chapters nine through eleven of Romans clearly state God is NOT finished with Israel or the Jewish people. Paul said in Romans 11:1-2, *"Hath God cast away his people (Israel)? God forbid. For I also am an Israelite, of the seed of Abraham, of the tribe of Benjamin.* **God hath not cast away his people** *which he foreknew."* No, God has not cast them away and replaced them with the church. He still loves Israel and has a plan for them which will unfold after the Church Age ends. Then, during the seven-year Tribulation, Israel will come to her Messiah, Jesus, and God will prepare her to be the head of nations. And at the end of the Tribulation, God will keep His promise by having Jesus, the son of David, the Jewish Messiah, rule from His throne in Jerusalem. God will also give Israel the entire land grant He

Destination Hell

promised them in Genesis 15:18-20 and Joshua 1:3-4, which has yet to be fulfilled.

The Seeker Sensitive and Purpose Driven Church both try to build their membership through marketing strategies. They are big on entertainment and motivation, with a light, friendly message where often the gospel is unrecognizable. They believe that smart marketing will draw the unsaved. Success is measured by the number of attendees. And those who do come to the saving knowledge of Jesus seem to remain perpetually immature.[41]

Sadly lacking is the Holy Spirit. It reminds me of Revelation where Jesus stood outside knocking on the door of the Laodicean church asking to get in. This is a carnal church that believes the flesh of man can do what only God's Spirit can. It waters down the gospel in hopes of offending no one and appealing to the unsaved, and in doing so denies the very saving power of God's Word.

On top of that, in John 6:44 Jesus said, *"No man can come to me, except the Father which hath sent me draw him."* The salvation of a soul is a supernatural event. It can't be achieved by man's clever campaigns or schemes. We plant seeds into the hearts of the unsaved. Someone else waters them. But it is God who makes the seeds root and grow. 1 Corinthians 3:7 is a reminder of this: *"So then neither is he that planteth any thing, neither he that watereth; but God that giveth the increase."* If we try to use the arm of flesh to do what only the Holy Spirit can, it will ultimately fail.

The Emergent Church is based on the belief that the church should change with the times so it can reach the current culture. Thus, it wants to reinvent itself. It is selective in what Biblical doctrines it teaches and does not believe in the inerrancy of God's Word. Rather, it believes that truth is "questionable."

It is big on "feelings" and "experiences" rather than the gospel. Its interests also extend to social and environmental issues. And its emphasis is more on relationships with each other than declaring God's Word. In some ways, it resembles seeker-sensitive churches. Its worship can include the use of icons, candles, scents, images, and repetitious mantras. It can even take on a mystical quality. Its "contemplative prayer" resembles Buddhist practices.[42, 43]

Since it has no official church doctrine and not all Emergent Churches are alike, it is possible some pastors are more faithful to Scripture than others. However, when the final arbitrator of truth is a person and not Scripture, then it's easy to imagine that a descent into apostasy is inevitable, if not already there.[44]

Destination Hell

A Palestinian Jesus was first mentioned by former PLO Chairman, Yasser Arafat, when he claimed Jesus was a Palestinian and not a Jew. It caught on in some circles, especially Muslim ones. Recently, Congresswoman Ilhan Omar also inferred this claim was true. Even some Palestinian Christians believe Jesus was not a Jew but a Palestinian. According to *themonastery* website, there are some scholars who actually debate this question![45]

The claim is so utterly ridiculous it defies description. Jesus is a Jew, from the line of David. He is the Lion of the tribe of Judah. Judah was one of Jacob's twelve sons, the very sons who formed the nation of Israel. This fact is repeated again and again in the Bible.

But why is it important? Why does it even matter? Because Jesus coming from the line of Judah was a fulfilment of Bible prophecy. God promised Abraham that the Messiah would come from his son, Isaac (who fathered Jacob). And God fulfilled that promise through Jesus. In order to be the Messiah of Israel He had to be a Jew. In order to be the Savior, He had to be a Jew. And in order to sit on the throne of David during the millennium, He must be a Jew.

This is foundational. And this is why there is so much anti-Semitism worldwide. Satan hates the

Jews because they are God's chosen people from which we have received the Ten Commandments, the prophets, the Scriptures and yes, our Messiah, Savior and King.

A word of caution. Antisemitism is dangerous because it touches the apple of God's eye (Zechariah 2:8). He who curses the descendants of Abraham (the Jews), God, in turn, will curse (Genesis 12:3). God made that covenant with Abraham and it's unconditional, meaning it is not based on anything Abraham or his descendants do or don't do, but only on God's Word and His faithfulness. I wouldn't recommend falling on the wrong side of this.

Chrislam is on the rise. It's a belief that Christians and Muslims worship the same God. "Unity meetings" between Christianity and Islam, place the writings of the Quran and Bible on equal footing. According to a Christian Coalition newsletter, 300 churches have added Islam to their Sunday school curriculum. These churches declare both the Bible and Quran honor Jesus even though the prophet Jesus in the Quran has no resemblance to our Jesus. According to Islam, Jesus is **Not** the Son of God, **Not** virgin born, and **Never** died on the cross.

Destination Hell

So, who is the Jesus of the Quran? Muhammad Hisham Kabbani, Founder and Chairman of the Islamic Supreme Council of America, said it well. I paraphrase his description: Jesus will return with the Muslim Messiah, Mahdi, to establish a New World Order. When he does, he will confess he never died on the cross, that it was all a fake. He will further confess that while he was away, he discovered the truth of Islam. Then he will destroy all crosses and become the Mahdi's executioner of every man, woman, and child who refuses to convert to Islam.

This is blasphemy. So is trying to co-mingle Islam with Christianity.

Christian wicca, Christian yoga, and Christian psychics are all oxymorons. I never thought I'd see this level of idolatry in the church. The Bible tells us not to be unequally yoked or to fellowship with unrighteousness because *"what communion hath light with darkness?"* (2 Corinthians 6:14). And that is what's happening here. People are trying to mix good and evil together and it just can't be done. But this is what happens when the church departs from the truth of God's Word. It finds itself on a slippery slope into the occult.

Christian wicca is a blending of Christianity and witchcraft. It borrows from wicca, the Bible, the

Kabbalah, and the gnostic gospels. The Trinity, according to them, is God, the Wiccan Goddess, and Jesus. The frightening thing is that it's popular with high school and college students.[46] Make no mistake. Satan wants our children, and this is a way to reach them.

And it's pure evil. Witchcraft is an abomination in the sight of God. Deuteronomy 18:10-12 makes that very clear, *"There shall not be found among you any one that maketh his son or his daughter to pass through the fire, or that useth divination, or an observer of times, or an enchanter, or a **witch**, Or a charmer, or a consulter with familiar spirits, or a wizard, or a necromancer* (one who consults the dead). *For all that do these things are an **abomination unto the LORD**: and because of these **abominations** the LORD thy God doth drive them out from before thee."*

God considers this sin of witchcraft so egregious that He commanded Israel, in Exodus 22:18, to kill all witches. Why? So, they wouldn't contaminate the nation and lead it into idolatry.

Paul tells us in Galatians 5:19-21 that witchcraft is a work of the flesh and those who practice it, as well as the other things listed, will not *"inherit the kingdom of God."* This should not be taken lightly.

Destination Hell

Micah 5 is a prophecy about Jesus, His birth in Bethlehem and future reign as King after the Tribulation. Verse 12 gives this warning: *"And I* (God) *will cut off* **witchcrafts** *out of thine hand; and thou shalt have no more soothsayers."* When Jesus returns as King of Kings and Lord of Lords, He is going to completely eradicate all witchcraft. The fact that this cleansing will happen before Jesus takes His rightful place on the throne of David indicates it seriousness and how much of an abomination it is in God's eyes.

But the wonderful thing is this, if those practicing witchcraft repent and receive Jesus, they will be forgiven and accepted as His own. He is so loving and kind and will not turn any away, no matter what they have done or how deep into the occult they have gone.

Christian Yoga combines ancient yoga positions, meditation and breathing with Christianity. Yoga's roots are found in spiritual Hinduism. Thus, those practicing yoga are practicing a form of Hinduism. The word "yoga" means, "to yoke or join." What exactly are people yoking to or joining when practicing these positions? They are yoking to or joining with the serpent power or kundalini spiritual force. And the serpent is just another name for Satan! Thus, yoga is not merely a physical exercise but a spiritual one, and that spiritual side is demonic.[47]

Mike Shreve, Christian author and evangelist, was a former guru and yoga teacher who had a yoga ashram (retreat) before coming to the Lord. He wrote *Seven Reasons I No Longer Practice Yoga*, which details the dangers of yoga and its occult connection. He's one who has lived it firsthand and understands its serious significance.

But there are other good books that expose yoga, the New Age, and the occult such as *The Second Coming of the New Age* by Steven Bancarz and Josh Peck And yoga, one of Satan's greatest success stories, has been the vehicle that has opened the door of the church to New Age ideas and the occult.

Christian psychics are suddenly appearing. This is just another name for fortune tellers and mediums, which the Bible condemns. Leviticus 19:31 says, *"Regard not them that have familiar spirits* (psychics*), neither seek after wizards, to be **defiled** by them: I am the LORD your God."* Here, God says that seeking a psychic, whether called Christian or pagan, will defile that person.[48]

Some of these so-called Christian psychics use cards similar to tarot cards to tell a person's future.

Destination Hell

There are also Christian psychics who offer online spiritual readings. Sylvia Brown, now deceased, was one such psychic who used Christian jargon and often spoke of being used by God and the Holy Spirit. She was, however, deep into the occult. Don't be fooled by the use of Scripture and familiar phraseology. Satan knows more Scripture than anyone except God. And he can appear as an angel of light.

1 Timothy 4:1-2 accurately describes what is happening here. *"Now the Spirit speaketh expressly, that in the **latter times** (end-times) some shall depart from the faith, giving heed to seducing spirits, and **doctrines of devils**; Speaking lies in hypocrisy: having their conscience seared with a hot iron."* How sad that so many pastors have opened their doors to the demonic!

Isaiah 5:20 is a sobering warning. *"Woe unto them that call evil good, and good evil: that put darkness for light, and light for darkness; that put bitter for sweet, and sweet for bitter!"* That word "woe" is *howy* in Hebrew and means, "oh, alas, an expression of grief." In other words, it will not go well for those who do this. They will experience grief and a sad ending.

It is heartbreaking to see how far the church has fallen. But Jesus warned about deception and false teachers in the last days (Mark 13:5-6; Luke 21:8). There is now a clearly defined apostate church. It compromises God's Word and promotes sin. Its leaders mock and even attack those who believe the Bible is the inerrant Word of God. It is a church that loves the world and wants to be loved by it. And in this quest to be loved and accepted, and not be cancelled by our culture, it cancels out God. James 4:4 tells us that to be friends with the world is to be an enemy of God. Never has there been such a drastic separation between goats and sheep, between the remnant and apostate church. Jesus said you will know them by their fruits, and that bad trees produce bad fruit (Matthew 7:16-17). And the fruits of the apostate church are repugnant to the Lord.

Tozer's words have never been more apropos: "We who preach the gospel must not think of ourselves as public relations agents sent to establish good will between Christ and the world. We must not imagine ourselves commissioned to make Christ acceptable to big business, the press, the world of sports or modern education. We are not diplomats but prophets, and **our message is not a compromise but an ultimatum.**"[49]

But Protestant institutions are not the only ones affected. Since the Catholic Church admits that tradition is equal to and sometimes above

Destination Hell

Scripture, and because many pagan practices are incorporated in their worship,[50] it was only a matter of time before the demonic teaching of Marxism infiltrated its halls via the Jesuits. Though the Jesuit order began as a vehicle to defend the faith, they gradually shifted direction until their main effort became the promotion of Marxism and Liberation Theology. Their prevailing belief is that "the Scriptures are scientifically inaccurate obscurantisms (uncertainties)."[51] One is reminded of Proverbs 14:12, *"There is a way which seemeth right unto a man, but the end thereof are the ways of death."*

Malachi Martin, a Jesuit, himself, as well as an eminent Catholic theologian, speaker of seventeen languages, member of the Vatican Advisory Council, advisor to three popes, and the Vatican's researcher on the Dead Sea Scrolls, tried to expose their Satanic cabal and activities in the Vatican. In his book, *The Jesuits: The Society of Jesus and the Betrayal of the Roman Catholic Church*, Martin claimed the order wanted to replace the church's teaching with communist doctrine. Martin also claimed that Pope John XXIII made a secret agreement, called the Metz pact, with the USSR to have two Russian-Orthodox prelates participate in the Second Vatican Council.[52] What they had to do in exchange, one can only guess.

To be sure, the Catholic Church has had a checkered past. Martin wrote about how an Illuminati-Masonic (Freemason) group had infiltrated the upper ranks of the Catholic Church and conspired to bring about a one world government. He talked about how prominent clerics worshipped Satan and that some clerical homosexual cliques had joined Satanic covens.

Martin also talked about a secret ceremony, which he called the *"enthronement of Satan,"* which took place at the Vatican in 1963. Its purpose: to ensure two outcomes, Satan's control over Rome and a demonically controlled end-time pope.[53] Pope Paul VI (pope from 1963-1978) called this ceremony, *"the smoke of Satan which has entered the Sanctuary."*[54] Monsignor Luigi Marinelli also backed this up in his 1999 book, *Gone with the Wind in the Vatican*, in which he talks of Catholic priests who made pacts with Satanists and served communion at Black Sabbath masses.[55]

Clearly, Satan has had a foothold in the Vatican for centuries through members of the Freemasons and Illuminati. Pope Pius IX, serving as pope from 1846-1878, called it the *"Synagogue of Satan."* And in 1884, Pope Leo went so far as to issue an encyclical damning these Masonic efforts.[56]

Destination Hell

As mentioned, eventually the Catholic Church came up with its own version of Kingdom Now theology when, in the 1960s, the Latin American wing of the church began preaching Liberation Theology. In addition to it being heavily Marxists, it advocates freedom from economic, social, and political oppression as part of salvation.[57]

And the use of force to ensure it was not off the table. It also upholds that Jesus was more a political revolutionary than Savior.[58]

And in spite of the creation of a modern Jewish state and the prophesies regarding Israel being fulfilled right before our eyes, the Catholic Church's position on the rapture, like some Protestant churches, continues to be based on the misguided writings of St. Augustine who allegorized the Book of Revelation. According to Tim Drake, a Catholic apologist, "The Catholic Church is 'amillennial,' meaning that it believes that Christ's second coming and the last judgment will happen at the same time. According to Colin Donovan, theologian at EWTN, the Church 'teaches that Christ already reigns in eternity (1 Cor 15:24-27) and that in this world his reign . . . is found already in the Church' . . . Therefore, we believe 'He will come again in glory to judge the living and the dead.' Our belief is that the rapture will take place at the end of the world, and not until then."⁵⁹

The Catholic Church also believes it will usher in the return of Christ by purifying the world. And though it does not believe in the millennial reign of Jesus, it believes **they** themselves fill that role and are currently reigning in His place, and even believes **they** oversee God's Kingdom on earth.

To better understand how wrong all these theologies are, we need to take a brief look at the Bible's definition of the Kingdom of God.

Jesus said in Luke 17:20 that, *"The kingdom of God cometh not with observation* (we can't see it) *Neither shall they say, Lo here! Or, Lo there! For, behold the kingdom of God is within you."* So, right off the bat, Jesus told us we won't be able to see His kingdom. Rather, the Kingdom of God is **within** us.

Jesus also said in John 18:36, *"My kingdom is not of this world."* That means it is a heavenly kingdom. Then Jesus told us who can see this kingdom. *"Except a man be born again, he cannot see the kingdom of God,"* (John 3:3). Jesus expounded on this in verse 5, *"Verily, verily, I say unto thee, Except a man be born of water, and of the Spirit, he cannot enter into the kingdom of God."* So, **only** those who are born-again can see the Kingdom or enter it.

Destination Hell

Then Jesus said in Matthew 5:3, *"Blessed are the poor in spirit: for theirs is the kingdom of heaven."* Who are the poor in spirit? They are those who are humble and know they are sinners. They know that spiritually they need a Savior. They are the ones who will possess the kingdom of heaven.

Paul added to this in Romans 14:17. *"For the kingdom of God is not meat and drink: but righteousness, and peace, and joy in the Holy Ghost."* Peace and joy are fruits of the Holy Spirit. Paul further added in 1 Corinthians 15:50, *"that flesh and blood cannot inherit the kingdom of God."* Again, Paul indicated that currently on earth the Kingdom of God is a spiritual kingdom and cannot be appropriated by human means. No revolution or political movement or pope can bring it about. Simple as that.

But while Jesus' kingdom is a heavenly kingdom, those who believe in Him **can** experience His spiritual kingdom on earth via the indwelling Holy Spirit. As born-again believers we have the Kingdom of God inside us. As such, we are ambassadors of God and represent His kingdom on earth. Thus, we are to exhibit the fruit of that Kingdom, which is love, joy, peace, longsuffering, gentleness, goodness, faith, meekness, and temperance, (Galatians 5:22-23).

We also have authority, outlined in Mark 16:17-18, to heal the sick and cast out devils. Additionally, we are to do the good works which God has already planned for us to do (Ephesians 2:10). But our most important mission is to share the gospel and point people to Jesus so they, too, can experience the Kingdom of God within them.

The Great Welsh revival of 1904-05 resulted in the closing of many bars not because Christians purchased them and shuttered them or turned them into ice cream parlors, but because people encountered the true and living God, and repented. They were changed from the inside and no longer wanted to go to bars, thus forcing their closure.[60]

Currently, God's spiritual Kingdom works from the inside out. That's how change occurs. The Holy Spirit changes a person from within. Then slowly that person's outward actions reflect his inner change. Trying to force change from the outside in is called tyranny.

Scripture is clear on when God's physical Kingdom will come to earth. Jesus, Himself, told us that it would be at the end of the Church Age. He talked about the signs of the end times, listing deception, wars, earthquakes, famines, and pestilences. Then He said this in Luke 21:31, *"when ye*

Destination Hell

see these things (these signs of the end times) *come to pass, know ye that the kingdom of God is nigh at hand."*

1 Corinthians 15:24 also confirms this. *"Then cometh the **end**, when he* (Jesus) *shall have delivered up the kingdom to God, even the Father;* **when he shall have put down all rule and all authority and power."** It is Jesus, Himself, Who is going to put down the evil institutions and evil political systems when He returns.

Revelation 11:15 tells us that the seventh trumpet will announce the coming of Jesus' physical Kingdom. *"And the seventh angel sounded; and there were great voices in heaven, saying,* **The kingdoms of this world are become the kingdoms of our Lord,** *and of his Christ; and he shall reign for ever and ever."* Notice, this speaks of two different kingdoms: the current worldly kingdoms and God's Kingdom which will replace the kingdoms of the earth.

Until then, the kingdoms of the world will remain evil and fallen because, as mentioned, they currently belong to Satan. He even offered them to Jesus in the wilderness. *"Again, the devil taketh him* (Jesus) *up into an exceeding high mountain, and sheweth him all the kingdoms of the world, and the glory of them; And saith unto him, All these things will I give thee, if thou wilt fall down and worship me,"* (Matthew 4:8-9).

Jesus didn't tell him they weren't his to give. He knew they belonged to Satan because Adam and Eve relinquished them in the garden when they fell. That's why Satan is called the god of this world (2 Corinthians 4:4) and the prince of this world (John 14:30).

Daniel 7:13-14 speaks of the future kingdom of Jesus. In these verses, Daniel describes a vision he had. *"I saw in the night visions, and, behold, one like the* **Son of man** (Jesus) **came with the clouds of heaven**, *and came to the Ancient of days, and they brought him near before him. And there was given him dominion, and glory, and a kingdom, that all people, nations, and languages, should serve him: his dominion is an everlasting dominion, which shall not pass away, and his kingdom that which shall not be destroyed."* This is when Jesus sets up His earthly kingdom, when He returns with His bride.

And when will we possess the physical Kingdom? When will we see Utopia on earth? Again, Daniel 7:27 is speaking of a time after the Tribulation. *"And the kingdom and dominion, and the greatness of the kingdom under the whole heaven, shall be given to the people of the saints of the most High, whose kingdom is an everlasting kingdom, and all dominions shall serve*

Destination Hell

and obey him (Jesus).*"* So, we will not experience a physical Kingdom of God on earth until we return with Jesus after the seven-year Tribulation.

How far will this apostate church fall? During the time of Hitler, some churches put swastikas on their doors. Can this type of thing happen again when the antichrist steps upon the world's stage? Yes. A church that has lost its mooring will be ripe for the antichrist and false prophet and be willing to accept their lies.

In Matthew 5:13, Jesus said believers are the salt of the earth. But what happens if we lose our saltiness? Jesus gave the answer, *"It is thenceforth good for nothing, but to be cast out, and to be trodden under foot of men."* This is what the apostate church has made itself, good for nothing.

So, if the Bible is the anchor which holds society in check, what happens when that anchor is severed? And what happens to society when the church relinquishes its role and is no longer salt and light? Answer: it becomes the counterfeit narrow road, a road marred by destruction and decay. Galatians 6:7 says it well, *"Be not deceived; God is not mocked: for whatsoever a man soweth, that shall he also reap."*

For too long, the apostate church has been sowing to the flesh, teaching false doctrine, as well as compromising with the world. Thus, it is not surprising to see its destructive effects as our nation descends deeper and deeper into sin.

Some Statistics:

Statistics can be mind-numbing. They can also be skewed so I have tried to use the most credible sources. But if statistics are accurate, they can tell an important story and serve as a barometer of a nation's health. Let's see how we're doing.

In George Barna's 2016 book entitled, *America at the Crossroads*, his investigation found that most Americans are concerned about what's going on in their nation and that they believe "they are living in dangerous and bewildering times."[61]

So right off we see that Americans believe something is amiss. They understand that this is not their grandparent's America. If people believe they are living in "dangerous and bewildering times" that means they are frightened and confused, and that's a sad commentary on any society.

How did we get here?

The biggest clue is that many Americans no longer believe the Bible is relevant. In fact, only 20% of

Destination Hell

Americans are practicing Christians.[62] And only 6% believe in a Biblical world view.[63] That says our godly foundation has eroded. A nation, a government, an institution is only as good as its foundation. When that foundation crumbles, the rest will fall.

People are leaving the church at an alarming rate. Currently, 150 million former American Christians have left the church. And 59% of Christian young adults from ages fifteen to twenty-nine no longer have any interest in religion.[64] Only 40% of those under forty believe Jesus is the only way to salvation,[65] while only 35% of those adults who remain in the church even share the gospel.[66]

From 1990 to 2004, American church membership only grew by 5% while Buddhism grew by 170% and Islam by 109%.[67] What does that say about our churches? It says they are weak, and that people are not being spiritually fed.

And no wonder. According to a 2008 Barna report, only 51% of pastors held a Biblical world view.[68] In addition, a 2021 study indicated that finances were the top issue for 60% of churches.[69]

Where does that put God, His Word, evangelism, and people? If so many pastors don't believe in the Bible and so many churches are concerned about budgets and bottom lines, how can they spiritually inspire anyone? In addition, won't these pastors and churches shy away from any meaningful messages, preferring, instead, to not "rock the boat" and offend anyone? This only perpetuates the cycle of offering easily digestible pablum which changes no one, instead of offering the Living Word, which is more powerful than a two-edged sword (Hebrews 4:12) and changes lives.

Because people are looking for meaning in their lives and not finding it in church, they have turned to other sources. Teens, especially, have been affected. Unaware of the danger, they are turning to the occult. According to Barna, seven million U.S. teens claim to have had an encounter with a spirit entity.[70] This explains why the number of wiccans in America doubles every two and a half years,[71] and is currently the seventh largest religion in the U.S.[72]

But adults are getting into the act as well. According to Gallop, 32% of Americans believe in the paranormal,[73] including 31% who are into astrology.[74] This is an invitation for demon activity and manifestations.

But there is good news, too. Committed Christians are still committed. It is the nominal Christians

Destination Hell

who are defecting.[75] This testifies to the fact that there is both a remnant and apostate church.

Now, let's look at some specific ways our culture has been affected.

Divorce:

According to the 2021 Hive Law report, the U.S. divorce rate is 44.6%. It also claims the divorce rate for committed Christians is 38%,[76] which is much higher than the rate cited in a report by *Got Questions*. Their report came out in April 2021 and was compiled in partnership with George Barna. It found that **less** than 30% of committed Christian marriages end in divorce. That's good news. However, this same report claims that the rate among nominal or cultural Christians is about 20% higher than the national average of 44.6%.[77] I don't understand why. But at the very least it again shows a stark difference between committed Christians (the remnant church) and nominal Christians (the apostate church).

Abortion:

This is a difficult subject and rends the heart. One must always keep in mind the awesome forgiveness of God. Those who have had abortions can and will be forgiven if they bring this sin to Jesus and put it under His blood. Then God will drop it into the sea of forgetfulness and remember it no more. How wonderful is that?

Nevertheless, the stats are disturbing. According to an article in *The Christian Post,* dated November 25, 2015, 70% of women who get abortions claim to be Christians. However, when you break it down to committed Christians verses nominal Christians, that rate becomes 20% for those who attend church weekly and only 6% for those who attend two or more times a week.[78] This matches a much earlier study (2001) by the Alan Guttmacher Institute which states 18% of born-again believers have gotten an abortion.[79]

Again, we see a dichotomy between committed Christians and those who are nominal. And the good news is this: American pro-life churches have gained 38% more membership in the past four decades while the mainline Protestant pro-abortion churches have lost that amount and more, though the stats only go up to 2013.[80]

And here is a shameful fact. For years, the U.S. has been funding abortions worldwide via the UNFPA or United Nations Population Fund which finances both involuntary abortions and sterilizations. President Clinton, in 1993, funded the UNFPA knowing it was a major part of China's

Destination Hell

mandatory population-control program.[81] Obama followed his lead and in just 2015 alone, his administration poured $75 million into UNFPA's coffers. Trump, to his credit, pulled this funding when he became president.[82] But now Biden declared, on January 28, 2021, that America is back in the abortion business and will be funding international organizations promoting abortion.[83]

What a stain on our moral conscience!

Sex outside marriage, and cohabitation before marriage:

This trend illustrates the decline in U.S. morals. Sex outside marriage has always been a reality but considered wrong. The difference now is that it's not only accepted by most people, but not even considered immoral. According to Pew Research, more adults have cohabited than have married. And the bulk of Americans believe cohabitation is acceptable even if it doesn't lead to marriage. And here's the clincher: the majority of Americans believe the same legal rights that apply to married couples should apply to those who cohabitate.[84] And two-thirds or 65% of Americans actually believe cohabitation is a good idea.[85]

How does this translate to the church? Hard to believe, but 41% of practicing Christians also believe cohabitation is a good idea.[86] And according to Pew, "58% of white evangelicals said cohabitation is acceptable if a couple plans to marry." This is especially true of young couples.[87] But no matter how acceptable it has become, it's still called "fornication" and flies in the face of Scripture. There are many passages that speak against it. A few are: Acts 15:20, Romans 1:29 and 1 Corinthians 6:13.

Substance Abuse:

Oh, how substance abuse, both alcohol and drugs, have devastated our nation! The toll is enormous. In 2017, The National Survey on Drug Use and Health found that 19.7 million Americans, twelve and over, had a substance abuse problem.[88] By 2021, that number was estimated to be 31.9 million.[89] Also, since 2000, there have been 700,000 deaths due to drug overdoses. And here's a surprise. Drug use by people over forty is increasing faster than in younger groups.[90]

Alcohol abuse is also on the rise. And as unbelievable as it sounds, some churches have actually formed home or life groups around "craft beer."[91] All this translates to illness, loss of life, the destruction of the family and individuals, loss of income and jobs, psychiatric disorders, and crime, including spousal abuse.

Destination Hell

Regarding the church, Pastoral Care Inc. gives sobering stats on alcohol and substance abuse. While not as high as the stats for the unchurched, it is still appalling. The one thing I question is the percentages assigned to born-again believers which are only about 10% to 15% lower than the world's, while evangelicals are almost 40% lower than the national average. I know born-again believers who are also evangelicals. So, I wonder why Pastoral Care separated the two groups or how they ran their survey or framed their questions. Still, I have included their stats since they seem to be the most up to date.[92]

Pastoral Care also said drug abuse was increasing among pastors as a way of dealing with the stress and difficulties of their job, but it does not provide the actual percentages.[93]

Pornography:

Pornography is a scourge on our nation. According to Barna and Covenant Eyes, over forty million Americans view porn regularly.[94] It has gone mainstream. A 2016 Barna Group study says less and less people find it objectionable. And it seems to be viewed equally by Christians and non-Christians. Young teens (90% of 13–17-year-olds) and young adults (96% of 18–24-year-olds) find nothing wrong with it. And many are engaged in sexting, which means they are receiving or sending texts with sexually explicit images of others or themselves.[95]

The average age a child is first exposed to porn is eleven. By age fourteen, 94% of American children will have been exposed. Youth pastors see this as a serious issue. But the problem doesn't end with them. Among adult male church goers, 68% frequently view porn, while 87% of Christian women say they have watched it at least once.[96]

And here is a sad fact: four in ten pastors watch porn every day,[97] while 50% of evangelical pastors have viewed it at least once during the year.[98]

Even sadder is the fact that priests and ministers have abused young people due to their own perversion. The Catholic Church has settled 17,000 cases of child abuse since the 1980s and paid $4 billion to their victims.[99] In 2019 alone, the U.S. Catholic Church paid out over $281 million in child sex abuse cases.[100] And in 2020, 1,200 members of the clergy in just the Catholic Dioceses of New York and California alone were named as "credibly accused," meaning there was credible evidence they had sexually abused a child.

But if you think it ends at the doorstep of the Catholic Church you would be wrong. According

Destination Hell

to the *Insurance Journal*, "the three companies that insure most Protestant churches in America" actually "handle 260 sex abuse cases a year."[101] And according to the O'Hara Law Firm, Protestant churches are just as guilty as Catholic churches of trying to hide these facts as well as moving suspected pedophiles to other churches.[102]

But this is just the tip of the iceberg. These are only the reported cases. How many go unreported because the victims are too ashamed or traumatized, and therefore suffer in silence?

To say the pornography industry is evil would be an understatement. But it's big business and difficult to snuff out. It has forty-two million websites, and its annual revenue exceeds that of the MLB, NBA and NFL combined![103] And like a cancer, it continues to grow.

All this immorality has led to more immorality. Now, same sex marriage, gender confusion, and horrendous child abuse via sex change hormonal therapy and operations are becoming more common and causing some of our precious young people to no longer know if they are a boy or girl. What a victory for Satan!

And here's a heartbreaker. Did you know America leads the world in both producing and exporting hard core pornography?[104]

So, what do these statistics show? It shows that the church has failed to be light and salt, thus allowing darkness to fall upon America and the world. How many pastors preach on holiness anymore? Or the need to live holy lives? Or on any of the above subjects? Not many. And what a missed opportunity to tell people that struggle with these issues that this is not the life God planned for them. And that God's love is big enough to see them through to the other side via the power of the Holy Spirit. And then help them through prayer, counseling, and providing accountability.

I wonder what harm has been done by failing to preach these messages. Has it become a subtle wink to some weaker in the body, and even in the world, which says these sins are not so bad? And what of the young people who look for guidance, even though they pretend they don't want it? Drugs, pornography, sexting, sexual promiscuity, and pedophilia have seared our national conscience. They have stolen our children's innocence and made them feel used and abused, depressed, alienated, and worthless.

Destination Hell

Is that why teen suicides have increased over the past ten years? It is currently their second cause of death.[105] The CDC has a slightly different number and puts the suicide rate for ten-to-twenty-four-year-olds as the third leading cause of death rather than the second. The American SPCC states that every day 5,400 young people from middle school age to high school age attempt suicide.[106] Our young people are our future, and we are losing them to gross immorality and godless Marxism. What kind of prospects do these stats say our future generations have?

At the very least they reveal the deep decline of American morality, including the church's. For years, America has been pivoting toward secular humanism and paganism. We have turned our back on God. By our laws and actions, we have spit in His face, the face of the very God who has blessed us mightily and made us one of the greatest nations on earth. What, then, is to happen to such a nation?

Our actions have provided God with ample justification to destroy us. Why He hasn't, demonstrates His mercy and longsuffering. But we are nearing the end of the Church Age. Soon, the remnant church will be raptured, leaving behind the apostate church along with the rest of the world. And sometime afterward, when the antichrist confirms a covenant with Israel, the seven-year Tribulation will begin and then God's judgment **will** fall.

But what about all the prophets who have prophesied that a great revival is coming? Surely that will bring everything back to the way it should be?

It's true that numerous American prophets have declared the coming of "the greatest revival in history." But many of these same prophets have been wrong in their other predictions. We saw this after the 2020 election and during the pandemic when many so-called prophets made pronouncements that never came true.

The gift of prophecy should be respected and never abused or taken lightly. Those who claim to have the mantle of a prophet need to be very very careful that what they prophesy is truly from the Lord and not from their own mind or heart.

It's interesting to note that one of the characteristics of the last days apostate church, as revealed in Pergamum and Thyatira, is the rise of false prophets. That does not mean there are no true prophets in these days. But one must remember that according to Deuteronomy 18:22, if a prophet's pronouncements didn't come true that

Destination Hell

prophet had *"spoken it presumptuously."* In other words, a prophet claiming to speak for the Lord must be 100% accurate. If not, that person has failed the test of a true prophet.

Some of these last-day prophets are self-appointed and have never received a mantle from God. Rather, they speak out of their own heart and mind. Others may be like the prophet Balaam who, for gain, power, or glory, have sold their services. Others, like in the days of Jeremiah and Ezekiel, may be operating under a familiar spirit or spirit of divination rather than the Holy Spirit. But whatever the case, it is something we need to be concerned about. And in God's eyes, it is serious.

And the punishment for prophesying falsely is harsh. In Deuteronomy 18:20, God said that if *"the prophet, which shall presume to speak a word in my name, which I have not commanded him to speak, or that shall speak in the name of other gods, even that prophet shall **die**."* These prophets were stoned to death! We don't do that now, but at the very least, these current false prophets are putting themselves on the wrong side of God.

This brings me to the current New Apostolic Reform Movement which is ripe with problems, and which has contributed to this confusion. This movement began about forty years ago under C.

Peter Wagner at Fuller Seminary. Its premise is that God's plan was for prophets and apostles to lead and govern churches, not pastors, evangelists, or teachers. Only under this governmental structure would the church fulfill the Great Commission. By receiving "new" revelations from God, these prophets and apostles would enable the church to establish dominion.[107] We have already seen that Dominion Theology is based on the erroneous belief that Jesus can't return until the church perfects the world.

Those who adhere to New Apostolic Reformation (NAR) thinking often emphasize experience and mysticism over Scripture. They also desire control over politics and culture. It is a disjointed movement, not centrally controlled, with the prevailing belief that apostles are spiritually superior and expressly endowed by God, and that once the church falls under their authority they will become even more supernaturally empowered.[108]

This movement is known by various names: Joel's Army, Manifest Sons of God, Third Wave, Latter Rain, Kingdom Now, Dominionism, Charismatic Renewal and Charismania, but the basic claim is the same, only prophets and apostles have "the power and authority to execute God's plans and purposes on earth."[109]

Destination Hell

And what is this plan of God's? It's for a "now" global church headed by these same prophets and apostles! One must wonder if these people are really looking to build God's Kingdom or their own. These same people are also the biggest proponents of the soon coming "greatest revival in history."[110]

Paul, in Romans 16:17-18, warns the church to avoid those who, through self-interest and selfish motives, cause division through conveying doctrines contrary to the gospel.

2 Peter 2:1 talks about how false prophets will come among the people, and *"bring in damnable heresies, even denying the Lord that bought them, and bring upon themselves swift destruction."*

And in 2 Corinthians 11:13, Paul talks about *"false apostles, deceitful workers, transforming themselves into the apostles of Christ."*

But this is nothing new. It has been going on throughout the Church Age. It even happened in Israel. While Jeremiah prophesized the downfall of Jerusalem at the hands of Babylon, other prophets claimed that all was well, and predicted this destruction would never happen. God's response in Jeremiah 23:21-22; 25-26 was: *"I have not sent these prophets, yet they ran: I have not spoken to them, yet they prophesied. But if they had stood in my counsel, and had caused my people to hear my words, then they should have turned them from their evil way, and from the evil of their doings. . .. I have heard what the prophets said, that prophesy lies in my name, saying, I have dreamed, I have dreamed. How long shall this be in the heart of the prophets that prophesy lies? yea, they are prophets of the deceit of their own heart."*

God was angry with these prophets who kept prophesying only good things and not what God wanted, because it kept His people from taking Jeremiah's warnings seriously and repenting. Consequently, they were not prepared for what was coming.

In Jeremiah 29:8-9, God continued to warn against false prophets. *"For thus saith the LORD of hosts, the God of Israel; Let not your prophets and your diviners, that be in the midst of you, deceive you, neither hearken to your dreams which ye cause to be dreamed. For they prophesy falsely unto you in my name: I have not sent them, saith the LORD."* Then in the very next verse, God again confirms that Jeremiah's prophesies were correct by promising Israel that the coming Babylonian captivity would only last seventy years.

Are we in a parallel time? A time when the church should be repenting, drawing closer to the Lord,

Destination Hell

and be concerned with winning souls because God's wrath is coming? I think so. I know it's a tough sell. People don't like to hear bad news. Even when Jesus predicted the destruction of the Temple and Jerusalem most people didn't believe it. But remember, only five of the ten virgins made it into the marriage supper, then the door was closed.

In Isaiah 30:9-11, God rebuked rebellious Israel for trusting in Egypt (symbolic of the world). He also faulted them for their contempt and disrespect of His Word, and said, *"this is a rebellious people, lying children, children that will not hear the law of the LORD: Which say to the seers, See not; and to the prophets, Prophesy not unto us right things, speak unto us smooth things, prophesy deceits."*

These people didn't want to hear God's Word. They wanted to hear only things that pleased them. They put their trust in false prophets and the world (Egypt), and it led to their destruction.

Then there was Ezekiel. His name means "God will strengthen." He was twenty-five when taken into Babylonian captivity. His book details how God is not only the God of love but the God of judgment. His chapter 13:1-10, 16-17 is especially relevant to our day. *"And the word of the LORD came unto me, saying, Son of man, prophesy against the prophets of Israel that prophesy, and say thou unto them that prophesy out of their own hearts, Hear ye the word of the LORD; Thus saith the Lord GOD; Woe unto the foolish prophets that follow their own spirit, and have seen nothing! O Israel, thy prophets are like the foxes in the deserts. Ye have not gone up into the gaps, neither made up the hedge for the house of Israel to stand in the battle in* **the day of the LORD** *(the Tribulation). They have seen vanity and lying divination, saying, The LORD saith: and the LORD hath not sent them: and they have made others to hope that they would confirm the word. Have ye not seen a vain vision, and have ye not spoken a lying divination, whereas ye say, The LORD saith it; albeit I have not spoken? Therefore thus saith the Lord GOD; Because ye have spoken vanity, and seen lies, therefore, behold, I am against you, saith the Lord GOD. And mine hand shall be upon the prophets that see vanity, and that divine lies: they shall not be in the assembly of my people, neither shall they be written in the writing of the house of Israel, neither shall they enter into the land of Israel; and ye shall know that I am the Lord GOD. Because, even because they have seduced my people, saying* **Peace, and there was no peace**; *and one built up a wall, and lo, others daubed it with untempered morter . . .. To wit, the prophets of Israel which prophesy concerning Jerusalem, and which see visions of peace for her, and there is no peace, saith the Lord GOD. Likewise, thou son of man, set thy face against the daughters of thy people, which prophesy out of their own heart; and prophesy thou against them."*

Destination Hell

WOW! This is saying that because false prophets prophesied that all would be well, that everything was fine, Israel didn't properly prepare for the calamity that was coming. And because of that, God was against these prophets. Aren't our prophets prophesying the same thing? The signs of the end times are all around us and still they are prophesying great revivals and how God's kingdom will be brought to earth by man's hand.

Note, these passages also mention *"the day of the LORD."* This phrase, in both the Old and New Testaments, refer to the end times.

Then Ezekiel 14:2-8 talks about Israel's elders, the religious and political leaders, coming to inquire of Ezekiel. When they do, God tells Ezekiel that they have idols in their heart, and He wasn't going to answer them. These men sought Ezekiel three times to get a word from God, and the only word they got was "repent." God does not hear an unrepentant heart. Psalm 66:18 says, *"If I regard iniquity in my heart, the Lord will not hear me."*

Is there a correlation of what has happened in our country? Do many of our spiritual leaders have idols in their heart? Has fame, wealth, the size of their churches become stumbling blocks? Is that why they can't hear from God? Is this why some pastors and elders, why even our government leaders, judges, etcetera do not hear from God or have their prayers answered? Is this why many prophets have missed God so completely with their erroneous prophecies? We cannot serve two masters. We cannot have idols in our heart and serve God. If we do, we will not hear from Him.

1 John 4:1 reminds us that we are not to believe everyone who claims to prophesy. Rather, we are to test the spirits *"because many false prophets are gone out into the world."* I believe it's time to test the spirits.

So, is the massive global revival that the prophets are talking about going to come? I believe the Holy Spirit will continue bringing people into the saving knowledge of Christ and that there may even be pockets of revival in various places and in various churches prior to the rapture.

But, no, I don't believe there will be a massive revival until **after** the rapture. Before I give my reasons, let me say I have been praying for one last great revival for over thirty years. I want there to be a revival, so I hope I'm wrong. I **want** to be wrong. But I am not a prophet and must go by what I believe the Word of God says.

Destination Hell
What I base this on:

Paul, in his letter to Timothy described what the last-days church would be like. And yes, he was talking about the church and not the world as indicated by several key phrases which I have highlighted. It is a sad and sobering picture. *"This know also, that in **the last days** (the end times) perilous times shall come. For men shall be lovers of their own selves, covetous, boasters, proud, blasphemers, disobedient to parents, unthankful,* **unholy***, Without natural affection, trucebreakers, false accusers, incontinent, fierce, despisers of those that are good, Traitors, heady, highminded, lovers of pleasures more than* **lovers of God; Having a form of godliness**, *but denying the power thereof: from such turn away. For of this sort are they which creep into houses, and lead captive silly women laden with sins, led away with divers lusts,* **Ever learning, and never able to come to the knowledge of the truth,***"* (2 Timothy 3:1-7).

This is the last days apostate church. They are unholy. This is noteworthy because while nonbelievers are unholy and not expected to be holy, believers are supposed to be. But here we see these believers are not holy, either. They are lovers of God but love pleasure and other things more. Thus, He is not preeminent in their lives. They still have a form of godliness, in other words, a form of religion, but deny the power, which I take to mean deny the power of the Holy Spirit who enables us to live a Christian life. These people talk the talk but don't walk the walk. And even though they may be sitting under various ministries supposedly learning something, it doesn't bring them to the Truth, which is Jesus.

Paul, in 1 Timothy 4:1-2 continued to warn Timothy about the coming church apostasy. *"Now the Spirit speaketh expressly, that in the* **latter times** (the last days) *some shall depart from the faith, giving heed to seducing spirits, and doctrines of devils; Speaking lies in hypocrisy, having their conscience seared with a hot iron."*

Paul goes on in 2 Timothy 4:2, exhorting Timothy to preach the gospel. Then Paul tells him what's going to happen to the church in verses 3-4. *"For the time will come when they* (those in the church) *will not endure sound doctrine; but after their own lusts shall they heap to themselves teachers, having itching ears; And they shall turn away their ears from the truth, and shall be turned unto fables."* That word "fables" in Greek is *muthos* and means, "a tale, fiction." So, in the last days, people are going to be listening to fiction, to lies and falsehoods.

Paul was not only speaking about what would happen throughout church history, but especially what would occur in the last days or "latter times."

Destination Hell

And we have seen this unfold before our eyes. Many people now go to church wanting to be entertained and hear a "feel good" message rather than sound doctrine. They are even listening to doctrines of demons which tell them things like wicca, yoga, and psychics are Christian, and that there are many roads to God.

Jesus said in Matthew 7:21-23, *"Not every one that saith unto me, Lord, Lord, shall enter into the kingdom of heaven; but he that doeth the will of my Father which is in heaven. Many will say to me in that day, Lord, Lord, have we not prophesied in thy name? And in thy name have cast out devils? And in thy name done many wonderful works? And then will I profess unto them,* **I never knew you; depart from me, ye that work iniquity.**" What a tragic day that will be for them!

Also, recall how in Revelation, Jesus laid out church history in His seven letters. The characteristics of the church kept *"from the hour of temptation* (Tribulation), *which shall come upon all the world, to try them that dwell upon the earth,"* (Revelation 3:10), are faithfulness to His Word, persecution, and weakness (few miracles). Nowhere is it characterized by a great revival.

Then there's Jesus' description of the last days. He said they would be like the days of Noah and Lot. And while Noah was a preacher of righteousness for decades, giving the people time to repent while he built the ark, there was no repentance, no revival. And regarding Lot, when the angels looked for ten righteous people in Sodom so he wouldn't have to destroy it, he couldn't find them. Both indicate there will be no revival prior to the Tribulation. But the greatest revival the world has ever seen will come after the rapture.

But what about the promise of the Holy Spirit's outpouring which was to come in two waves? Only the first was fulfilled. What about the second?

Both Joel 2:28-32 and Acts 2:17-21 talk about this second outpouring of the Holy Spirit. And both say it will occur before the Day of the Lord, which does not refer to only one event, but encompasses the Tribulation, God's judgment and His physical return to earth as King.

Acts 2 repeats the promise God made in Joel. It says, *"And it shall come to pass **in the last days**, saith God, I will pour out of my Spirit upon all flesh: and your sons and your daughters shall prophesy, and your young men shall see visions, and your old men shall dream dreams: And on my servants and on my handmaidens I will pour out **in those days** of my Spirit; and they shall prophesy:* ***And I will shew wonders in heaven above and signs in the earth***

Destination Hell

beneath, blood and fire, and vapour of smoke: The sun shall be turned into darkness, and the moon into blood, before that great and notable day of the Lord come. And it shall come to pass that whosoever shall call on the name of the Lord shall be saved."

The only difference between Acts 2 and Joel 2:28-32 is that Joel calls the day of the Lord "terrible" rather than "notable." Both words are important and mean different things. That word "terrible" in Hebrew is *yare* and means, "to fear, cause to frighten, make afraid, revere." It denotes something terrible, something horrifying that makes people afraid while at the same time it denotes something worthy of worship, veneration, and reverence.

On the other hand, notable is *epiphanes* in Greek and means, "to shine, become visible, give light." Do these contradict each other? No. Rather, they give a full picture of the Day of the Lord. It will be a fearful, terrifying, and awe-inspiring day for those who don't know Jesus, but wonderful for those who do because He will finally be revealed and will shine on earth, ridding it of evil and ushering in a time of great peace and joy.

So, when will it happen?

Both Joel and Acts give the same clues. It will happen when there will be wonders in the heavens and earth. It will happen when there will be *"blood, and fire, and vapour of smoke;"* when the sun is darkened and the moon looks like blood.

Since the Bible explains itself, it gives the timeframe of when this wonderful revival will occur. It's in Revelation 6:12-14 which describes the early part of the seven-year Tribulation. The sixth seal judgment is opened by Jesus and here's what happens: *"And I* (John) *beheld when he* (Jesus) *had opened the sixth seal, and lo, there was a great earthquake; and the* **sun became black as sackcloth of hair, and the moon became as blood: And the stars of heaven fell unto the earth,** (signs in heaven) *even as a fig tree casteth her untimely figs, when she is shaken of a mighty wind. And the heaven departed as a scroll when it is rolled together; and every mountain and island were moved out of their places* (more wonders and signs in heaven and earth)."

The Tribulation will be a horrendous time on earth, but God in His mercy will pour out His Spirit on all those left after the rapture and will give them an opportunity to come to Him. What a wonderful promise! These Scriptures state that before Jesus returns after the Tribulation, there will be one last great revival! And all those who

Destination Hell

sincerely call upon Him will be saved. How gracious is our God! How merciful!

But how will God accomplish this? Again, Revelation tells us. First, God will seal 144,000 Jewish witnesses, called "servants of God." And 12,000 will come from every tribe of the twelve tribes of Israel except for Dan (Revelation 7:4-8). God will also send two witnesses who prophesy and have the power to keep back the rain, turn water into blood, smite the earth with plagues, and kill anyone who tries to stop them (Revelation 11:3-6). And finally, God will send an angel and have him *"fly in the midst of heaven, having the everlasting gospel to preach unto them that dwell on the earth, and to every nation, and kindred, and tongue, and people,"* (Revelation 14:6).

It's interesting to note that after the 144,000 are sealed by God in Revelation 7:4-8, the very next verse (Revelation 7:9) describes a massive praise and worship service in heaven, implying that multitudes have been saved prior to losing their lives in the horrendous events that were occurring on earth. It says, *"After this (after the sealing of the 144,000) I (John) beheld, and lo, a great multitude, which no man could number, of all nations, and kindreds, and people, and tongues, stood before the throne, and before the Lamb, clothed with white robes, and palms in their hands."* This sounds like the "greatest revival in history" to me!

This is the length our good and kind and merciful God will go in order to give everyone a chance to come to Him. He desires that none should perish. He wants to give everyone a chance before the "Great and Terrible Day of the LORD."

Gary Stearman, in his article entitled, *The Symmetry of Biblical History*, explains how "God operates in terms of foreordained patterns that resonate with the themes of prophecy, yet to be fulfilled."[111] In other words, Biblical history is often cyclical.

This pattern is seen in the verses of Joel and Acts. The first great outpouring of the Holy Spirit or the 1st Pentecost fell upon Jews who then when out and evangelized the world. The 2nd Pentecost will also fall upon Jews, the 144,000 who then go out and evangelize the world. The 1st Pentecost came when the world was pagan and prior to the destruction of Jerusalem in 70 A.D. and its corrupt political and religious leaders. The second great outpouring or 2nd Pentecost will come after the rapture of the church when the world is pagan and prior to the destruction of the corrupt world and religious system of the antichrist.

Destination Hell

But has America really become pagan? Yes. And becoming more so every day. Let's look at some proofs.

In 1980, the Georgia Guidestones, a Stonehenge-like structure, were erected in Elbert County, Georgia. It unabashedly declared the same demonic and pagan aspirations of the Illuminati, the Freemasons, various secret societies and of those who seek a New World Order. It advocated global governance, population control (under 500 million), and eugenics (DNA tampering and selective breeding to create a more desirable human).[112]

It also promoted "environmentalism—exalting the creation over the Creator and rights of humans," and advocated for a new spirituality, the Religion of Reason.[113] This is the same religion of reason and science that secret society members, Sir Walter Raleigh and Sir Francis Bacon espoused.

Since then, the world has seen an explosion of Gaia worship. In Gary Stearman's article, *Gaia Worship is Thriving*, dated August 2014, he chronicled the rise of the "green" religion; how more people have begun to credit the earth for giving life. He also talked about the National Religious Partnership for the Environment and how its "goal is to integrate green beliefs with our traditional religious beliefs."[114]

In February 2017, witches all over America gathered at midnight (EST) to curse President Donald Trump. They also planned to meet each night, as the crescent moon diminished, to further curse him in hopes of ridding the country of him and his administration.[115] I'm not suggesting that evil groups have not met in the past to bring down governments or leaders. But what was different about this was their openness and blatant flaunting of their intentions.

Also in 2017, Anthony Levandowski created the Way of the Future Church, a church that worships artificial intelligence as god. He said, "If artificial intelligence is a billion times more intelligent than humans, what else would you call it (but God)."

According to a News Punch 2018 article by Baxter Dmitry, Oxford University declared Satanism to be the "fastest growing religion in America."[116]

Then in 2019, *Prophecy Watcher* came out with an article by Carl Teichrib entitled "Report from the Toronto Parliament of the World's Religions" in which he recorded his observations after attending that Parliament in November 2018. What was obvious was the sheer number of pagans represented. In fact, according to Teichrib, the very first day was spent, "reminding us how our loyalty and duty must be to Mother Earth."

Destination Hell

Teichrib witnessed native Americans calling on their ancestor spirits, Wiccan priestesses praying, pagan workshops, rants on the evils of "white, Euro-centric Christianity," a woman, claiming to be a Baptist minister, using Buddhist techniques to curse our leaders, and the overwhelming message that, "we are nobody's savior except our own." And all this was delivered in a tone of rancor and hatred.[117]

Then there's the Harry Potter books which have left a huge scar on our nation. The U.S. military currently has so many recruits who grew up with these books and are devoted witches, that the military "is allowing them to have their own witchcraft services." Tony Garland, high priest of his coven, boasts it's always packed with "basic military trainees" who "are studying witchcraft in his circle."[118]

Also, instead of Utopia on earth, 2 Timothy 3:1 talks of "perilous times" in the last days. And 2 Timothy 3:13 tells us that in these last days things are going to get worse. *"But evil men and seducers shall wax worse and worse, deceiving, and being deceived."*

So, the Bible tells us the world will only get darker not better. It also tells us that even the church will deteriorate, becoming less able to endure sound doctrine (2 Timothy 3:1-13; 2 Timothy 4:3-4).

In Matthew 24, Jesus, when speaking to His apostles about the end times, talked about wars and rumors of wars, about famines, pestilence, and earthquakes. Then He said this in Matthew 24:11-12, *"And many false prophets shall rise, and shall deceive many. And because iniquity shall abound, the love of many shall wax cold."*

Unfortunately, all the above is only the tip of the iceberg. Bearing that in mind, the weak and persecuted remnant church is hardly the one to spearhead the "greatest revival in history." It is far more likely to come via the 144,000 Jewish evangelists set on fire by God, the two witnesses who can do miracles and display incredible signs and wonders, and the flying angel who proclaims the gospel throughout the world. Then millions will *"call upon the name of the Lord and be saved."* How wonderful!

But as wonderful as that is, the fact remains these people will still have to go through a horrendous time on earth. Most will be martyred or die from these events. This is not what we want for our family, friends, neighbors, or co-workers. So, now is the time for the body of Christ to wake up; to draw closer to God; to leave churches that don't

Destination Hell

preach the true gospel; to pray earnestly for others; and when opportunity permits, to share the gospel with the unsaved and warn them so that God's fishing net will be filled and these people will be spared the coming wrath.

Ephesians 5:15-16 reminds us to, *"walk circumspectly, not as fools, but as wise, Redeeming the time, because the days are evil."* Let it be so, Lord!

The Broad Way

Henry G. Bohn, in his 1855, *A Handbook of Proverbs*, wrote that "the road to hell is paved with good intentions." The truth is this road is paved with rebellion against God since after the Fall rebellion became the natural inclination of our hearts. As fallen people living in a fallen world, everyone over the age of accountability is condemned, which means separation from God and an eternal future in hell and the lake of fire. The only remedy is Jesus. John 3:18-19 says, *"He that believeth on him (Jesus) is not condemned: but he that believeth not is **condemned already**, because he hath not believed in the name of the only begotten Son of God. And this is the condemnation, that light is come into the world, and men loved darkness rather than light, because their deeds were evil."*

Since salvation is not corporate as some cults would have us believe, and doesn't fall like snow, involuntarily covering everyone beneath it, the only way to get off this enormous road to hell is by **personally** believing in Jesus and accepting what He did. It involves free will and a conscious decision. But many will not accept this costly but free gift because it means giving up their evil lifestyle. This is exacerbated by the fact that the whole world is under Satan's control.

Thus, the road to perdition is massive. Jesus acknowledged this in Matthew 7:13-14 when He said, *"Enter ye in at the strait gate:* **for wide is the gate, and broad is the way, that leadeth to destruction***, and many there be which go in thereat: Because strait is the gate, and narrow is the way, which leadeth unto life, and few there be that find it."*

America has been on this superhighway for some time. Evil men with evil agendas have pushed our great nation to the brink and have taken many people along for the ride.

World domination has been Satan's plan for centuries. He hates God, and uses his skill, intelligence, and power to thwart God's plans and destroy the things He loves. To that end, Satan has powerful, secret groups working behind the scenes, with people positioned in high places. His first attempt was in Babylon with Nimrod, but it didn't stop there.

I described these secret societies and their impact on our nation in my book, *The Coming Deception,* and will include a small portion here since it's important to understand what is happening now,

Destination Hell

and why our own government wants to destroy us and our nation.

First, we need to comprehend the dual nature of America's foundation. One group wanted to create a *New Atlantis*, the other, a *New Jerusalem*. When Puritans, who saw themselves as a "kingdom of believers," embarked on the Mayflower to establish a *"New Jerusalem"* in America and share the gospel, Satan's followers were busy establishing a *"New Atlantis."*

To jump start it, Sir Walter Raleigh, a member of an occult secret society, organized and financed the Roanoke Colony.[119] It failed. Then came Jamestown, established by the Virginia Company of London, a company also founded by members of secret, occult societies and whose membership included Sir Francis Bacon. Their goal was conquest, trade, enrichment, and the creation of a springboard for a one world government modeled after the mythical high-tech, pagan *Atlantis*, also considered the "Golden Age of Osiris (Nimrod)." America was to become the launching pad for the New World Order.[120] All this factors into American Freemason ideology.[121]

Both Sir Walter Raleigh and Sir Francis Bacon played major roles in Britain's colonization of North America, and both were members of the same occult society, School of Night.[122] Bacon went on to become a Freemason and eventually headed England's branch[123] as its first Grand Master. Associated with Bacon was Dr. John Dee, Queen Elizabeth I's astrologer who sought secret knowledge through contact with demons.[124] It was Dee who introduced England's royalty to the occult.

American Masonry can be traced to Sir Francis Bacon's England of 1561-1626. Since then, a Luciferian network has been working to implement Satan's plan.

Manly P. Hall, (1901-1990) who was a 33rd Degree Freemason, author, astrologer and mystic, described Masonry as, "a fraternity within a fraternity—an outer organization concealing an inner brotherhood of the elect . . . it is necessary to establish the existence of these two separate yet interdependent orders, the one visible and the other invisible. The visible society is a splendid camaraderie of 'free and accepted' men enjoined to devote themselves to ethical, educational, fraternal, patriotic, and humanitarian concerns. The invisible society is a secret and most august fraternity whose members are dedicated to the service of a mysterious arcanum arcanorum (a secret or mystery). In each generation, only a few are accepted into the inner sanctuary of the work."[125]

Destination Hell

Hall also said, "The rise of the Christian Church broke up the intellectual pattern of the classical pagan world. By persecution . . . it drove the secret societies into greater secrecy: the pagan intellectuals then reclothed their original ideas in a garment of Christian phraseology, but bestowed the keys of the symbolism only upon those duly initiated and bound to secrecy by their vows."[126]

Masonry is an organization of lies and deception. Using Christian phraseology, the higher ups deceive their members as well as the world-at-large. Even so, their true nature and purpose are clearly reflected by Masonry's own Supreme Council when describing the levels of membership. It calls the 1st to 11th degree of their membership, 'slaves of **Lucifer**,' and the 12th to 22nd 'pontiffs of **Lucifer**.' As for those who become a 33rd degree Mason, they refer to themselves as being 'a sovereign of **Lucifer**'."[127]

While members of the lower ranks are kept in darkness, if an initiate reaches the highest level, it all becomes clear. Manly P. Hall said it this way, "When the Mason . . . has learned the mystery of his Craft, the seething energies of **Lucifer** are in his hands." Thus, when Masons bow before The Worshipful Master and recite their vows during their various initiations, they are making those vows to Satan. In addition, high ranking Masons understand that when they pray or refer to the Lord or God, they are referring to Satan. In addition, many belong to the Illuminati and are Satanists who claim to possess the Light of Lucifer. Additionally, many in the Illuminati claim to be descendants of the Nephilim.

Albert Pike, Sovereign Grand Commander of the Scottish Rite (a branch of Freemasonry) and one who had achieved Masonry's highest degree, openly stated, "The true and pure philosophic religion is the belief in **Lucifer**."[128]

Note the continuous references to Lucifer. These secret societies are not benign organizations. Their aim is to control the world's governments, including America's. Manly P. Hall left no doubt of this by saying, "Men bound by a secret oath to labor in the cause of world democracy decided that in the **American colonies** they would plant the roots of a new way of life. Brotherhoods were established to meet secretly, and they quietly and industriously conditioned America to its destiny for leadership in a free world."[129]

Beginning with Sir Walter Raleigh and Sir Francis Bacon, secret societies have been quietly working to bring about their *New Atlantis*, their idea of Utopia, a perfect society without the God of the Bible. And from that time to this, our history is

Destination Hell

marred with their handiwork. Their goal of a religion of reason and science are etched in the Georgia Guidestones, which were discussed in the last chapter.

Half of the signers of the Declaration of Independent were Masons, as was America's first president, George Washington. Other U.S. presidents, both Democrat and Republican, were members, as well as heads of banks, newspapers, media, corporate CEOs, politicians, and heads of state. And their ranks continue to grow.

Washington D.C. itself is full of Masonic symbolism. Designed by a Masonic architect, it is laid out in a pentagram. Many federal buildings have Masonic cornerstones, and all "bear a Masonic plaque."[130] The back of the U.S. dollar also includes Masonic symbolism, which refer to the New World Order.[131]

Manly Hall openly admitted this when he said, "Not only were many of the founders of the United States Government Masons, but they received aid from a secret and august body existing in Europe, which helped them to establish this country for a peculiar and particular purpose known only to the initiated few. The Great Seal is the signature of this exalted body—unseen and for the most part unknown—and the unfinished pyramid upon its reverse side is a trestle board setting forth symbolically the task to the accomplishment of which the United States Government was **dedicated from the day of its inception.**"[132]

The Luciferian elites have made great progress in ushering in the *"New Atlantis."* The influence of their secret societies can be seen everywhere from the European Parliament building called the "Tower of Eurobabel," to the statue of the goddess, Europa, riding a bull outside EU headquarters in Brussels.[133] And powerful organizations such as the U.N., Bilderbergs, Club of Rome, and Trilateral Commission are all populated with Freemasons or members of other secret societies, and make up the "shadow government." All have the same goal: to bring about a New World Order based on socialism and communism.

Indeed, in 2017, when 4000 world leaders met in Dubai for the World Government Summit, an "Arch of Baal" was erected in honor of the occasion.[134] Baal was considered the most powerful of the ancient Canaanite gods. They called him the "giver of life." What does that say about those leaders or where they believe their power lies? It was not the Creator, the God of Abraham, Isaac, and Jacob they honored, but a pagan deity of stone.

Destination Hell

But make no mistake, these people are influential. Magazine editor, David Rothkopf, who wrote about the global elites, claims that between six to seven thousand wealthy globalists "run the world's governments, largest corporations, powerhouses of international finance, media, and religions."[135]

No wonder they hate nationalism. As long as people love their country and believe in national sovereignty, how can they bring about a one world government which will also include a one world religion? It's a package deal.

David Spangler, a leader in the New Age Movement, gave insight into what the One World Religion will look like when he said, "No one will enter the New World Order unless he or she will make a pledge to worship **Lucifer**. No one will enter the New Age unless he will take a **Luciferian Initiation**."[136]

Again, we see the reference to Lucifer.

Remember the *Communist Manifesto* and *Humanist Manifesto* were taken from the demonically inspired *Illuminati Manifesto*. Their common seventeen goals have already been listed in the previous chapter. Their end objective is to rule mankind and the world by destroying all religion and governments and setting up their own.[137]

That necessitates the destruction of America as a superpower. Apparently, as the springboard to the *New Atlantis*, it has served its purpose and must be leveled in order to accommodate a larger power — that of a One World Government. To that end, those behind-the-scenes-elites have worked to abolish private property and inheritances, destroy Christianity, patriotism, family life and marriage, create chaos, discord, confusion and increase the power of bureaucracies.[138]

Is it any wonder why so many politicians, both Democrat and Republican, are not working for our good or the good of America? Why, in fact, they are deliberately destroying our country? As globalists, they need to weaken our nation for a one world government to be possible. They also need to destroy our faith in the God Who created us.

The Bible tells us that a house divided cannot stand. That's what we are seeing, America divided as both foundations, one founded on godly principles, the other on forbidden secret knowledge, vie for dominance. And because so much of the church has lost its light and saltiness, members of these demonic societies now dominate America.

Destination Hell

Some signposts of their handiwork and the decline of America:
1) The disbanding of the Legion of Decency and further depravity of the movie industry
2) the sexual revolution of the '60s
3) removal of prayer in school
4) *Roe v. Wade* and the legalization of abortion
5) the legalization of same-sex-marriage

The Legion of Decency:

The Legion was founded by Catholic Archbishop John McNicholas in 1934. Later, Protestant groups joined to help regulate a film industry that seemed incapable of regulating itself. Films flagged as objectionable or indecent by the Legion meant millions would refuse to see it, thus affecting the movie's bottom line.

Up until the early '60s, the Legion of Decency had a substantial effect on the movie industry. But by the mid '60s, its influence had waned, and in 1965, it was reorganized into the National Catholic Office for Motion Pictures (NCOMP). Later, the NCOMP morphed into other entities, but they never achieved the same clout as the Legion. Its final form, The Office of Film and Broadcasting, terminated operations in 2010,[139] leaving Hollywood to further disintegrate into a total cesspool.

Sylvia Bambola

The ill effects of Hollywood and the entertainment industry cannot be overemphasized. Neuromarketing is the big thing and has been for years. It is subliminal messaging designed to manipulate people. Hollywood is a master at it and has used both subliminal and overt messaging to peddle their demonic ideology.

Early on, they portrayed Christians as buffoons or mentally unstable, thus trying to promote a disdain for Christianity. They then began portraying parents as incompetent fools, while children appeared smarter and wiser, thus promoting disrespect for parental authority and mocking the traditional family structure. Then the messages became even more overt, promoting premarital sex followed by adulterous sex, homosexuality, and lesbianism, then the sexualizing of children. Now, we are bombarded by messages and images of violence and the occult.

But Hollywood has always been comfortable with the occult. Many have sold their souls for fifteen minutes of fame. And while Hollywood has always had its share of practicing Satanists, they are now coming out of the closet in droves, thus guaranteeing their movies will continue to be filled with vice and immorality.

Destination Hell

A side note: A holly tree is both ornamental and evergreen. Slow growers, they can reach heights of fifty feet, and live up to three hundred years. Druids viewed them as symbols of eternal life and fertility. Believed to have magical properties, its wood was used to make sorcerers' wands. That's why, in the 1920s, the motion picture industry named itself, "Hollywood."[140] And it has indeed become a "sorcerer's wand."

But Satan also has his hand in the music industry. Hard rock, by their own admission, is dominated by Satanists. And much of rap music glorifies sex, violence, and disrespect toward both women and police. Television is no better, nor are secular books that promote sin and hopelessness.

Regarding the book industry, recently, the ABA, the American Booksellers Association, issued a pathetic and spineless apology for their "serious, violent incident." Just what was this "serious, violent incident"? It was mailing flyers promoting an anti-trans book entitled, *Irreversible Damage: The Transgender Craze Seducing Our Daughters*. Written by Abigail Shrier, it was originally hailed as "one of the most important books of our time."[141] Its censorship provides an ominous warning for the book industry and free speech.

Through neuromarketing, subliminal messages in movies, books, music, TV, video games, and advertisements have had a devastating effect. A 163-billion-dollar industry, neuromarketing is based on science, and it works. Their studies define how to manipulate people's brains for a desired outcome whether it's behavioral or psychological. It can affect how you spend your money, what products draw you, how to evoke certain emotions through smell, sight, and sound.

The sexual revolution:

This revolution of the 1960s was a turning point for our nation. It was a time of "sex, drugs, and rock 'n' roll." Attitudes toward morality and sex shifted, impacting homes and marriages. It also fueled feminist groups and energized the fledgling gay rights movement.[142] At the same time, Bob Dylan was telling "everyone" to get stoned, and they did. Young people, especially, began experimenting with illicit drugs beginning with marijuana and LSD, followed by amphetamines, barbiturates, cocaine, then heroin in the '70s.[143] By the late '60s, hard rock, a subgenre of classic rock, became more and more popular, with many of its singers being practicing Satanists.

Destination Hell
The removal of school prayer:

Not surprising, the '60s also saw the removal of school prayer after atheist Madalyn Murray O'Hair filed a lawsuit against Baltimore's school board. The 1963 case, *Murray v. Curlett*, was upheld by the U.S. Supreme Court in a vote of 8 to 1. And here's the tragedy. Not one Christian church or Christian organization presented a case to the courts supporting school prayer![144] It's worth noting that from 1941-1971, the Supreme Court was controlled by Masons. And four Mason Supreme Court judges were able to influence the Court's decision to remove prayer and God from our schools.[145]

The legalization of abortion and same-sex marriage:

In 1973, the U.S. Supreme Court declared abortion was protected under the constitution in the landmark case, *Roe v. Wade*.[146] And since 1973, over 62 million precious babies have been murdered in America,[147] making us a nation of blood and one that has made a covenant with death.

And on June 26, 2015, the Supreme Court, in *Obergefell v. Hodges*, declared that according to the Fourteenth Amendment, same-sex couples had a fundamental right to marry, changing the time-honored Biblical definition of marriage.[148]

It's clear that most of the seventeen strategies listed in the *Illuminati, Communist,* and *Humanist Manifestos* have already been achieved. It's also clear that our nation is on the road to perdition.

Jesus said you would know a good tree and bad tree by their fruits (Matthew 7:16-20).

Let's look at the fruits produced.

Children are a gift from God (Psalm 127:3-5). Satan knows this. He also knows they are every nation's future. That's why one of his primary aims is to destroy them. And he starts in the womb. One of his greatest American success stories is *Roe v. Wade*. To ensure its continuing triumph, he keeps abortion a hot button topic, pushing back against any sign of its being weakened.

Months ago, in the dead of night, a far-left group called INDECLINE invaded Eureka Springs, Arkansas, in order to drape the sixty-five-foot statue, Christ of the Ozarks, with a blasphemous banner, "God bless abortions." To add insult to injury, they plan to put this message on t-shirts and sell them as a fund raiser for Arkansas Abortion Support Network.[149]

Destination Hell

Currently, there's a push by leaders in liberal cities to include abortion in their "paid leave" policies. By slipping it into their "bereavement leave" for women who have had miscarriages or stillborn deliveries they are, in effect, requiring taxpayers to fund it.[150]

Satanists have supported abortion for years, even teaming up with Planned Parenthood in 2017 to help them expand their Missouri clinics. And in 2020, the Satanic Temple came out and tied abortion to their official rituals.[151] So, when Texas passed their "heartbeat" law, they were outraged.

What that law codifies is that abortions after six weeks are illegal, and after that specified time, citizens may take legal action against those who perform them or those who aid others in performing them. Portland's city council, along with Mayor Ted Wheeler, immediately sprang into action by proposing a ban on Texan goods as well as travel to their state.[152]

Right behind them was the Satanic Temple who protested that this violated their "religious freedom" by impeding their right to have official ritual abortions. They claim these "rituals" should be protected under Religious Liberty laws. Their spokesman, Lucien Greaves, believes this is a "battle of competing religious viewpoints."[153]

We must understand that what Satanists are fighting for here is the right to perform **human sacrifices**! They are killing unborn babies in Satanic rituals. And the added shock is how brazenly the Satanic Temple admits this. That should horrify everyone.

The Texas abortion ban has also created a frenzy among liberal lawmakers. On September 24, 2021, to the cheers of Speaker Pelosi, the U.S. House Democrats passed the most extreme pro-abortion bill of all time. If passed in the Senate, this radical bill will legalize "partial-birth abortion, dismembering babies, decapitating babies, and targeting babies in the womb for any reason."[154]

But if Satan can't destroy our children in the womb, he will try other means. Since the 19th century, Satan has been infiltrating our schools. Though many dedicated and sincere teachers remain, he has successfully inserted his anti-God, anti-Christian lackeys as staff, teachers, principals, and school board members. He has also successfully incorporated his ideology and philosophies into official school curriculum.

This became evident by the '60s. Colleges and universities began offering liberal courses that questioned morality. Suddenly, topics like "situational ethics" sprang up. So did the push to replace

Destination Hell

Biblical morality with the faulty science of evolution as a controlling foundation.[155] The attitude was if we are just an accident of nature, the product of something that crawled out of the primordial ooze, why shouldn't we make up our own moral codes?

Colossians 2:8 cautions us against this very thing. *"Beware lest any man spoil you through philosophy and vain deceit, after the tradition of men, after the rudiments of the world, and not after Christ."*

But the church took no notice. As a result, we now have colleges producing students incapable of honest and respectful debate, and who need "safe spaces" where they can retreat with their "blankies and playdough" to keep from hearing ideas they don't like. And some colleges even encourage students to use totalitarian tactics to silence differing opinions.

Early indoctrination is key. It's one of the cornerstones of communism. A young tree is easier to bend than an older one. That's why Vladimir Lenin said, "Give me just one generation of youth, and I'll transform the whole world."[156]

Hitler also understood this principle when he said, "Let me control the textbooks and I will control the state. The state will take youth and give to youth its own education and its own upbringing. Your child belongs to us already."[157] The Hitler Youth program and League of German Girls were implementations of this philosophy.

America's public schools are pushing their evil agenda on younger and younger children. And while they outspend almost every other nation, real education is suffering. Pew Research provides a dismal picture. In 2015, American students tested 24th in both science and reading, and 39th in math. That means twenty-four and thirty-nine other countries did better than our children in those areas.[158]

If California is any indication, these scores will not improve anytime soon. Their new guidelines for teaching math, which originally suggested it "upholds white supremacy and that numbers are racist," (since removed) will dumb down their math classes. Using philosophies found in Critical Race Theory to "apply social justice principles to math lessons," it will suspend the grading of students in favor of simply allowing them to "view their learning as a process." California also plans to dispense with all accelerated math programs.[159]

This did not sit well with 746 mathematicians and scientists who sent an open letter to the California Department of Education claiming their proposed

Destination Hell

changes and "one size fits all" approach would most certainly "place K-12 public school students at a disadvantage compared with their international and private school peers" and ultimately "cause lasting damage to STEM education in the country and exacerbate inequality by diminishing access to the skills needed for social mobility."[160] Will this letter change anything? Doubtful.

But if ideology is the measuring rod, then our public schools have gotten their money's worth. While most older Americans are still proud of their county, according to *Issues & Insights*, most young people are not. In fact, only 36% of them claim to be proud of America.[161]

Not surprising, college students and young adults were socialist Bernie Sanders' biggest supporters in his bid for the Presidency. During the Clinton-Sanders race, a whopping 59% of them favored Sanders,[162] as did 57% in the Sanders-Biden contest.[163] That means an incredible number of our young don't value the freedoms America offers. Instead, they are enamored by socialism even though this ideology has failed the world over. It has impoverished the nations that tried it and left them with tyrannical overlords. Millions were killed or imprisoned during the iron-fisted reign of Lenin, Stalin, Mao Zedong, Nicolae Ceausescu and

Pol Pot, all communist dictators. And yet, this is what our young want to bring to America.

Even so, these and other liberal views continue to be crammed down our children's throats. An LA Alexander Hamilton High School history teacher was forced to remove her objectional classroom flags. Featured were a Palestinian flag, Black Lives Matter Flag, a transgender flag, and two flags that said "F…the Police" and "F…Amerikkka."[164] What were they doing there in the first place?

Then a teacher at Marysville Middle School was ordered to remove a Thin Blue Line flag that conveyed support for law enforcement while other teachers were allowed to hang Black Lives Matter and LGBT pride flags.[165]

And in Florida, a teacher became unglued over her students supporting another student's right to bring a Trump flag to class. She called the flag carrier, "a racist." Then told her class, "Trump brings out racism in trashy people."[166]

This is not the only case of a teacher bullying a student because he/she embraced a different philosophy. Nor it is the first story of unsuitable educators occupying positions they shouldn't. Sadly, there are many of them.

Destination Hell

But this one is unbelievable! Theology professor, Curtis Freeman, at Duke University and Director of its Baptist House of Studies said, "Evangelical Christianity is the greatest threat to human existence today. It must be laid waste." He also compared Christian fundamentalists to the Taliban. And this is a **theology** professor teaching young adults about religion?[167] God help us!

And what about the bullying by teachers and administrators of those students not in lockstep with their latest Covid positions? There are stories of teachers segregating students who don't wear masks or are not vaccinated. There is even a story of a sixteen-year-old Wyoming student who was fined $500 for refusing to wear a mask, then arrested, during which time her entire school was locked down for over an hour.[168] Other students have been shamed by their teachers for noncompliance. And still others have been forced to wear colored arm bands indicating they have not been vaxed.

How bad is it? Look no further than the recent dustup between parents and their local school board. When parents criticized the Covid mandates and the push to institute Critical Race Theory (CRT) in their schools, U.S. Attorney General Merrick Garland quickly came out denouncing them and instructed the FBI to investigate these detractors. Then, on the heels of Garland's pronouncement, Viola Garcia, National School Boards Association president and CEO Chip Slaven, co-signed a letter to Biden imploring him to use federal agencies, as well as the Patriot Act, against outspoken parents who oppose school Covid mandates and the teaching of Critical Race Theory. The letter claimed these parents should be investigated for "domestic terrorism and hate crimes threats." To accomplish this, their letter suggested Biden use the Secret Service, FBI, DHS, and DOJ. The National School Boards Association represents all U.S. public school boards.[169]

Then, in an ironic twist of fate, it leaked out that Garland's son-in-law, Xan Tanner, is co-founder of Panorama Education, the very company selling CRT books to schools and who stands to make millions![170] What was Garland's next move? He sent federal agents to a school board meeting in Fairfax to intimidate the disgruntled parents.[171]

Because this is an obvious conflict of interest, Garland was hauled before congress on October 21, to explain himself. Sometime after, a whistleblower came forward to refute Garland's testimony that the FBI was not targeting parents. The whistleblower's documents showed "the FBI's counterterrorism unit was adding a 'threat tag' to parents who protest at local school boards."[172]

Destination Hell

But nothing changes. If you think AG Garland backed down, you'd be wrong. On November 16, the FBI's SWAT team showed up at Sherronna Bishop's house. A Colorado mother of three, and activist against election fraud, she has also protested critical race theory and mask mandates at her school board. In addition, her website informs other mothers of what's going on in their children's schools.

So, what happened? At 9:30 a.m., the FBI's SWAT team battered down her door, handcuffed both her and her husband while two of their children watched in horror. Then the FBI searched their house. No charges were ever brought against her, indicating this was an intimidation tactic to silence her and serve as a warning to other protesting parents.

Many retired FBI agents are outraged that their beloved department has sunk so low. In going after a law-abiding citizen whose only crime was exercising her right of free speech, they fear the FBI, once known for its honor and integrity, has become the White House's "political shock troops."[173]

But there are plenty of others who aid and abet this craziness. The American Medical Association came out with their guide on "advancing Health

Equity" with promotes Critical Race Theory.[174] And California's Governor, Gavan Newsom, signed Bill-AB 101, making his state, beginning in the 2029-2030 school year, the first to require the taking and passing of a CRT based course for graduation.[175]

And get this: Democrat Terry McAuliffe, when running for Virginia Governor, said while debating his rival, Republican Glenn Younkin, "I don't think parents should be telling schools what they should teach."[176] What? Parents shouldn't care about what their children are doing in school? Or what they are learning? We have already seen how educators and the education system have betrayed us. The very people entrusted to teach our children have violated that trust and misused their position to further their own agendas. For that reason, parents should get more involved not less!

Then to add insult to injury, Miguel Cardona, Education Secretary, testified before a Senate Committee acknowledging that parents are "important stakeholders" in their children's education, but they **should not be the "primary" ones**. Rather, "educators must determine the programs."[177] Again, we've seen where that leads.

Destination Hell

In response to all this, Republican House Leader, Kevin McCarthy, drafted the "Parents Bill of Rights," hoping to stop the current infringement on parental rights, but the Democrats immediately blocked it.[178]

But there is good news. Since the National School Boards Association request to Biden to sic the FBI, DHS, DOJ, and the Secret Service on protesting parents, twenty-six states have cut ties with them.[179]

But having our children deceived politically is not enough for some educators. They want them corrupted in every way possible by promoting sexual immorality and gender confusion. All this is grooming and recruiting our children to accept sexual advances and deviant forms of sexual behavior as normal. So, it wasn't that surprising when the San Francisco Gay Men's Chorus came out with a song called, *"We're coming for Your Children,"* that boldly declared they plan to indoctrinate and seduce our children into the LGBTQ lifestyle, though they deleted their video six days later.[180]

Some teachers are actively recruiting students into LGBTQ clubs according to a leaked recording of two seventh grade California teachers. During the October 2021 CTA Conference, these teachers shared how they deceive parents by calling these clubs "equity clubs," and how they find recruits by "spying on students' online searches and activity as well as eavesdropping on their conversations to identify and recruit sixth-grade students into these LGBTQ clubs whose membership rolls are kept hidden from parents." The school responded by suspending all these clubs.[181] Praise God!

Then recently, Allyn Walker, assistant professor of criminal justice and sociology at Old Dominion University, came out "openly suggesting pedophilia is natural and should not be considered wrong." She was placed on leave.[182]

The entire list of other inappropriate behavior by educators is too long to include, but here are just six:

- A Florida Broward County School Board member chaperoned the field trip of elementary students to a gay bar.[183]
- Loudoun County School covered up the rape of a fourteen-year-old girl by a transgender boy using the girls' bathroom. To add insult to injury, they had the girl's father arrested for bringing it up at a school board meeting. The rapist was transferred to a different school where he sexually assaulted another girl. "And so far, the only

Destination Hell

person convicted of a crime is the victim's father."[184]

- Jacob Engels, a Gateway Pundit contributor, attended an Orange County School Board meeting where he used his time to read portions of *Gender Queer*: a memoir by Maia Kobabe. The book was carried by and featured in the Boone High School library during Pride Month. Engels was able to read only one section of the sexually graphic interactions of homosexuals before the chairman ordered him to stop, then had him escorted out by police when he refused.[185] Apparently, it was appropriate material for high school students but not for adults.

- Recently, parents exposed a Hudson Ohio School Board when they discovered their high school kids were reading, *642 Things to Write About*, then instructed to "write a sex scene you wouldn't show your mom." To his credit, the Hudson Mayor, Craig Shubert, gave the board an ultimatum: resign or be criminally charged for distributing child pornography.[186]

- Parents in Minnesota discovered that the Richfield School Board had approved a sex ed program that required their children to act out both transgender and gay roles. Among other things, this K-12 3Rs sex education program teaches "gay sex, gender ideology, abortion, racial justice, and more, and utilizes visuals and role-playing activities."[187]

Over 100 obscene and sexually explicit books were discovered by parents in the North Carolina, Wake County, public elementary, middle, and high schools. Criminal charges have been filed by parents against the school board.[188]

New York and California are already trying to decriminalize sex between children and adults. And members of NAMBLA (North American Man/Boy Love Association) a homosexual-pedophile organization, now call themselves "minor-attracted persons" and claim to champion sexual freedom for children.[189]

Even social media has bought into gender bending. One example is Facebook, who in 2014, created a drop-down menu offering fifty-eight different gender choices.[190]

Parents are also buying into this. Recently, a Los Angeles mother noted in her 2021 Christmas card that her kindergarten-age daughter was now a "son who is non-binary." She then followed it up with an op-ed piece in *Today*.

Destination Hell

As a result of all this, our children are anxious and confused. Some no longer know if they are male or female and are getting hormone therapy and surgeries to artificially change their sex. The American College of Pediatricians has been very vocal about the dangers of this. They state, unabashedly, that artificially altering one's sexuality most often leads to unhappiness and depression. They even called this "CHILD ABUSE." And when these children become adults, their suicide rate is twenty times higher than the national average.[191]

Because these types of things have been going on for years, is it any wonder that according to a study by Arizona Christian University, 30% of millennials identify as LGBT?[192] It was a small study of only six-hundred people from eighteen to thirty-seven years old, but if accurate what does that mean in terms of numbers? Statista.com claims there were 72.1 million U.S. millennials in 2019. Thirty percent of that translates to 21.6 million!

Recently, Arkansas tried to protect the children in their state by passing the "Save Adolescents From Experimentations Act" or SAFE which prohibits physicians from performing genital surgeries or administering puberty blockers to minors. Asa Hutchinson, the Republican Governor, vetoed it, but the state legislature overrode his veto causing the ACLU to file a lawsuit. The bill's enforcement was then blocked by Judge Jay Moody. Arkansas Senator Tom Cotton strongly favored the SAFE Act and spoke out against this flagrant child abuse.[193] Unfortunately, few voices joined him. In fact, those speaking for this gross mutilation of our children far exceeded those opposed.

Even the famous are promoting the same radical ideas pushed in schools. Popular Canadian recording artist, Celine Dion, began a gender-neutral clothing line for babies and toddlers. Her company, CELEINUNUNU, was created in conjunction with NUNUNU, a popular line featuring Satanic symbols on their clothing such as pentagrams, death flags, human skulls, caps with devil's horns and the all-seeing eye. Dion's mission statement is to "free newborns from gender binarity (two genders)."[194]

And what about DC Comics' casting of Superman's seventeen-year-old son, Jonathan, as bisexual? Not only is he bisexual but "woke." Among young Jonathan Kent's missions will be "fighting wildfires caused by climate change and protesting the deportation of refugees."[195]

It's obvious that there are many in industry, government and our institutions of learning who have an ominous agenda: control schools and use them for communist indoctrination; destroy

Destination Hell

concepts of morality and promote obscenity and pornography; promote all manner of sex as normal; destroy religion; destroy the family; encourage the raising of children by the state; promote violence as a legitimate means of protest.[196]

We have given our children over to be taught by godless secular institutions and are surprised when we discover they disrespect our values, have lost faith in God, hate this country, themselves, and each other, have no foundation, have seared consciences, and can, without any noticeable remorse, do something as unthinkable as kill their fellow students, which recently a fifteen-year-old Michigan high school student did when he walked into his school and shot twelve people, killing four.[197]

To Satan's delight, our children are being destroyed before our eyes. And while he is doing it, our lawmakers remain silent. Where are they? Don't they have children of their own? Why are they not speaking up? More importantly: WHERE IS THE CHURCH? The silence is deafening. And how this must break God's heart!

But the population at large isn't doing well, either. Since 2020, violent crime in the U.S. has risen in almost every category. According to Fox News, in just a six-month period, murders rose 16%, assaults 9%, domestic violence 2%, auto theft 21% and gun assaults 5%,[198] while the FBI's claim is that 2020 saw a 29.4% increase in murders.[199] And during this time we've seen some of our cities burn, businesses destroyed, the police ambushed and disrespected.

In the face of all this, the radical left want to defund the police. Why? Because then it will be easier to create their own national police force. Allowing, and even promoting terror, chaos, and dysfunction will spike the crime rate. That's what Hitler did in order to make it easier for him to recruit unemployed ex-military, and in March 1921, create the infamous Brownshirts, also called Storm Troopers or *Sturmabteilung* (SA) the "assault division." It became the strong arm of the Nazi Party.[200] The liberal elites want to create their own Brownshirts. In some ways they already have through Antifa, which is well funded as evidenced by their sophisticated body armor, helmets, gas masks and goggles.

If the elites can create a federalized police force, one answerable only to them, it will ready the planet for the One World Government and enable it to enforce the dictates of the one who will run it.

Destination Hell

John Adams knew what he was talking about when he said, "Our Constitution was made only for a moral and religious people. It is wholly inadequate to the government of any other."[201] There are not enough police to manage an immoral people who desire to do evil and hurt others. The only means of controlling such a society is through a despot, and one is coming soon.

The cumulative effects of all this are horrifying. Andrew Powell, in his article, *What the devil? U.S. turns to dark side as Americans make Satan mainstream*, encapsulates what's going on in America by citing, in one paragraph, actual events: "(the erecting of) Satanic statues, witches casting spells, drag queens reading to kids, open pedophilia on streaming services such as Netflix, sex dolls with real child's likeness, cannibal restaurants, Satanic rituals at all-American event like the Super Bowl, radical leftist groups outright saying they want to destroy the nuclear family, a daughter of politicians wishing a Happy New Year to the Church of Satan, a chemical named 'Luciferase' in the COVID-19 vaccine."[202]

More and more people are becoming open about their ties to Satan. When Christian Bale won his Oscar, he thanked Satan for his success, though some say he was joking. In Phoenix, Arizona, a woman said a satanic prayer on the local KNVX station. And in Alaska, Satanic prayers were said prior to a city council meeting.[203]

While Satan is elevated, some in the media compare Christians to the Taliban. I suppose that should come as no surprise. Jesus said the world would hate us because it first hated Him, (John 15:18).

The U.S. State Department's, *International Religious Freedom Report*, claims that 25% of the world is religiously intolerant. That affects 75% of the earth's inhabitants.[204] And 80% of this intolerance is directed toward Christians.[205]

A recent example is the story of the Canadian Pastor, Tim Stephens, who was jailed for conducting outdoor services during Covid, then held for seventeen days in solitary confinement.[206] Another, is the demolition of crosses all across China in 2020, their intimidation of Christians, and their outlawing home churches, all according to their five-year plan to "re-create" spiritual beliefs and make them conform to Communist Chinese ideology.[207]

Even our own government is hostile to Christianity. One example was exposed on October 23, 2013, when Fox News posted an article to their website written by reporter Todd Sterns. The article

Destination Hell

covered a view held by some military higher-ups regarding evangelicals and the Tea Party, and how that view is creeping into the military at-large. Sterns wrote, "Soldiers attending a predeployment briefing at Fort Hood say they were told that evangelical Christians and members of the Tea Party were a threat to the nation and that any soldier donating to those groups would be subjected to punishment under the Uniform Code of Military Justice."[208]

And more recently, Santa Clara County, California, imposed $2.8 million worth of Covid fines on Pastor Mike McClure of Calvary Chapel for keeping his church open for services during the pandemic. Santa Clara is defying the U.S. Supreme Court's ruling that forbids government entities from levying "harsh penalties and restrictions" on houses of worship not imposed on other "essential" businesses. It's still being thrashed out in court.

Censorship in America:

For years, liberals have claimed the high road. *They* are the true lovers of mankind. *They* are not haters like conservatives. But the mask has fallen off and it's become obvious they love only those who agree with them, while at the same time destroying those who don't, thus **they** are the "intolerant" ones.

Our government is now colluding with Big Tech to censor free speech under the guise of protecting us from "disinformation." In a recent briefing, White House Press Secretary, Jen Psaki, said that the government would be instructing Facebook regarding what is allowable on their platform. She claimed the White House maintained contact with social media organizations and that "we're flagging problematic posts for Facebook."[209] It's all for our benefit, of course, so the public is not misled. Notice that governments always claim that everything they do is "for our good."

So, what are these *"problematic posts"*? Answer: They are any posts that dispute the current COVID narrative and that question the outcome of the election. People are being de-platformed every day for this type of "disinformation." In other words, the elites, and only them, will control the narrative. And the narrative they especially want to control is information regarding the pandemic and the 2020 election.

These same issues were flagged when, on August 13, 2021, NBC News reported that the Department of Homeland Security (DHS) had just come out

Destination Hell

with a new terrorism advisory, listing the following as terror threats:
- **Opposition to COVID Measures**
- **Claims of election Fraud**, Belief Trump Can Be Reinstated
- 9/11 Anniversary and Religious Holidays[210]

In addition, DHS said it, "will continue to identify and evaluate calls for violence, including **online activity associated with the spread of disinformation, conspiracy theories, and false narratives,** by known or suspected threat actors and provide updated information, as necessary."[211]

What exactly constitutes a conspiracy theory or disinformation is unclear. But DHS has certainly thrown a wet blanket over free speech. And with these vague definitions, DHS can, in the future, shift them like sand to mean anything they want.

Then the following month, DHS Secretary, Alejandro Mayorkas, doubled down at a September 21st Committee hearing when talking about violent extremists and their "ideological motivations." He said these motivations include, "racial bias, perceived government overreach, conspiracy theories promoting violence, and false narratives about unsubstantiated fraud in the 2020 presidential election." Again, the terms "perceived government overreach" or "conspiracy theories" or "false narratives" about the 2020 election were not defined. Mayorkas is talking about predicting "future crimes . . . based on behavioral patterns," rather than actual crimes.[212] This is an open invitation for any upcoming totalitarian regime to arrest anyone they choose based on artificial criteria.

Mayorkas also wants the public to inform on anyone they think harbor such "motivations."[213] This is what Hitler asked his citizens to do, too, and eventually turned his nation into a country of informants.

It's clear through these pronouncements that the COVID protocols, and especially the vaccines are a big deal to the elites and our government. Jen Psaki and the DHS left no room for doubt. That they would silence free speech over it, is appalling. Those who speak out against them or question the information coming out of Washington are now considered "potential terrorists."

But it's not just our government. Companies and various institutions are also jumping on the bandwagon to denounce any opposition as coming from dangerous "extremists."

PayPal joined the chorus by announcing no longer will "extremists" and "anti-government voices"

Destination Hell

have "donate" buttons on their site.[214] VISA and MasterCard are also doing their part in other ways.

Big Tech, from Facebook to Mailchimp, are expanding their counterterrorism plans to expose "domestic right-wing organizations."[215] Notice, no one seems concerned about **left-wing** extremists.

Then, on September 29, 2021, YouTube announced it would ban all "harmful vaccine content."[216]

Apple also will begin spying on our phones for potential "child pornography,"[217] but we know it won't stop there. Soon enough, they will be trolling for "terrorists." The Democratic National Committee and other like-minded groups are already striving toward this end. They want "fact-checkers" to work with SMS carriers. That means checking our private emails and texts to see if we are spreading any "disinformation."[218]

But recall that DHS also labeled those who questioned the election as being "potential terrorists." This is the saddest assault of all. Americans have always been free to vote for who they wanted without apology or explanation. And in the past, both Democrats and Republicans have questioned elections and demanded recounts. It's part of our treasured "right to vote" process.

But all that has changed. The liberal elites are denouncing all Trump supporters. For some time, they have claimed these supporters are akin to Nazis. Now, they have gone a step further by declaring that Trump supporters need to be "deprogrammed."[219]

In a tweet, a *New York Times* reporter even called Trump supporters "enemies of the state," then took it down after some blowback.[220]

And then there's this. The liberal Center for American Progress recently sent a letter to the Federal Communications Commission regarding "reshaping" the U.S. media. The letter contained this incendiary question: "Are we going to **have to shoot Republicans** to reclaim our democracy?"[221] Since when does it become okay for one political group to suggest killing members of an opposing political group?

Going back to vaccines: Why are the elites so focused on them?

The elites are adamant that everyone gets vaccinated. Why? People who have had Covid have natural immunity and don't need the shot. Others want to opt out for health or religious reasons. Still others don't want to be injected with an experimental, untested substance. We've seen

Destination Hell

measures, implemented or proposed, that affect our freedoms and free speech, but none harsher than those concerning the Covid vaccination. The elites are obsessed with it.

Recently, "woke" former officials came out declaring the need for a "NO-FLY" list for those who refuse to get vaccinated.[222] And John Asplund, Superintendent of School District 205 in Galesburg, IL, plans to hand out yellow ID badges indicating that the person wearing it has gotten his shot.[223] Edward Starr, city manager at Montclair, California, has ordered government workers to wear masks at work or place stickers on their badges to show they are vaccinated.[224]

There are other stories like this such as colleges suspending students who refuse to get vaccinated; high schools refusing to allow unvaccinated students to attend their prom, etcetera, but are too numerous to include.

All these things are designed to make us conform, then to separate the non-conformists. Dividing people into groups follows Hitler's pattern of dehumanization. First, you separate them verbally, claiming one is good, one is bad. Then you point to the "bad group" as the ones causing all the problems. It's **their** fault that things are like they are. Then you separate them physically, either in camps or confined places like ghettos. Then you separate them from life by coming up with a "Solution" that enables them to be killed efficiently. As mentioned, Hitler did it, and this is what the proponents of the New World Order will eventually do.

Does that sound farfetched? Then check this out. It's perhaps the scariest information of all. A National Guard's August 16, 2021, post (since removed) advertised job openings for **"Internment/Resettlement Specialist."** The job description included, "supervise confinement and detention operations; provide external security to facilities; provide counseling-guidance to individual prisoners within a rehabilitative program; and manage and maintain prisoners/internees and their programs."[225]

In 2010, the U.S. Army published a training manual entitled FM 3-39.40 that included how to detain **civilians** and the type of detention camps allowed on U.S. soil. This same document described these camps and the procedures and techniques to be used on detainees. Included among them were "search, silence and segregate." Of particular interest is "silence." How and why are the "internment specialists" to silence a detainee? Answer: by muffling them with a "soft, clean cloth tied over their mouth" in order to

Destination Hell

"prevent detainees from communicating with one another or making audible clamor such as chanting, singing, or **praying**."[226]

WOW! Now why would the National Guard need interment and resettlement specialists? And why would they need to "rehabilitate" or "silence" those who "chant, sing or pray"? I'm suddenly picturing loaded cattle cars rolling into facilities fenced by barbed wire. We've seen this before.

But here's an interesting side note: While Americans are required to follow all the Covid restrictions, those crossing our border illegally are not.[227] They are not even tested to see if they have Covid while many citizens are required to be tested regularly in order to work at their jobs! How can this be? Since when do non-citizens have more rights than citizens? To add insult to injury, Biden is requiring all truck drivers crossing U.S land borders to be **fully vaccinated** and the deadline is January 22, 2022. The CEO of the American Trucking Association, Chris Spear, said that will affect 37% of his truckers and be "catastrophic," implying it will seriously affect our supply chain.[228] This is the definition of insanity, especially since Biden is giving a free pass to thousands of illegals who he is bussing throughout our country in the dead of night. Talk about possible Covid spreaders!

And there's this: Republican Congresswoman, Mariannette Miller-Meeks introduced a bill requiring illegal immigrants to test negative for Covid before Customs and Border Protection released them into our country. But House Democrats BLOCKED it even though members of our Border Patrol are required to get vaccinated.[229]

In addition, after all the scare tactics regarding the unvaccinated harming the vaccinated, the irony is that according to several recent reports, it's the vaccinated who are the super spreaders and not the other way around. One such study by Oxford University Clinical Research Group that came out August 10, 2021, found that "vaccinated individuals carry 241 times the load of COVID-19 viruses in their nostrils compared to the unvaccinated."[230]

According to Dr. McCullough, well-known cardiologist, internist and epidemiologist, this raises questions about the cause of post-vaccination surges in countries with high percentages of their population vaccinated. McCullough also questions the safety of patients treated by vaccinated healthcare workers and the potential of these workers to infect them.[231]

Then in December 2021, Dr. McCullough came out with a warning against using Covid vaccines in the young. A renown and respected cardiologist, he

Destination Hell

fears that if injected, an "extraordinary number" will have "permanent heart damage." Less than a week later, Jim Hoft of the Gateway Pundit reported that New York's Suffolk County Eastport-South Manor Central School District sent an email to all parents introducing them to the new hire, Doctor Melina Khwaja. And what is her principal role? Answer: to bring all districts up to speed in grades K-12, regarding *"sudden cardiac arrest."* It's believed that New York is ready to mandate Covid vaccines for all attending students. Just what are they expecting to happen when they do?

That same month, Jim Hoft of Gateway Pundit again broke news by citing the December 14, 2021, study by Nature Medicine, which was analyzed by researchers at Oxford University. Oxford's findings: 1 in 100 vaccinated people have died or been hospitalized with cardiac arrhythmias.

And then there's this. According to Kay Smythe's article dated December 20, 2021, in The National Pulse, Pfizer is laying out $6.7 billion to purchase a **cardiovascular biopharma company** called Arena. Based in Utah, Arena, while researching bowel disease treatment has also been working with United Therapeutics in researching **pulmonary arterial hypertension** one of the very issues related to Covid-19 vaccines!

On the heels of all this, Julian Conradson (December 29, 2021) and Jim Hoft (December 31, 2021) published reports in the Gateway Pundit revealing additional damning information. Discussed were two recent studies both claiming the Covid vaccines "cause more illness than they prevent." The first study, by a team of Danish researchers, claim that the vaccine is ineffective against Omicron within two months after vaccination. It also ascertained that those inoculated with the Pfizer vaccine had 76.5% more chance of a breakthrough infection after 90 days than the unvaccinated. The study also declared that "the spread of the new Omicron variant was 'likely' caused by super-spreader events among young, **vaccinated** individuals." And here's the heartbreak: "the FDA granted an extension to Pfizer's EUA (Emergency Use Authorization) despite recording an astounding 1,200-plus vaccine related deaths in just the first 90 days of its availability."

The second report by the Canadian Covid Care Alliance, a group of 500 independent health care professionals which include both doctors and scientists, also declared, after doing an in-depth analysis, that "Pfizer's COVID-19 inoculations cause more illness than they prevent." That includes increased risk of death. They also concluded that Pfizer "failed to follow established,

Destination Hell

high-quality safety and efficacy protocols for vaccine development." In addition, the vaccines "offered less than 1% benefit."

Then the CDC announced that beginning December 31, 2021, it will no longer use the PCR test to determine if someone has Covid. The reason: the test cannot distinguish between the Covid virus and common flu. That means many many people who tested positive for Covid actually had the flu. That also explains why 2020 U.S. flu cases disappeared entirely! It also indicates that during the beginning of the pandemic until now, Covid cases have been drastically inflated. You can't make this stuff up!

Interestingly enough, Bill Gates seems to think there is a role for vaccines in population control.

It's no secret that many prominent globalists like Bill Gates are interested in reducing the world's population. His ideal is around 500 million. Sound familiar? It's the same figure suggested on the Satanic Georgia Guidestones. It's also the same figure suggested by the elitist Club of Rome that believes the "ideal sustainable population is hence more than 500 million but less than one billion."[232]

David Brower, first Executive Direct of the Sierra Club, also agreed with depopulation and came up with a plan. "Childbearing (should be) a punishable crime against society, unless the parents hold a government license . . . All potential parents (should be) required to use contraceptive chemicals, the government issuing antidotes to citizens chosen for childbearing."[233]

It's obvious the elites want to reduce population. It's part of their global master plan. In lieu of this, one must wonder if vaccines are a means of "thinning the herd." Already, 300 healthy athletes around the world have suffered cardiac arrest or died after being vaccinated.[234] On July 16, 2021, the CDC itself posted 11,405 vaccine deaths on their VAERS website which is their official site for tracking adverse effects of medications, vaccines, etcetera. In addition, they cited 190,000 other issues connected with the Covid vaccines which included: hospitalizations, urgent care visits, office visits, anaphylaxis, and Bell's Palsy.

By July 19, 2021, VAERS showed the death rate to be 12,313 but later that day, the CDC changed the numbers to read 6,079 deaths.[235] This should tell us the numbers in all categories (death, hospitalizetion, sickness, etc.) are not to be trusted and are much much higher. According to VAERS, by December 24, 2021, the number of Covid vaccine adverse incidences rose to 1,000,227 which included over 22,000 developing serious heart

Destination Hell

problems. The number of deaths due to the Covid vaccine rose to 21,002.

In addition, the European Union website, on November 2021, cited 30,551 Covid vaccine deaths and 1,163,356 adverse reactions.[236] And recently, the UK reported 300,000 cases of sudden heart problems, calling it "pandemic stress" without even trying to determine if they are vaccine related.[237]

In the meantime, Pfizer is fighting a Freedom of Information Act request to review their experimental test data on patients prior to the unrolling of their vaccine, and are asking the FDA to seal these documents for 55 years. The FDA happily agreed, then asked a judge for an additional twenty years by claiming it needs 75 years to go over all the requested documents.[238, 239] Makes one wonder if they are hiding anything.

Fortunately, the court rejected this request and instead, ordered the FDA to release vaccine FOIA documents monthly. Twelve thousand were to be released by January 31, 2022, then 55,000 every thirty days thereafter. According to Julian Conradson, reporting for the Gateway Pundit on January 7, 2002, their initial 500 pages revealed there were "over 1,200 vaccine deaths withing first 90 days."

In the past, these vaccines would have been pulled from the market long ago. The fact that they have not is unbelievable. To understand just how unbelievable, consider that in 1976 the government stopped vaccinating for swine flu after only **53 people died** from the vaccine.[240]

Sooner or later this concept of population control was bound to emerge in politics. Thus, it was not surprising that Pennsylvania Democrat Christopher Rabb introduced a bill that would not only limit the number of children a couple can have (three) but required forced sterilization of the man once that limit was reached or when he turned forty, whatever happened first. If the man didn't comply, anyone could turn him in and receive a $10,000 reward.[241] Rabb later back tracked.

One important component of population control is abortion. The National Library of Medicine stated their position clearly in a paper about the "Role of Abortion in control of global population." It stated that "abortion is essential to any national population growth control effort."[242]

In connection with this, it's interesting how heavily the Gates' foundation is into vaccines. At the exclusive TED2010 Long Beach, California Conference, Gates spoke about reducing CO_2 emissions in his speech entitled, "Innovating to

Destination Hell

Zero!" and said this, "First we got population. The world today has 6.8 billion people. That's headed up to about 9 billion. Now if we do a really great job on **new vaccines**, health care, reproductive health services, we lower that by perhaps 10 to 15 percent."[243] Lower what? Lower the population! He's talking about using vaccines, healthcare (abortion) and birth control to lower the world's population. Since then, so called "fact checkers" have tried to spin it by saying Gates meant reduce population growth rate not population. But how can vaccines reduce population growth rate when they are designed to keep the population strong and healthy? It doesn't make sense. But I'll let the reader decide which is the correct interpretation.

Additionally, over the last ten years, Gates' foundation has donated nearly $10 billion to create and administer vaccines in developing countries.[244]

Is there more to this vaccination issue?

Aside from linking vaccines to population control, is there any other connection that make it so important to the elites? The answer seems to be, "yes."

Vaccines will allow our bodies to become "computers" by implanting some form of data storage and collection device accessible to governments; devices able to control buying and selling. Already, a Swedish company, Epicenter, has come out with a microchip, when embedded in a person's hand or arm, can verify vaccination status, and by extension, a person's ability to travel, where he/she can shop, at what restaurant he/she can eat, etcetera. It's the size of a "grain of rice" and serves as a Covid passport. But it won't stop there. The globalists want all our information.

And Bill Gates is at the forefront. He funded MIT's development of a quantum dot tattoo which contains "an enzyme called **Luciferase**." In addition, its Microsoft patent number (obtained March 26, 2020) is WO/2020/060606, which is interesting since the mark of the beast, according to Revelation, is 666.[245]

You're talking about a global digital ID system that will contain all our personal and banking information and be connected to a Chinese style "social scoring system" that can raise or lower our social credit score depending on our words, behavior, beliefs, and lifestyle, thus impacting how much digital currency we will be allowed to have and use.[246]

Judging by what China is doing, it would work this way: those malcontents who complain about their government or criticize any of their policies

Destination Hell

or question their latest propaganda, would be penalized and their social credit score, lowered. And if they offend too often, their score could be lowered to such a point as to make it impossible to buy anything. Conversely, the score of those who support the latest party line will climb, making them eligible to receive bonus points and additional digital currency.

That means those who believe in a sovereign border, that we should be energy independent, that looting and burning a city should be called criminal instead of a "summer of love," that mandating a vaccine for citizens but not for those crossing our border illegally is wrong, who believe in free enterprise, personal responsibility and liberty, who love their country, who believe a Christian baker shouldn't have to bake for an LGBTQ wedding or don't believe that a man can be a woman, will be labeled an extremist or malcontent and have lower social credit scores.

It's obvious that a global digital ID system is vital for the coming New World Order when no one can buy or sell without it.

Is that why inflation is rising? For all this to work, America's economy must tank, and the "petro-dollar" replaced. Already, it is believed that Saudi

Arabia and Russia made an agreement to stop transacting in U.S. dollars.[247]

Is that also why vaccines are so important to globalists? Are they trying to perfect a prototype of a digital ID system deliverable through vaccines by mandating that every person on planet earth get a shot?

Not long after the Covid vaccines came out, Dr. Fauci began hinting a booster may be needed in order for someone to be considered "fully vaccinated"? By early December 2021, Albert Bourla, CEO of Pfizer, declared that he believed a "fourth dose" was needed.[248] A few days later, Fauci came out with his own pronouncement that Americans should expect yearly boosters and they will "just have to deal with it."[249] But take it to the bank, this is just the beginning. It won't end here. Eventually, additional vaccines or boosters will be required forever. And while the population of the world is used as a guinea pig to perfect a vaccine that can deliver this global digital ID system, many will die from the experiment.

Miscellaneous other controls in the works:

According to Breitbart, the Democrats have inserted in their large and expensive infrastructure bill, a provision for a new program to track our cars

Destination Hell

and milage in order to collect more taxes.[250] But if the program can do that, it means it can also track the whereabouts of every driver, meaning the government will know just where we are going and where we have been.

And according to PNW, Biden wants to inspect our banking and other financial transactions exceeding $600.[251] That means they will know how we are spending our money and what we are spending it on. So far, he's getting a lot of pushback. Even so, effective January 2022, businesses like PayPal, Cash App, and Venmo are required by the IRS to report customer transactions that **exceed $600 a year**! That should pretty much include everyone! Now, couple things like this with facial recognition software that is used by more and more stores and companies, and it's easy to see how fast Big Brother is evolving.

This is the Utopian New World Order that Prince Charles, Klaus Schwab, Bill Gates, and their cronies want to bring about.

It's clear to see that America is in a freefall. The tentacles of the secret societies run deep. And they have been trying to destroy our republic by overwhelming it with one crisis after another, then incrementally replacing it with socialism or communism.

That explains why open borders are essential and why our government wants unvetted millions to pour across them. And that is why massive spending is necessary. It will make our nation's debt unsustainable. That's also what defunding the police is about. So is allowing the thugs of Antifa and Black Lives Matter to loot and destroy our cities. It's all designed to overwhelm and collapse our systems and leave a void to be filled by the New World Order.

What's going on globally?

The New World Order's motto: "order out of chaos" is revealing. It explains why Rohm Emanuel said, "Never let a good crisis go to waste." This is their M.O. Use a crisis to solidify power. If there is no crisis, create one, then come up with a solution. And the solution usually involves the loss of liberties because a crisis allows those in power to step in and initiate things they would normally be unable to do.

This tactic has existed for ages and has been employed by people seeking power. Journalist, satirist, and cultural critic, H.L. Mencken (1880-1956) understood that when he said, "The whole aim of practical politics is to keep the populace alarmed (and hence clamorous to lead them to safety) by menacing it with an endless series of

Destination Hell

hobgoblins, all of them imaginary."[252] And making it work is an "iron" coalition of money, scientists, lawyers, lobbyists, and politicians whose strings are pulled by secret societies.

In my book, *The Coming Deception*, I detail many of the organizations that are working toward creating a One World Government and that information is too lengthy to repeat in full, so I will only touch on a few points.

The U.N. is one of the biggest proponents of the New World Order. The now deceased U.N. General Assembly's first president, Paul-Henri Spaak, made this outrageous statement: "We don't want another committee, we have too many already. What we want is a man of sufficient stature to hold the allegiance of all the people and to lift us up out of the economic crisis into which we are sinking. Send us such a man, whether he be God or **devil**, we will receive him.[253]

What kind of society would welcome help from a devil? The kind that has lost its spiritual mooring and has become morally bankrupt!

In 1980, the U.N. formulated a plan for the New World Order. In 1996 it detailed how to implement that plan in a 420-page document called, *Our Global Neighborhood*. And in 2015, it came out with its *Agenda 2030* with plans to transform the world and solve all its problems.[254]

While no cross or other religious artifacts are displayed in or on U.N. grounds, a statue of Zeus stands near the entrance of the main lobby. Remember, Jesus called Zeus, "Satan," (Revelation 2:13). Recently, a second statue appeared outside U.N. headquarters. It's a "beast" called the "Guardian of International Peace and Security." With its snarling mouth, huge wings, and tail, it looks like something out of a horror movie or . . . the Book of Revelation.[255] And it hardly evokes "peace and security." Also, in the U.N. meditation room, there is a trapezoid-shaped altar like the trapezoid altar found in a Masonic lodge, and represents Nimrod's unfinished work at Babel.

Both socialism and communism were birthed out of a desire for a New World Order. Rockefeller made loans to the Bolsheviks during their revolution, as did the Morgan banks. In addition, J.P. Morgan's companies helped finance the American Communist Party.[256]

In his book, *The Committee of 300,* Dr. John Coleman said this of the Illuminati, "In the Committee of 300, which has a 150-year history, we have some of the most brilliant intellects assembled to form a completely totalitarian, absolutely controlled

Destination Hell

'new' society—only it isn't new, having drawn most of its ideas from the Clubs of Cultus Diabolicus. It strives toward a one world government."[257]

Phyllis Schlafly in her book, *A Choice Not An Echo*, describes a secret Bilderberg meeting in 1957 held in the King and Prince Hotel near St. Simon's Island, Georgia. "Those who came were not the heads of states, but those who give orders to heads of states—in other words, the kingmakers."[258] The strategy of the Bilderbergs is to bring "Order out of chaos." To achieve this, they must break down all our systems and create new ones. And they are willing to manufacture a crisis when needed.[259]

Many "movers and shakers" of our world are part of one or more of these organizations. In 1975, thirty-two U.S. Senators and ninety-two U.S. Representatives signed a "Declaration of Independence" stating, "we must bring forth a New World Order." One can only imagine how much that number has grown!

Now we're hearing about "The Great Reset." What is it? It was so named in June 2020 when the World Economic Forum (WEF) held its 50th annual meeting. Organized by Prince Charles, its primary focus was on rebuilding the post-COVID economy and society. Later, Charles admitted that "The present pandemic is a golden opportunity for radical change."[260]

No surprise to Tyler Durden, the pseudonym for a group of editors writing for Zero Hedge and who believe, "the lockdowns, mandates and vaccines were never about safety and were always about control — from social control to population control."[261]

During WEF's 50th annual meeting, Klaus Schwab, the Forum's CEO, laid out three pillars of the Reset.

First, establish a "stakeholder" economy. Who are the stakeholders? Investors, trade associations, governments, employees, customers, suppliers, and communities. In other words, good-bye free trade and capitalism. Businesses would have to answer to an array of people who had their own vested interests and agendas.

Second, it would be based on "green" principles. You are talking about CO_2 emissions, carbon footprints, etcetera. You are talking about the "Green New Deal" that will bankrupt every industrialized nation in an effort to redistribute wealth.

Destination Hell

Already a company has come out with a credit card that monitors CO2 usage called "Doconomy" or DO for short, and collaborates with Mastercard. In addition to monitoring our carbon footprint, it can also cut off our spending when we reach our "carbon max."[262] But just who will assign our "personal carbon allowances"? I imagine those who head the New World Order. And of course, it will all be "for our good." The claim is that monitoring our carbon footprint is voluntary, at least for now. But we know where that's headed.

Since globalists will use global warming to redistribute wealth, and since they perceive America to be the worst offender and largest user of the world's carbon-based resources, the U.S. will need to be regulated by the international community and pay for their greedy crimes through carbon taxes.[263]

Biden and the Democrats already want to create a Civilian Climate Corps (CCC). Its funding (in the billions) is included in the 2021 Reconciliation Bill introduced by Bernie Sanders.[264]

While its aims sound good, one can see where this will eventually lead. I don't think it's a stretch to see a future where non-elected CCC officials will dictate what people can and cannot do on both private and public lands, all in the name of "climate control." What these elites fail to understand is that God controls the climate. He has the last say, not man. Nearly fifty verses in Scripture attest to this. Job 5:10, Job 28:25-27, Leviticus 26:4 and Matthew 5:45 are just a few.

Third, Klaus Schwab wants to "harness the innovations of the Fourth Industrial Revolution." Just what is that? Schwab himself defines it: "The Fourth Industrial Revolution will lead to a fusion of our physical, biological and **digital** identities." He's talking about implants, people being chipped and even merged with machines. In his book, *Shaping the Future of The Fourth Industrial Revolution*, which came out two years prior to the 2020 forum, Schwab made it even clearer. "Fourth Industrial Revolution technologies will not stop at becoming part of the physical world around us— **they will become part of us.**"[265]

Schwab is also an advocate of population control, believing the world's population should be around one billion. He also said, "You'll own nothing" and "you'll be happy about it."[266] So, if no one is going to own anything, who will? The Schwabs of the world? That's what happened in the Soviet Union. The common people got poorer, and the oligarchs (the elites) got richer.

Destination Hell

This is communism. Pure and simple. And that implies the end of private home ownership and small business. Is it any wonder that during the forced Covid lockdowns, small businesses were hit the hardest? According to Yelp, 60% of U.S. businesses that closed because of Covid will never reopen.[267]

That is tragic. Think of the many who lost their livelihoods, years of sweat equity, their dreams? Remember, the World Economic Forum called the pandemic a "perfect opportunity." Is this why in October 2019, the World Economic Forum and the Bill and Melinda Gates Foundation did a "simulation" called "Event 201" involving a global pandemic, the control of individual liberties, and economic downturns? A simulation that became reality just a few months later?[268]

How to implement the Great Reset was also discussed. Several key goals need to be reached. They are: 1) replacement of the dollar as the global currency 2) creation of a "cashless" society 3) weaken Christianity and its influence "by enforcing rules of punishment for intolerance" 4) limit travel 5) track the population 6) remove borders 7) destroy patriotism, and 8) reprogram the young.[269]

Other secondary but important measures were gun control, socialized medicine, cheap labor, high taxes, increasing the poverty level, and increasing national debts worldwide until they become unsustainable. Rest assured, the elites are busy working on all of them. Recently, a "gun confiscation bill" was inserted into the 2022 National Defense Authorization Act. It would enable a military court to confiscate guns from ex-service personnel and make it illegal for them to own one.[270]

But this is just the beginning. Expect more chipping away of our Second Amendment. Already the CDC have declared gun violence a "public health threat," and will study the matter. And Biden has called gun violence a "public health epidemic."[271] It seems they are getting ready to make their move.

A glimpse into the future:

If you want a small glimpse of what the New World Order will look like, then look no further than Australia, the poster country for Utopia. It employed some of the most draconian measures during the height of the pandemic. Even as late as July 2021, it refused to relax its edicts and after only 239 new cases of COVID popped up, Sydney immediately implemented an outdoor mask

Destination Hell

mandate, and restricted residents' travel to only three miles from their homes. What? Where is the science in that? In addition, the premier of New South Wales, Gladys Berejiklian, requested 300 military personnel to help impose the restrictions. You are talking about a military police force! Only thirteen people died during the July outbreak. And while one life is too many to lose, how is it possible that thirteen deaths require such tyrannical tactics?[272]

Then about two weeks later, The Minister for Health and Medical Research, Brad Hazzard, informed parents that their children would be required to be vaccinated, and that wasn't optional. In addition, parents were not allowed to be with them. In other words, Hazzard was telling parents that over 20,000 of their children would be forced into a stadium and injected and they couldn't even be there![273]

Australia was now on a roll. In August, health officials revealed their plan to build "Mandatory Quarantine Facilities," called "Wellcamp," to "house rule-breakers who have been ignoring lockdown orders, and keep them from leaving." On August 27, 2021, Queensland's Minister of Trade, Annastacia Palaszczuk, explained that this 1000-bed quarantine facility was needed "to keep you safe." In the meantime, their Gestapo-like-military police went door-to-door to make sure no one was violating the mandates. And this while only four new Covid cases in Queensland were reported, bringing the total in that state to twenty-six![274]

By September, Australia was using facial recognition and a geolocation app to enforce quarantines of returning travelers, and Premier Steven Marshall thought "every South Australian should feel pretty proud that we are the nation's pilot."[275] Also by September, Australian officials began using the term, "New World Order." Dr. Kerry Chant, Chief Health Officer of New South Wales said, "we will be looking at what contact tracing looks like in the **New World Order** and yes, it will be in pubs and clubs and other things."[276] Health Minister, Brad Hazzard, also used that phrase earlier on July 9, 2021 when he spoke of the pandemic and said, "We've got to accept that this is the **New World Order.**"[277]

By early September 2021, Australian officials were either talking about or had initiated quarantine camps; private, in-home electronic surveillance; control of online accounts; plastering quarantine notices on doors; and denying various services to those who had not been vaccinated.[278]

Destination Hell

Is it any wonder that these tyrannical Australian officials had no problem "ambushing" those who peacefully demonstrated against these extreme measures? That's what happened when people began protesting their inability to work and feed their families. Videos show Gestapo-type-police firing on unarmed crowds with rubber bullets and tear-gas. Even when the crowds dispersed and people tried to flee, they were shot in the back. The police had "begun deploying a new quick—strike tactic to disperse the crowd—rush the unsuspecting protesters and light them up with rubber bullets."[279]

Meanwhile, private citizens are being terrorized, daily. An Australian man was stopped and savagely beaten because, according to the new lockdown regulations, he was shopping too far from his home. It turned out they had mistaken him for someone else.[280] And a twelve-year-old girl was pepper sprayed for failing to wear a mask.[281] Another incident involved two Australian officials who showed up at a woman's house because of her "posting things on social media." Some of these postings concerned an upcoming protest. The officials "instructed" her to stay home.[282]

Then Gladys Berejiklian, Premier of New South Wales, warned that even after the Covid lockdowns ended, life for those not vaccinated "will be very difficult indefinitely."²⁸³ A few days later, Berejiklian resigned due to corruption charges.²⁸⁴

In the meantime, Australian police asked the government to ban all Melbourne flyovers so cameras couldn't capture the massive size of the anti-government protests.²⁸⁵ People were fed up.

Even so, Victoria's officials ramped up their mandatory quarantine program and told citizens they would be receiving random phone calls at their home, after which they had only five minutes to respond with a selfie. Failure to do so would bring a health official to their door.²⁸⁶

By November, Australian governors were threatening people with the seizure of their homes and bank accounts if they failed to pay their "COVID violation fines."²⁸⁷ During that same time, a Victoria lawmaker introduced two draconian bills authorizing the fining of individuals to the tune of $90,000 for violating public health orders and fining businesses $455,000. In addition, it authorized jail time of up to two years for non-compliance of Covid orders.²⁸⁸

A few weeks later, after nine new Covid cases popped up, the military was ordered to "relocate Covid-19 positive" people along with their "close contacts" to the Darwin quarantine camps.²⁸⁹

Destination Hell

Twenty-six-year-old Hayley Hodgson is someone who has been there. Without legal process or recourse, she was forcibly transported to the Howard Springs camp after her friend tested positive for Covid. There she was detained for two weeks even though promised a release once she tested negative and though constantly testing **negative**. And here's the kicker: as of November 2021, the current number of deaths in her area is **zero** yet authorities are putting people in quarantine camps![290]

And if that weren't enough, Jim Hoft, in his December 21st Gateway Pundit article, reported that beginning in February 2022, Australia will employ "vaccination hunters to track down the unvaccinated." Anyone over fourteen who is not vaxed will be fined up to 3600 euros or $4104 (1 euro = $1.14). This will bankrupt people and enable the government to confiscate their homes and property in payment of these fines.

Then on January 6, 2022, Michael Gunner, Northern Territory Chief Minister, announced that all those not fully vaccinated will now be required to stay indoors and unable to go to work until the following week. This was done to prevent the mild Omicron variant from spreading. The question is, will it be lifted? Or will some other excuse be made to continue the "lockdowns?"

If you think this will never happen in the U.S. or elsewhere, think again. The CDC now asserts it has the authority to apply the same enforcement tactics currently employed by Australia. It's already in the works. Congress has given Health and Human Services powers which the HHS then "delegated" to the CDC to "establish quarantine and isolation protocols." Think "Wellcamp." In addition, the CDC claims their powers also include the ability to utilize state and local police as enforcers.[291]

The National Defense Authorization Act (NDAA) already gives our government the authority to imprison any American citizen it deems a terrorist. And in 2006, a $385 million contract was awarded to Kellogg Brown and Root for the building of American detention facilities.[292] And you can be sure that when the time is right, the government will fill them.

And according to an article in The National Pulse by Kay Smythe, dated December 18, 2021, The New York Legislature will vote in early January 2022, on a six-year-old proposal, Bill A416. If passed, it will give the NY Governor or his/her delegates (local health departments, etcetera) the ability to detain any person or groups of people they believe pose a "significant threat to public health" and indefinitely remove them from public

Destination Hell

life. These people can be detained in a facility and forced to accept vaccinations and medical treatments against their will. The Bill only allows a 60-day confinement period but has the provision to be extended an additional 90 days, then another 90 days, then another 90 days, and on and on. Due to all the backlash, the Bill has since been taken down, but expect it to be resurrected again in the future.

Already, we can see glimmers of it. Recently, the Washington State Board of Health has proposed draconian Bill WAC 246-100-040. If passed it will authorize the involuntary detention of its citizenry, ages five and up, in "internment camps" for failure to get vaccinated.

Welcome to the New World Order!

The elites are well on their way to fully implementing their New World Order, their *New Atlantis*. They are diminishing America as a superpower and are working on destroying its Constitution, implying our laws should be made by a multi-national governing body. In other words, America should surrender its sovereignty to a body of unelected and unaccountable globalists like those in the U.N.

The elites are also busy destroying families in order to make the state the complete control agency; enlarge bureaucracies; centralize government; transition from a republic to a totalitarian (socialist or communist) government; control the media in order to control the message and push their propaganda; indoctrinate the young through the public school system and colleges; then create a crisis, or several, to invent a need for a strong federal government to "fix things."

And all this must be cloaked in palatable, even lofty-sounding words such as abortion becomes reproductive freedom, same sex marriage becomes marital justice, etcetera. But above all, demonize those who disagree or won't conform. Make them appear less than human and objects of derision and scorn so the rest of society will hate them and silence the opposition.

And with each manufactured crisis, acquire more power since people will be willing to give up additional freedoms to solve the problem. That means more restrictions, laws, government controls until, like the frog in the pot that doesn't know it's being boiled to death, we have lost all our freedoms and are ruled by tyrants.

In addition, popularize paganism and the religion of materialism. Dr. Michael Lake describes this

Destination Hell

religion in his book, *The Shinar Directive,* and lists these belief components:
- Man is just an animal
- There is no creator
- There is no god, except for yourself
- There are no absolutes
- There are no consequences for what we do[293]

All the above contain the playbook of the New World Order and One World Religion. The world is getting ready for antichrist. It's interesting to note that the three major religions, Christianity, Judaism, and Islam, are currently all awaiting their messiah.

But there is one more piece of the puzzle. Klaus Schwab's plan to join mankind with machines. How is that progressing?

I've covered this in my book, *The Coming Deception,* and will only repeat a few things here.

Man has been corrupting God's creation for some time. Plants, insects, animals, none have escaped. Hybrids are everywhere. Even our food supply is corrupted. GMOs (Genetically Modified Organisms) fill the produce sections and shelves of our food stores. Scientists are doing things to God's wonderful creation that are unthinkable.

And these scientists have already created kits that can modify human DNA and make a human into something else, something "other." The kit is called CRISPR-Cas9, short for, "clusters of regularly interspaced short palindromic repeats." Simply put, it's the altering of DNA to modify gene function. It's playing god. And now every person on earth can play god, too, because CRISPR has become available as a home-do-it-yourself-kit. It comes in a small box with four or five pre-filled injectable syringes which, when administered in a specific sequence, can alter DNA. Right now, it's being touted as something good because it can possibly target serious diseases such as Alzheimer's, leukemia, and cancer.[294] But that's how it always starts. Satan is no dummy. Get the foot in the door then come out with the real agenda, which is to corrupt mankind, change him into something detestable to the Creator.

In 2006 the Department of Health commissioned Case Law School to create guidelines concerning "trans-humans" and "bioethics."[295]

Joseph Infranco, lawyer for the Alliance Defense Fund, said, "We are well beyond the science fiction of H.G. Wells' tormented hybrids in the Island of Doctor Moreau. We are in the time where scientists are seriously contemplating the creation of human-animal hybrids."[296]

Destination Hell

Even the government has joined the effort. JASON, the highest think-tank of the Pentagon, believing that creating Human 2.0 is the next arms race, said that if they didn't enter the bio-tech war soon it would be too late, and that they needed to create a new species of man for the battlefield. In the Pentagon's 2011 budget, millions were allocated to redesign human DNA to create super battlefield soldiers.[297]

DARPA, the Pentagons' Defense Advanced Research Projects Agency, with a budget of $2 billion a year, has become "the world's largest funder of 'gene driven' research."[298] In 2013, DARPA requested a bid for Project ST13B-001, which involved "mammalian genome engineering," in other words, mixing animal and human DNA.[299]

Dr. Leon Kass, Chairman of the President's Council on Bioethics from 2001 to 2005, warned that, "All of the boundaries are up for grabs. All of the boundaries that have defined us as human beings, boundaries between a human being and an animal and between a human being and a super human being or a **god**."

And that's the bottom line. Transhumanists want a Utopia without God. In fact, they want to be god. And they readily admit it. Their aim is to drastically increase human lifespan as well as increase human intelligence, strength, and ability. In other words, they want to create a "super race." They view this as the "next step in evolution" and are willing to do just about anything to achieve it.

Nick Bostrom, professor at Oxford and a proponent of transhumanism, makes their position clear, "Transhumanists view human nature as a work-in-progress, a half-baked beginning that we can learn to remold in desirable ways. Current humanity need not be the endpoint of evolution. Transhumanists hope that by responsible use of science, technology, and other rational means we shall eventually manage to become post-human beings with vastly greater capacities than present human beings have."[300]

Zoltan Istvon, Former Presidential Candidate for the Transhumanist Party, simplified it by saying, "Transhumanism's number one goal is to not die and to become godlike through technology."[301]

Here are just a few experiments that have been or are currently being done: creating human-pig embryos, cross species experiments, cloning extinct or endangered species, and homosexual reproduction.[302] Other experiments include adding a silk gene to goats, injecting mice with a bovine growth hormone gene to create a "super mouse", pigs with mice DNA,[303] mice with human brains, and fusing human cells with rabbit eggs[304] The latest is mixing human and monkey DNA to increase the size of the monkey's brain.[305]

And this is just the tip of the iceberg!

What will the elites' new posthuman world look like?

It's frightening, but I'll let the proponents of transhumanism speak for themselves.

"The new species or 'posthuman' will likely view the old 'normal' humans as inferior, even savages, and fit for slavery or slaughter." George Annas, Professor at Boston University[306]

Author Noboru Kawazoe gives us additional insight into these new "superior" humans. "After several decades, with the rapid progress of communication technology, everyone will have a 'brain wave receiver' in his ear, which conveys directly and exactly what other people think about him and vice versa. What I think will be known by all the people. There is no more individual consciousness, only the will of mankind as a whole."[307]

And would you be surprised to learn that "there are already those in the Transhuman movement calling for concentrations camps for those who fail to make the transition"?[308] Will they be sent to "Wellcamp"? Why not? People like Elon Musk (CEO of SpaceX) declared that in the future only people who are cyborgs, who are connected to artificial intelligence, will be **relevant**.[309] So, obviously there will be those who are "irrelevant." And the next question is: "What do you do with them?"

The picture becomes clear. This is the elites' idea of Utopia: a depopulated earth, super humans who will live forever and be masters over the rest—those "inferior authentic humans." It is a Luciferin plan, plain and simple. And the elites, those members of secret societies, are working hard to ensure this agenda becomes reality even though some people, like Stephen Hawking, predict that AI (Artificial Intelligence) could be the "end of the human race."[310]

But AI has already infiltrated our lives. Some form of it is used in everything from car production to healthcare. Already the concept of human and robot babies is being explored. Artificial Intelligence researcher, Dr. David Levy, believes that "cells can be manipulated to create a baby with human and robot DNA."[311] Is this what Klaus Schwab meant when he said, **"technologies will become part of us"**?

Destination Hell

What these elites fail to understand is, *"the earth is the Lord's and the fullness thereof,"* (1 Corinthians 10:26). God owns everything. And in Genesis 1, seven different times He commanded that each species produce "after his/their kind." Since seven is the number of perfection or completion, God was saying His creation was perfect and this was His perfect means of filling the earth. The DNA of species was never to be mixed to produce hybrids. And NEVER was man's DNA to be altered since man was made in God's image.

Revelation 11:18b talks about how God will destroy those who destroy His creation, which is exactly what the transhumanists are doing. There is a time coming when all accounts will be settled.

What other signs are there that these are the end times?

First, lawlessness:

According to Jesus, the end times will be like the days of Noah and Lot (Luke 17:26-28) which were characterized by lawlessness (Genesis 6:13).

We have already established that the statistics on violent crime reveal an uptick. But in addition to individual crime, lawlessness has spread across America through groups like Antifa and Black

Lives Matter. These groups have also spread throughout Europe and other countries. And for the most part, the media looks the other way. A case in point: the riots in St. Paul, Minneapolis after the death of George Floyd that lasted from May 26, 2020, to June 7, 2020. The media called it "mostly peaceful." This "mostly peaceful" uprising ended by destroying 330 buildings and leaving a **five-mile** trail of destruction. The damage in dollars is estimated to be $82 million. Shops were burned or looted. Almost two-dozen pharmacies were robbed and, according to the Drug Enforcement Administration, $15 million worth of narcotics ended up on the city's streets. And by year's end, violent crime had increased in that area by 21%.[312]

And Shillman Journalism Fellow, Daniel Greenfield, claims that due to Black Lives Matter, the "number of black murder victims rose 62% in one year."[313]

But riots also occurred in other parts of the nation. Shops were robbed, destroyed, and their owners sometimes injured as they tried to protect their property. And those in authority, the ones elected to keep their community safe, did absolutely nothing to protect their citizens!

Destination Hell

Natural Disasters:

Jesus also said the end times will be marked by natural disasters. So, are we seeing them?

According to the U.N.'s World Meteorological report of September 1, 2021, over the past half century, "extreme weather events" have increased by a factor of five which averages out to one each day.[314]

Also, reports indicate that June 2021 was the "hottest in recorded history." Temperatures in places like Washington state and Oregon spiked to over one hundred degrees. Droughts in the southwest dried-up reservoirs, seriously impacting farmers and ranchers. Twelve states saw a combined total of eighty-six wildfires,[315] while other states, like New York and Pennsylvania, were flooded by rain.

Reports of world-wide flooding and drought are also common. So are the reports about the increase of tornados, hurricanes, earthquakes, and volcanic eruptions.

Regarding tornados: according to NOAA, the National Oceanic and Atmospheric Administration, EF-O tornados have increased.[316] EF-Os are weak tornados with wind speeds of sixty-five to eighty-five miles per hour. NOAA credits this "increase" to better instruments and tracking devices.

But then, in December 2021, the "Quad-State Tornado" hit four states. December rarely sees more than one tornado in these areas. Now, they saw 44, causing damage over a 230-mile long and three-quarters of a mile wide course. Less than a week later, another tornado hit "half of the lower 48." Downed trees produced power outages, roofs were ripped off, vehicles overturned like toys. Also during that time, the National Weather Service logged in a record breaking 55 different reports of hurricane winds in one day.

Although hurricanes in general have also increased, Drs. Vecchi and Knutson from NOAA Geophysical Fluid Dynamics Laboratory say it's "likely that the increase in Atlantic tropical storm and hurricane frequency in HURDAT (Hurricane Databases) since the late-1800s is primarily due to improved monitoring."[317]

Earthquakes greater than 8.0 in magnitude have also greatly increased since 2004. Scientists credit this to "mere chance."[318]

And *The Watchers* website claims that volcanic activity is increasing and that we are seeing

Destination Hell

activity in volcanoes formally thought to be dead.[319] On the other hand, the Smithsonian's Global Volcanism Program claims it doesn't "see any evidence that volcanic activity is actually increasing."[320] But NPR claims that climate change will increase volcanic activity.[321]

If this all sounds confusing, it is. Many sites claim no increase in natural disasters while others claim they are increasing[322] and put the blame on climate change which, in turn, other sites claim is not occurring. But the "Big Gun," the World Economic Forum, the one most elites listen to, says natural disasters **are** increasing and again, it's because of climate change. They also say AI can help.[323]

Whatever the current truth, natural disasters **will** increase as the birth pains Jesus spoke about become more severe. There will be a "convergence" of all these things to create great distress on earth signaling that the Church Age is about to end. And all this already has and will continue to impact food production, which will lead to famines. The earth is groaning and it's not because of climate change.

These happenings, politically, economically, morally, spiritually, and in nature, point to the fact that America is on the edge of the abyss. Even if tomorrow we got the most capable president imaginable, and all the members controlling congress had integrity, would that bring America out of this crisis? No. It might delay things but not change them. No one man or political party can change what's happening here. Because I love my country, I like the slogan, "Make America Great Again." But if we really want to make her great again, we need to put Jesus back in charge. Patriotism isn't repentance. We can raise up an entire nation of patriots and it wouldn't change our destructive underlying issues. Without revival, judgment will fall.

So, how will God react? First, we need to understand that God is holy. When Isaiah saw God on His throne he was overwhelmed by his own sinfulness, and said, *"Woe is me! for I am undone: Because I am a man of unclean lips, and I dwell in the midst of a people of unclean lips,"* (Isaiah 6:5). The apostle John had the same reaction when he saw Jesus. John said, in Revelation 1:17, *"And when I (John) saw him (Jesus), I fell at his feet as dead."* John was so overwhelmed, he passed out!

And because God is so holy, He cannot abide evil, and sooner or later His justice must be satisfied by way of judgment.

Nahum 1:2 is sobering. *"God is jealous, and the LORD revengeth; the LORD revengeth, and is furious;*

Destination Hell

the LORD will take vengeance on his adversaries, and he reserveth wrath for his enemies." This is the facet of God no one wants to talk about. But it's just as real and relevant as the aspect of God's love. There comes a time when God moves in wrath. Exodus 34:7 tells us that God will *"by no means clear the guilty."* While Proverbs 11:21 says, *"the wicked shall not be unpunished."* And Hebrews 10:31 says, *"It is a fearful thing to fall into the hands of the living God."*

There will be no escape. No one gets a free pass. Those not covered by the blood of Jesus will be held accountable for their sins. But God is so merciful. No matter how evil their lifestyle or how far from Him they have wandered; no matter how deep or dark their sins, God will forgive them and accept them if they come to Him in genuine repentance.

Who can understand God's love? It's a love so great that He desires none should perish. He loves even the worst sinners, and His grace and mercy can and will cover all their sins. Proverbs 28:13 says, *"He that covereth* (hides/conceals) *his sins shall not prosper: but whoso confesseth and forsaketh them shall have mercy."*

But for those nations and people who stay on that broad way and don't repent, God's judgment will fall, and they will experience His wrath. Since He *"is the same yesterday, and today and forever,"* (Hebrews 13:8) and He changes not, (Malachi 3:6), all we need do is look at what He has done in the past to see what He will do in the future.

Several prophets foretold that both the Assyrians and Babylonians would destroy Israel. Among them were Micah and Jeremiah. God's anger can be clearly felt in Micah 1:2-5: *"Hear, all ye people; hearken, O earth, and all that therein is: and let the Lord GOD be witness against you, the Lord from his holy temple. For, behold, the LORD cometh forth out of his place, and will come down, and tread upon the high places of the earth. And the mountains shall be molten under him, and the valleys shall be cleft, as wax before the fire, and as the waters that are poured down a steep place. For the transgression of Jacob (Israel) is all this, and for the sins of the house of Israel.* **What is the transgression of Jacob?"**

Micah lists them.
1) idolatry
2) evil works by those in power
3) abuse of power for benefit or enrichment
4) oppression of those without power
5) false prophets who use divination to gain wealth or power
6) people following false prophets

Destination Hell

Prior to these judgments, Israel's government and religious system became corrupt. Their primary interest was enriching themselves. They abused the people below them, and by their actions led the nation into idolatry. The prophets were no better. They used divination for their own gain, and people listened because their messages were pleasant. While the prophets were saying, "peace, safety, and prosperity," God was saying, "conflict, death, destruction."

America is now committing the same sins that forced God to destroy Israel:
1) idolatry—love of money, lovers of self (2 Timothy 3:2-7); the worship of Molech—the killing of children (shedding of innocent blood); sexual immorality, and pride (Romans 1:22)
2) blatant evil committed by those in authority
3) abuse of power for benefit or enrichment
4) the sin of unjust balances or perverted judgment. There is now a two-tiered justice system; one for the elites (the privileged and connected) and one for the rest of us.
5) false prophets who speak out of their own minds and hearts for gain
6) People following false prophets and believing there is a utopia coming rather than the judgment of God.

In both Micah and Jeremiah, Israel's sins are called "wounds" or "bruises." And they were said to be **incurable** (Micah 1:9, Jeremiah 30:12). God declared them to be death wounds. There would be no recovery. Their nation was beyond saving. Israel was so far gone that the only thing God could do was destroy them, hence their destructtion and captivity by Assyria and Babylon.

America should have been judged years ago. God has been patient with us. He has stayed His hand, I believe, in part, because we have been friends of Israel and God said that whoever blesses Abraham (the Jewish people) will be blessed and whoever curses Abraham, will be cursed, (Genesis 12:2-3). But that is changing. The Democrat Party is increasingly hostile to Israel. Recently, the House, in the 2022 Budget Bill, eliminated U.S. funding for Israel's Iron Dome, their major defense tool against rocket assaults. But after a huge backlash, they reinserted it.[324]

Then a few days later, the Democrat Congress proposed another bill which would turn over "Jerusalem's Jewish Quarter, Western Wall and Christian Holy Sites to Palestinians," and declared them "occupied territories."[325] Eventually, the Democrats will succeed in completely alienating us and Israel, thus taking away our last vestige of protection from God's inevitable wrath.

Destination Hell

If God judged His own chosen people, the nation of Israel, for their continual sins and rejection of Him after He gave them warning after warning after warning, what makes America think we are not going to be judged when we have thrown God out of our schools, courtrooms, government, families, and personal lives?

Instead of honoring the God who poured His grace on us, we have continually turned away from Him to become the largest distributor of pornography, the loudest advocate for abortion, the largest users of illicit drugs, the population with the highest number of STDs (sexually transmitted diseases), the nation with the highest number of teen pregnancy, the nation with one of the highest divorce rates, and with the highest percentage of single-parent households.[326]

Oh, how the mighty have fallen!

In addition, we have spit in God's face by enacting immoral laws. We have erected idols of materialism, money, pleasure, sex, and hedonism. We have become a pagan nation no longer fearing or honoring the God of creation.

The Bible says to whom much is given much is required, (Luke 12:48b). Thus, because America has been given so much, God requires much from us. Failure to do so, and instead, abusing God's grace, will eventually lead to the end of His mercy, then to the ultimate pronouncement of judgment. America and many of its people are traveling on the "broad way," the road to destruction, leading those on it to hell on earth and the seven-year Tribulation, then to the hell of the underworld, and finally to the hell in the lake of fire.

In the light of all this, I believe God is saying: **"America, your 'wound is incurable' and judgment is coming."**

Hell on Earth—the Seven Year Tribulation

The seven-year Tribulation will be bone chilling; a horror movie times a hundred. All the elements are there: terror, carnage, flight, disaster, suffering, death. But before that, something wonderful happens: THE RAPTURE! I've already covered this in my book, *12 Questions New Christians Frequently Ask,* but because of its importance, will include most of it here. It truly is our "blessed hope."

Is there really going to be a rapture?

The rapture question garners more dissention and downright anger as few other questions. And this puzzles me since it doesn't affect one's salvation. I think sometimes this vitriol stems from a mistaken belief that the rapture is escapist theology which will put the church to sleep and keep it from obeying the Great Commission.

Nothing can be further from the truth. Knowing what lies ahead for those left behind will make Christians more faithful in witnessing and praying for others. Because they love God, their family, friends, and neighbors, they won't want them to face the horrendous events that will unfold.

Another common indictment concerns the very word "rapture." Since it's not in the Bible, it must be invalid or even heresy. But other commonly accepted words such as Bible, Trinity, and Christianity are not mentioned, either. And while the word "rapture" may not explicitly be in Scripture, it is implied. 1 Thessalonians 4:17 speaks of the rapture and uses the term "caught up" which is *harpazo* in Greek and means "to seize, catch, pluck, pull, take by force." But when the Bible was translated into Latin, *harpazo* became *rapiemur* which is rendered "rapture" in English.

Still others scoff because the rapture seems too fantastic. Both Jude and Peter predicted this. Jude 17-18 says, *"But beloved, remember ye the words which were spoken before of the apostles of our Lord, Jesus Christ; How that they told you there should be* **mockers in the last time,** *who should walk after their own ungodly lusts."* And 2 Peter 3:3-4 says, *"Knowing this first, that there shall come* **in the last days scoffers**, *walking after their own lusts, And saying, Where is the promise of his* (Jesus') *coming? For since*

Destination Hell

the fathers fell asleep, all things continue as they were from the beginning of the creation." Both Scriptures speak about the last days/time, meaning the end of the Church Age. People already are and will continue to mock the concept of a rapture. Even so, that doesn't change God's Word or negate His promise.

It's important to note that the rapture doesn't kickstart the Tribulation. Rather, the Tribulation begins when the antichrist confirms a covenant between Israel and other signatories. This means there could be days or even years between the rapture and the beginning of the Tribulation.

But to answer the question, "yes," there really is going to be a rapture which, by extension, brings us to the next question. When?

There are three main theories as well as some minor ones.

The three major ones claim the rapture will occur pre-Trib, mid-Trib or post-Tribulation. Pre-Tribulation rapture believers say the rapture will occur before the Tribulation begins. Mid-Tribers say it will happen in the middle, and post-Tribers believe it will happen at the end when we are caught up in the air, then do an immediate U-turn and come back to earth with Jesus.

The rapture should not be confused with the Second Coming of Christ. That's where people miss it. They lump these two together. The second coming of Jesus is preceded by a series of specific signs. The rapture is not. It could happen any time. And I believe it will happen prior to the Tribulation, therefore I believe in a pre-Tribulation rapture.

Why?

For one thing, all of Daniel's seventy-weeks pertain to Israel not the Church. Daniel was a Jewish captive living in Babylon. After praying for his people, the angel Gabriel appeared and gave him the following prophecy regarding the Jewish Messiah (Jesus) and what would happen to Israel. Gabriel began by saying, *"Seventy weeks are determined upon **thy people** (Israel) and upon thy holy city,"* (Daniel 9:24), confirming that this prophecy concerns **only** Israel and the city of Jerusalem.

Gabriel went on to say that Messiah will be killed, but not for himself, that Jerusalem will be destroyed, and the antichrist will make a seven-year covenant with the Jewish people but will break it midway when he desecrates the Temple. Jesus did, indeed, come and die, not for Himself but for sinners, and both the Temple and Jerusalem were destroyed in 70 A.D.

Destination Hell

Then, between the 69th and 70th week of Daniel, there is a pause. This is the Church Age or Age of Grace. Sometime after it ends, Daniel's clock will resume, marking the start of the 70th week or seven-year Tribulation and the appearance of the antichrist. It's called by various names including Jacob's Trouble (Jeremiah 30:7), the end time, the indignation, the day of the Lord. It's a time when God judges the earth and deals with Israel as He prepares her to become the head of nations.

But Scripture tells us that the body of Christ is not appointed to wrath. And since the seven-year Tribulation is all about God's wrath, the church will not be here.

With all this confusion, why study the rapture at all?

Because, as mentioned, the Bible calls it *"that blessed hope"* (Titus 2:13) and it's meant to encourage us. Also, it's a reminder to be ever ready to meet the Lord and live our lives fully for Him. In addition, we can use it to encourage others. Finally, considering how terrible the Tribulation will be, it's an added incentive to pray diligently for others so they, too, will be spared.

Sylvia Bambola
What did the apostles and early church fathers believe?

Ken Johnson, Th. D., author, lecturer of Bible prophecy and ancient history, addressed this in his book, *Ancient Church Fathers, What the Disciples of the Apostles Taught*. In it, he documented that not one ancient church father taught a mid or post-Tribulation rapture, while many taught and wrote of a pre-Tribulation rapture such as:
- Shepherd of Hermas 150 A.D.—the name of a respected and popular Christian document
- Irenaeus 170 A.D.—Bishop of Lyons, France
- Tertullian 207 A.D.—presbyter (an administrative official) in Carthage, North Africa
- Cyprian 250 A.D.—Bishop in Carthage, North Africa
- Ephraim the Syrian 373 A.D.—the name of a respected Christian document

The apostles and disciples themselves believed they were living in the end times and that the rapture would take place before the Tribulation. Some disciples even believed it would happen before John the apostle died because Jesus said in Matthew 16:28 that some would not die before seeing the Son of Man come into His kingdom.

Destination Hell

They didn't understand that John would see this in a revelation on the Isle of Patmos.

So, what changed? As mentioned, in 70 A.D., Jerusalem was destroyed, then the Jews dispersed. Years went by, the apostles died, Israel remained scattered, and still no rapture. And because the church had no other way to explain it, they allegorized Revelation and the rapture teaching, saying it revealed spiritual truths but was never meant to be taken literally. This idea gradually took hold.

Then, in the 5th Century, St. Augustine, a prominent theologian of the Catholic Church, established his doctrine of amillennialism which claimed the age he was living in was the Millennium. He asserted that the Tribulation had already occurred, that Israel was no longer relevant, and the church would progressively purify the world. When it was sufficiently cleansed, Jesus would return. After Augustine, other theories emerged.

What does the Bible say?

Paul was given the mystery of the rapture. In 1 Corinthians 15:51-52 he said, *"Behold, I shew you a mystery; we shall not all sleep, but we shall all be changed, in a moment, in the twinkling of an eye, at the last trump: for the trumpet shall sound, and the dead shall be raised incorruptible, and we shall be changed."*

In 1 Thessalonians 4:16-17, Paul further described this event. *"For the Lord Himself shall descend from heaven with a shout, with the voice of the archangel, and with the trump of God: And the dead in Christ shall rise first: Then we which are alive and remain shall be caught up together with them in the clouds,* **to meet the Lord in the air:** *and so shall we ever be with the Lord."*

This clearly tells us that Jesus does not return to earth during the rapture, while at His second coming, He will, along with His army (Revelation 19:14). But we see no army in the above Scripture. Rather, we see Jesus remaining in the clouds while the dead in Christ and the living believers meet Him in the **air**.

And just before that happens, Jesus will give a shout. That word "shout" means "to summon, command, a call." I believe that command will be, *"come up hither."* Also, the voice of the archangel will be heard. In the ancient Jewish wedding when a bridegroom came for his bride, there would be a shout, usually from the groomsman saying, *"behold the bridegroom commeth; go ye out to meet him"* (Matthew 25:6).

Destination Hell

So, 1 Thessalonians was written to tell us about the wonderful rapture and how it takes place. While 2 Thessalonians was written to reassure the Thessalonians that the rapture had not occurred.

In 1 Thessalonians 1, Paul praised the church for their steadfastness, endurance, patience, and firm faith amid the persecution and crushing distresses and afflictions they were experiencing. Things were tough. Because of this, a rumor circulated that they were in the Tribulation and had missed the rapture.

How does Paul respond? 2 Thessalonians 2:1-3 tells us. *"Now we beseech you, brethren, by the coming of our Lord Jesus Christ, and by our gathering together unto him* (the rapture), *That ye be not soon shaken in mind, or be troubled, neither by spirit, nor by word, nor by letter as from us, as that the day of Christ* (the Tribulation) *is at hand. Let no man deceive you by any means: for that day shall not come, except there come a **falling away** first, and that man of sin be revealed, the son of perdition."*

From this we learn the Tribulation won't come until there is a falling away and the antichrist is revealed. In Greek, that word for "falling away" is *apostasia* and has these meanings: "a defection from truth; a divorce, a writing of divorcement; to physically remove." So, we have a play on words, indicating that people (the apostate church) will leave the Truth (Jesus) and God will divorce them, then physically remove those He has not divorced—in the rapture. **Then** the Tribulation will come.

It's interesting to note that early Bible translators believed *apostasia* referred only to a physical departure rather than a spiritual one. In fact, in the 4th Century, when Jerome translated the New Testament into Latin, he translated *apostasia* as *discessio*, meaning "the departure." Other translators like Wycliffe (1384), Tyndale (1526) and Geneva (1608) followed suit by translating it "departing first" all denoting something physical. Then the King James translators changed all that in 1611 by using the phrase "falling away."

But *apostasia* really says it best because I believe all three meanings will be realized: a spiritual departure, a divorce, then a physical departure.

Now, regarding the antichrist, 2 Thessalonians 2:6-7 tells us this man of sin will be revealed only after the restrainer is taken out of the way. *"For now ye know what withholdeth* (what is restraining) *that he* (the antichrist) *might be revealed in his time. For the mystery of iniquity* (lawlessness) *doth already work: only he who now letteth will let, until he* (who restrains) *be taken out of the way."*

Destination Hell

Obviously, the Holy Spirit is the restrainer. But the Holy Spirit will not be taken out of the world, only out of the **way**. Even so, the restraining influence of the church must and will be removed. Part of the church's function is to prevail against the gates of hell, and to be salt and light in a dying world. After the rapture, evil will grow worse and worse. The antichrist will be revealed and given power to make war with the saints. Think how amazing the rapture is! The world will be a mess and we, His bride, will be removed, given our glorified bodies, and joined with Jesus, forever!

Though evil will be unrestrained, the Holy Spirit will continue to be active by emboldening the 144,000 and two witnesses, as well as drawing people to Jesus. The Bible tells us that multitudes will come to Christ during the Tribulation. It will truly be a time of great revival. In fact, it will be the greatest revival the world has ever seen.

We are not appointed unto wrath.

In Luke 17:26-30, Jesus likened the day of His coming to the days of Noah and Lot. In both cases, they were removed before God's wrath fell: Noah into the ark of safety where God Himself shut the door, while Lot and his family were physically removed from Sodom before its destruction.

But there is a warning in the actions of Lot's wife. Though she was told not to look back during her flight, she disobeyed, revealing her attachment to Sodom. She loved it more than she loved the things of God. She is a picture of the apostate church, those who love the world, are tied to it, and live worldly lives. And like Lot's wife, they will be left behind.

I find Luke 9:62 interesting. Here, Jesus said, *"No man, having put his hand to the plough, and* **looking back***, is fit for the kingdom of God."* Someone who has committed himself to Christ cannot return to the world or love it as Lot's wife did.

And so it will be in the last days. We will be rescued before everything hits the fan. Yes, we may go through hard times, but before God pours out His wrath on this evil world, we **will** be physically removed and placed in a heavenly ark of safety to be forever with Jesus.

1 Thessalonians 5:9 says, *"For God hath not appointed us to wrath, but to obtain salvation by our Lord Jesus Christ."* Here, that world "salvation" in Greek is *soteria* and means "rescue and safety," as well as "deliver, health, salvation, save, saving." Another play on words. It means we are saved from our sins and rescued from the wrath to come.

Destination Hell

Luke 21:36 tells us to, *"Watch ye therefore, and pray always, that ye may be accounted **worthy to escape** all these things that shall come to pass, and to stand before the Son of man."* Notice the words "worthy" and "escape." "Worthy" in Greek is *kataxioo* and means, "to deem entirely deserving," while that word "escape" is *ekpheugo* and means "to flee out, to run away, escape, to **vanish**." Thus, if we are a genuine born-again believer, a bride without spot or blemish because we are covered by the blood of Jesus and our sins are forgiven, we will not be here during the Tribulation. Notice, nowhere does it imply we will be protected through it or given power to endure it. Scripture is clear. **If** we are found worthy, we **will** escape. We will actually **vanish** before the Tribulation begins.

1 Thessalonians 1:10 says we are to, *"wait for his Son from heaven, whom he* (God) *raised from the dead, even Jesus, which **delivered** us **from** the wrath to come."* That word "delivered" (*rhuomai*) means "rescued." Again, note, we are delivered *from* the coming wrath not *through* it, implying we won't be here.

We have already seen that in Revelation chapters 1-3 Jesus addressed seven churches. As previously mentioned, these churches existed during John's day. But they also symbolized stages in church history and their characteristics. In addition, the churches of Smyrna and Philadelphia depict the remnant church, the one raptured, while the others represent the apostate church, the one left behind.

Further Scriptures regarding God's wrath:
- Ephesians 5:6, *"Let no man deceive you with vain words* (false doctrines) *for because of these things cometh the **wrath** of God upon the children of disobedience."*
- John 3:36, *"He that believeth not on the Son . . . the **wrath** of God abideth on him."*
- Romans 5:9, *"Much more then, being now justified by his* (Jesus') *blood, we shall be saved from **wrath*** (God's wrath) *through him* (Jesus)."
- Romans 1:18, *"For the **wrath** of God is revealed from heaven against all ungodliness and unrighteousness of men, who hold the truth in unrighteousness."*

If God's wrath is reserved for the ungodly, the unrighteous, the unbelievers, is it reasonable to imagine Jesus would pour out his wrath on His bride? I think not. On the other hand, doesn't God want to raise up a church without spot or blemish? Yes, and Ephesians 5:26-27 tells us how He wants to do it. *"That he might sanctify and cleanse it* (the church) *with the washing of water by the word, That he might present it to himself a glorious church, not having spot or wrinkle, or any such thing; but that it should be holy and without blemish."* Thus, Jesus wants to

Destination Hell

prepare His bride by the washing of water (Jesus is the living water) and by the Word (Jesus is the Word). John 15:3 says, *"Now ye are clean through the word which I have spoken unto you."* It's God's Word and Holy Spirit that changes us.

It's clear Jesus doesn't want to cleanse us, his bride, through wrath, by bludgeoning us in the Tribulation, then taking us home, battered and bruised. Furthermore, would the rapture be a *"blessed hope"* (Titus 2:13) if we had to experience the wrath of God? If we had to face death at every turn? Or endure the horrendous things that will occur? Would it be a *"comfort"* as described in 1 Thessalonians 4:17-18? Hardly.

One of the biggest arguments mid-Tribers give is that the first half of the Tribulation is the wrath of man and Satan, not of God. They believe the rapture will occur just before God's wrath falls in the second half of the Tribulation. But that's not accurate. Jesus is the One who opens the seals, which then opens both the trumpet and bowl judgments. It is by His hand alone that judgment falls even though He uses Satan and sinful man to accomplish some of it. Thus, the full seven years of Tribulation is the Lamb's wrath.

In Revelation 6:16-17, the unsaved people living during the first half of the Tribulation clearly understand who is responsible for what's happening when they say, *"to the mountains and rocks, Fall on us, and hide us from the face of him that sitteth on the throne, and from the **wrath of the Lamb**; For the great day of **his** (Jesus') **wrath** is come; and who shall be able to stand?"*

Mid-Tribers also believe Jesus won't rapture us until the mid-point because the first half won't be that bad, and it's only from then on things really heat up. Yes, the second half will be worse, but the first half is terrible, too.

Revelation talks about seven seal, trumpet, and bowl judgments occurring during the seven years of trouble. In the seal and trumpet judgments alone, which occur during the first half of the Tribulation, great disaster is unleashed through wars, famines, pestilence, the slaughter of believeers in Jesus, and massive earthquakes. Nearly half of the world's population die, and a good part of the earth is destroyed. So that argument doesn't ring true, either.

Some Biblical types and shadows of the rapture:

The Bible is multilayered with numerous types and shadows. Enoch is such a type. He is a picture of the rapture. Hebrews 11:5 tells us Enoch, *"was translated* (changed, removed) *that he should not see*

Destination Hell

death." Genesis 5:24 says, *"And Enoch walked with God: and he was not: for God **took** him."* That word "took" in Hebrew is *laqach* and means "to get, fetch, snatch away." It's so like the Greek word *harpazo*. But *laqach* also means "to marry, take a wife." Enoch represents the Gentile Church. His translation or rapture represents the rapture of the church. Just as Enoch walked with God, so those Christians who walk with God will be raptured. And just as Enoch was symbolic of God's wife, so the church is the Bride of Christ.

Moses, at Mt. Sinai, (Exodus 19:19-20) is another foreshadowing of the rapture. *"And when the voice of the trumpet sounded long, and waxed louder and louder, Moses spake, and God answered him by a voice. And the Lord came **down** upon the mount Sinai, and the Lord called Moses up to the top of the mount, and Moses went **up**."* In short, God came down and Moses went up, just like Jesus will come down amid the clouds and call us up.

Also notice how similar Exodus 19:19-20 is to 1 Thessalonians 4:16-17, *"For the Lord himself shall descend from heaven, with a shout, with the voice of the archangel, and with the trump of God: and the dead in Christ shall rise first: Then we which are alive and remain shall be caught up together with them in the clouds, to meet the Lord in the air: and so shall we ever be with the Lord."*

The Moses scenario is also similar to Revelation 4:1. *"After this* (after John received the seven letters to the churches) *I looked and behold,* **a door was opened in heaven**: *and the first voice which I heard was as it were of a* **trumpet** *talking with me; which said,* **Come up hither** *and I will shew thee things which must be hereafter."*

Revelation 4:1 is the rapture. Note the open door to heaven and the voice that sounded like a trumpet and then the command to, *"come up hither,"* after which John was immediately in God's presence. This mirrors both 1 Corinthians 15:52 and 1 Thessalonians 4:16 which speak of the rapture and describe the sound of a trumpet. Remember, God's voice sounded like a trumpet when He called Moses up to Mount Sinai. And 1 Thessalonians 4:16 specifically mentions *"the trump of God,"* not a man's trumpet.

Then John spends the entire seven-year-Tribulation in heaven while the horrific events are played out before him on earth. There is no mention of the church after chapter four. Why? Because the church is no longer on planet earth. Rather, the focus shifts to Israel and the evil Gentile world systems.

Destination Hell
Other pictures of the rapture and end times:

The seven feasts of the Lord reveal God's plan and timetable. The first three have already been fulfilled by Jesus: Passover, Unleavened Bread, First Fruits. We are currently in the Feast of Pentecost, which is the Church Age. Only three feasts remain: Rosh Hashanah or Feast of Trumpets, Yom Kippur or Day of Atonement, and Succoth or Feast of Tabernacles.

Although the rapture is imminent and can occur anytime, I don't rule out its occurrence on the Feast of Pentecost thus signaling the end of the Church Age. I say this because God is a God of order. He moves in cycles with His mysteries imbedded in types and foreshadowing. According to Jewish tradition, during the Feast of Pentecost there is a celebration called "decorating the bride" when they believe a window or portal in heaven is open for a short time. It officially ends the spring grain harvest and time of the "former rain," those rains that water spring crops, versus the "latter rain" or late rains that water the fall crops. It's an easy comparison to the harvesting of God's church from the earth and the end of the "former" outpouring of the Holy Spirit or "former rain." The close of the spring harvest was also the time Boaz, a type of Christ, claimed Ruth, a Gentile, for his bride.

So far, there have been five different dispensations throughout history, marking God's divine order: the Age of Innocence when Adam and Eve were in the Garden (Genesis 1-2); The Age of Conscience, from the time of the Fall to the flood (Genesis 3-7); The Age of Human Government, the time after the flood (Genesis 8-50); Age of the Law, which covers the time of Moses to Christ; and the Age of Grace, the current Church Age. Interestingly, Pentecost has marked three of them: Government (when God gave Noah the sign of the rainbow, according to the *Book of Jubilees*), Law (the giving of the Torah to Mosses),[327] and Grace (the birth of the Church in the upper room). So, it could well mark the beginning of the Apocalyptic Age or seven-year Tribulation which leads to the final dispensation, The Kingdom Age.

Pentecost is the only feast without a fixed date. It is simply fifty days after the offering of the *omer* (the first fruits of the barley harvest, which can change every year). And because our calendar doesn't use the offering of the omer to determine the true day of Pentecost, it could well satisfy Jesus' prophecy in Matthew 24:36 when He said no man will know the day or hour of His coming for His church.

Other scholars believe the Feast of Trumpets, when a hundred trumpet blasts sound over a two-

Destination Hell

day period, is the better candidate. That's because a trumpet is mentioned in both 1 Corinthians 15:52 and 1 Thessalonians 4:16. But as stated, Thessalonians talks about the "trump of God" not a trumpet of man, so I don't believe it's a good fit.

But whatever the case, both the Feast of Pentecost and Feast of Trumpets come before the Day of Atonement (Yom Kippur), which is a type of the Tribulation, and Succoth or Feast of Tabernacles, which is a type of the millennial kingdom when God tabernacles with man, again indicating the rapture will occur before the Tribulation.

Adding to the rapture picture are the three major harvests in Israel: barley, wheat, and fruit.

Barley, the first harvest, is a soft grain and winnowed by throwing it into the air so as not to crush the kernels. It's a picture of the believers in Jesus, whose hearts and minds are tender toward God. It's a picture of God harvesting His church through the rapture prior to the Tribulation.

Then comes the wheat harvest. Because wheat is a hard grain, it must be threshed to remove the chaff (shell). In Bible times, it was often threshed by a sled-like board with its bottom embedded with rocks. A man stood on the board while it was harnessed to an ox then dragged over the wheat.

In Latin, that threshing board is called a *"tribulum."* It's a picture of the harvest of believers during the Tribulation after they are threshed, their hearts softened, and they have come to the Lord.

And finally, we have the fruit harvest, most notably the grape harvest. Grapes are crushed. It speaks of the final harvest when unbelievers are gathered, then crushed in the winepress of God's wrath. Revelation 14:19 says, *"And the angel thrust in his sickle into the earth, and gathered the vine of the earth, and cast it into the great winepress of the wrath of God."* What an awful picture! But the truth is, God doesn't want to crush anyone in His winepress, yet justice demands He do so.

But the law of gleaning reveals His tender heart. In Bible times, owners left the four corners of their fields unharvested for gleaners—the poor and widows—as a means for them to obtain food. In Matthew 24:1-31, Jesus, talking about the end of the Tribulation, said in verse 31, *"he* (the Son of Man) *shall send his angels with a great sound of a trumpet, and they shall gather together his elect from the four **winds**, from one end of **heaven** to the other."* What a beautiful picture of God gleaning the fields after the Tribulation so that not one precious kernel (soul) will be overlooked!

Destination Hell

To avoid confusion, note "winds" is *anemizo* and means "the four quarters of the earth." And even though the word "heaven" is used instead of "earth," it does not imply that the angels will be looking for believers outside the earth. Rather, that word "heaven" is *ouranos* and means, "sky, happiness, gospel, Christianity, a mountain, as lifting itself above the plain." I think it's safe to say the angels are gleaning the earth looking for surviving believers in Jesus; those who had stayed above or out of the reach of antichrist.

One of my favorite types and shadows of the rapture is imbedded in the ancient Jewish wedding, which has many parts and can take a year or longer. First, the bride is purchased. A bride price is agreed upon and paid by the bridegroom, just like Jesus purchased His bride with His blood. Then the marriage contract is drawn up. It details the obligations and responsibilities of both the bridegroom and bride. The New Testament is our marriage contract. It lays out Jesus' responsibilities to us and ours to Him. He saves us from eternal damnation. He protects us. We hide His Word in our heart. We obey His voice, etcetera.

In the Jewish wedding, the bride must accept or reject the offer via a verbal declaration. In like manner, we must accept or reject Jesus' offer of salvation, and voice it. Romans 10:9 says, *"if thou shalt **confess with thy mouth** the Lord Jesus and shalt believe in thine heart that God hath raised him from the dead, thou shalt be saved."*

Then, once the bride accepts the offer, the groom gives her gifts. Ephesians 1:13-14 tells us that after we believe the salvation message, we are *"sealed with the holy Spirit of promise, which is the **earnest** of our inheritance."* Here earnest means "pledge given in advance as security for the rest," like an engagement ring. Then the nine gifts of the Spirit are given (1 Corinthians 12:4-11).

After the gifts, the bridegroom returns to his father's house to prepare the bridal chamber. In John 14:2-3, Jesus said, *"In my Father's house are many mansions: if it were not so I would have told you. I go to prepare a place for you. And if I go and prepare a place for you, I will come again, and receive you unto myself; that where I am there ye may be also."*

Because our bridal chamber is in heaven, we must go there to complete the wedding. And it's the father who tells his son when it's time to bring his bride home. That's why Jesus said in Matthew 24:36, *"But of that day and hour* (the rapture when Jesus comes for His bride) *knowest no man, no, not the angels of heaven, but my Father only."*

Destination Hell

While the bridegroom is away preparing, he and his bride are legally married and can only be separated by a bill of divorcement. Again, we see why that word *apostasia* not only refers to a defection from truth, but a divorce, a writ of divorcement, in addition to being physically removed. Jesus will divorce those who have defected from the truth, and take those who have not, to the bridal chamber to consummate the marriage.

And while the bride is waiting for her groom, she must keep herself pure. When he finally returns, it's usually unannounced and at night. He then takes his bride to the bridal chamber where the couple will remain for seven days: a perfect picture of the raptured bride hidden away in the heavenly bridal chamber during the seven-year Tribulation.

At the end of seven days, the bridegroom brings out his bride and they join their guests for a marriage feast. Revelation 19:9 says, *"And he saith unto me. Write, Blessed are they which are called unto the marriage supper of the Lamb."*

Who are the "saints or elect" referred to during the Tribulation?

This refers to the 144,000 and those, both Jew and Gentile, who accept the Lord after the rapture. The words "elect" and "saints" are often used in the Old Testament to refer to the Jews. Isaiah 45:4 calls Israel *"mine elect."* Isaiah 65:9 also called Jacob and his seed, *"mine elect."* And Deuteronomy 33:3 says, *"all his saints* (those sacred, holy) *are in thy hand."* While I Samuel 2:9 says, *"He will keep the feet of his saints."* These are but a few examples in the Old Testament, all referring to Jews.

In the New Testament, the word "elect," as in Colossians 3:12, speaks of believers in Jesus. There are also many references to "saints" which also refer to believers. So, when Matthew 24:22 says, *"except those days should be shortened, there should no flesh be saved: but for the elect's sake those days shall be shortened,"* it refers to both Jews and Gentiles who accepted Jesus after the rapture and during the Tribulation.

What happens after the rapture?

All those left are on that broad way heading to hell. Meanwhile in heaven, believers will appear before the judgment seat of Christ. Revelation 11:18 speaks of this. *"And the nations were angry, and thy wrath is come, and the time of the dead, that they should be judged, and that* **thou shouldest give reward unto thy servants the prophets, and to the saints, and them that fear thy name, small and great**.*"* Additionally, both 1 Corinthians 3:13-15 and 2

Destination Hell

Corinthians 5:9-10 talk about the judgment seat of Christ.

This judgment seat is "bema." That word refers to a raised platform. In Roman times a judge sat on a bema, watching the athletes as they ran a race to ensure they followed the rules. Then, when the race was finished, he awarded the appropriate prizes. It's a perfect description of Jesus judging His church. Hebrews 12:1 says, *"let us run with patience the **race** that is set before us."*

All believers are running a race, and the Bema Judgment will not be a time of condemnation, but a time of rewards. Jesus will hand out crowns according to how we lived our lives for Him. Some believe there will be a span of time between the rapture and the beginning of the Tribulation, giving Jesus time to do this. Then, after the award ceremony is over, they will enter the bridal chamber for the full seven years of Tribulation.

Also, after the rapture, God transitions His focus from the church to Israel. Romans 11:25 says *"blindness in part is happened to Israel, **until the fullness of the Gentiles** be come in."* During the Tribulation, this blindness will be removed.

Micah 7:1-6, speaking of the end times, gives a bleak picture of what it will be like immediately after the rapture. *"Woe is me! for I am as when they have **gathered** (to remove, take away, fetch) the summer fruits, as the grape gleanings of the vintage: there is no cluster to eat: my soul desired the first ripe fruit. **The good man is perished out of the earth**: and there is none upright among men: they all lie in wait for blood; they hunt every man his brother with a net. That they may do evil with both hands earnestly, the prince asketh, and the judge asketh for a reward* (a bribe): *and the great man, he uttereth his mischievous desire: so they wrap it up. The best of them is as a brier: the most upright is sharper than a thorn hedge: the day of thy watchmen and thy visitation cometh: now shall be their perplexity. Trust ye not in a friend, put ye not confidence in a guide: keep the doors of thy mouth from her that lieth in thy bosom. For the son dishonoureth the father, the daughter riseth up against her mother, the daughter in law against her mother in law; a man's enemies are the men of his own house."*

Chaos and darkness have fallen upon the earth.

Two cautionary tales:

The parable of the ten virgins in Matthew 25:1-13 is a warning. Five of the virgins were wise and five were foolish. All ten fell asleep waiting for the bridegroom to come like so many in the body who are tired of waiting for Jesus to return. Five had extra oil and five ran out. Oil speaks of the Holy

Destination Hell

Spirit. Not having oil signifies they were not operating under the power of the Holy Spirit, thus were **carnal** Christians. Could these ten virgins represent the two end-time churches: the carnal, lukewarm, apostate church and the faithful remnant church praised by Jesus? I think so.

In the end, only five went with the bridegroom to the marriage and the *"door was shut,"* so like when God shut the door of Noah's ark. When the five foolish virgins shouted, *"Lord Lord, open* (the door) *to us,"* Jesus' answer was, *"I know you not."* And like Lot's wife, they will be left behind.

We see something similar in Matthew 24:40-43. Jesus is talking about the end times and says, *"Then shall two be in the field; the one shall be **taken**, and the other **left**. Two women shall be grinding at the mill; the one shall be **taken**, and the other **left**."* Another warning that during the rapture Jesus will take His bride and leave the rest, and that while we wait, we should keep our garments clean and not love the world or hold too tightly to our lives.

What are the reasons for the Tribulation?

Here are the main ones. Notice, none include purifying the church.

The Tribulation will reveal God's amazing character, His goodness, patience, and omnipotence. He is in total control! And even though it will be horrendous, over and over God shows His mercy by giving people opportunities to repent and turn to Him. He does this by sending two witnesses from heaven, by the 144,000 Jewish evangelists, and by the flying angel who proclaims the gospel throughout the world.

The Tribulation will also expose Satan for who he is, a deceiver and murderer, especially after the demon possessed antichrist comes to power.

As mentioned, during this time God will transition His attention from the church to Israel. He will also focus His attention on the sinful world, its sinful systems, and the sinful people who have rejected Him. He will purge the earth by fire and other judgements in preparation for His 1000-year reign.

Paul wrote in Acts 17:31 that, *"He hath appointed a day, in which he will judge the world in righteousness."* That "day" is the seven-year Tribulation.

Daniel 9:24 also gives the following reasons for the Tribulation or 70th week:
- To finish transgression
- To make an end of sins
- To make reconciliation for iniquity

Destination Hell

- To bring in everlasting righteousness
- To anoint the most Holy One (which is Jesus as King of Kings and Lord of Lords)

John's rapture:

As previously mentioned, Revelation 4:1 (*"Come up hither"*) is the rapture, signaling the end of the Church Age. John then found himself in the presence of God. Revelation 4:2-3 describes what he saw. *"And immediately I was in the spirit: and behold, a throne was set in heaven, and one sat on the throne. And he that sat was to look upon like a jasper and a sardine stone: and there was a rainbow round about the throne, in sight like unto an emerald."*

I love evangelist, teacher, and author, Perry Stone's commentary on this. He mentions that the sardine (sardius) and jasper stone were the first and last stones on the breastplate of Israel's high priest. In addition, Reuben (Jacob's firstborn) is represented by the sardius, and his name means, "behold a son," and Benjamin (Jacob's last son) is represented by the jasper and means, "son of the right hand" Both names are symbolic of Jesus as the "Son," Who sits at the "right hand of God." What a wonderful picture!

But that's not all. Perry Stone goes on to say that the emerald rainbow is not only the sign of God's covenant with Noah, but that an emerald was the fourth gem on the breastplate and represented the tribe of Judah, the very tribe from which Jesus came. Also, in ancient Jewish weddings, emeralds were the common wedding stones of the wealthy. It's a beautiful picture of Jesus as Bridegroom and John representing His bride, the church.

Also notice that while the jasper stone was the last stone on the high priest's breastplate, it was the first gem John mentioned, indicating he first saw Jesus sitting at the right hand of God. What an amazing sight that must have been! To see Jesus in all His glory! In addition, John doesn't call the jasper and sardius a gem, but a stone. That word stone is *lithos* and means, "a stone, a stumbling stone."

So, John also saw Jesus as "a stone (the Rock) and a stumbling stone." 1 Corinthians 10:4, as well as countless other Scriptures, tell us that Jesus is our Rock (stone), while Romans 9:33 specifically calls Jesus a *"a stumbling stone and rock of offence."* But those who believe in Him have nothing to worry about. To them, He will be their firm foundation: reliable and strong. And so He was to John, his reliable and strong foundation.

On the other hand, those who reject the Son of God should worry. Isaiah 8:14 talks about this *"stone of*

Destination Hell

stumbling and rock of offence," referring to how God will be a comfort to those who fear Him but great sorrow to those who don't.

Peter quoted Isaiah when talking about Jesus and unbelievers. *"And **a stone of stumbling, and a rock of offence**, even to them which stumble at the word* (of God)*, being **disobedient**: whereunto also they were appointed,"* (1 Peter 2:8).

So, when John saw the "Stone" it pointed to the fact that to believers, Jesus is not only their husband but their solid rock. However, to unbelievers, He is the Judge, the stumbling stone, the very stone that will crush them.

Then John noticed twenty-four elders sitting on thrones all dressed in white and wearing gold crowns. These elders fell on their faces and tossed their crowns at Jesus' feet saying: *"Thou are worthy, O Lord, to receive glory and honour and power: for thou hast created all things, and for thy pleasure they are and were created,"* (Revelation 4:10-11). What a sight! John was standing in the very presence of the God of all creation! His majesty and power had to be overwhelming.

There was a scroll in God's hand and John heard an angel ask, *"Who is worthy to open the book, and to loose the seals thereof?"* The angel was really asking,

"Who is the rightful heir?" Revelation 5:3 says, *"no **man** in heaven, nor in earth, neither under the earth was able to open the book, neither to look thereon."* That's when John began to cry.

The heir had to be a man. And we are told He is none other than the Lion of the tribe of Judah, the Root of David. It's Jesus, the Son of man, our Kinsman Redeemer. But when John looked, he saw a Lamb who had been slain, indicating why the Lamb was worthy to open the scroll. He had paid for it with His blood. And the Lamb was in the midst of the throne, surrounded by the four beasts who worshipped Him—indicating He is God.

Revelation 5:7 says, *"And he* (the Lamb) *came and took the book out of the right hand of him that sat upon the throne."* And when He did, all heaven burst into praise and worship, *"Worthy is the Lamb that was slain to receive power, and riches, and wisdom, and strength, and honour, and glory and blessing,"* (Revelation 5:12).

Because this scroll was sealed, it implies it is a legal document. In ancient Israel, property contracts were often sealed this way. Copies were stored in the Jewish Temple until the debtor proved that any debt made against his property was satisfied. Wills of affluent Romans were also sealed with seven seals. Thus, we can deduce that the scroll Jesus

Destination Hell

holds is a legal will involving property; the very title deed to earth, the one legally held by Satan during his time as "covering cherub" then rescinded due to his rebellion. It's the one that gave Adam and Eve authority over the earth before the fall; the one Satan was able to obtain again by default.

Now, Jesus is ready to appropriate His rightful inheritance. Because, as the second Person of the Trinity, He left the glory of heaven and became our Kinsman Redeemer, a man, and died for the sins of the world, He paid the debt on this property (the world) in full and can legally claim it.

And He, the Lamb, was the one who *"prevailed to open the book and to loose the seven seals thereof,"* (Revelation 5:5), meaning Jesus breaks all seven seals. The entire Tribulation wrath is contained in this scroll. It contains all the judgments that will be poured out for seven years.

Seven is the number of completion, perfection, and fullness. Thus, the seven seals, seven trumpets and seven bowls or vials complete God's perfect judgment and usher in the millennial reign. Jesus is about to break the back of sinful, unrepentant man, and pound the planet in judgment.

Sylvia Bambola
The enormity of the Book of Revelation:

Revelation talks about things that had already happened, was happening in John's day, and what will happen in the future. Chapter one is about Jesus, who He is, His death, burial, and resurrection. Chapters two to three are about seven churches, as well as the entire Church Age. Chapter four is the rapture. In chapter five, Jesus takes the scroll in preparation for the seven-year Tribulation. Chapters six to eighteen refer to that Tribulation. Chapters nineteen to twenty-two cover the disposal of both the antichrist and false prophet, the chaining of Satan, the millennial reign, the great White Throne Judgment, and the creation of a new heaven and earth.

The clock is set, the covenant signed.

Daniel 9:27 tells us the exact moment the Tribulation begins. It is when the antichrist *"shall* **confirm** *the covenant with many for one week."* It's interesting to note that the word "confirm" is *gabar* and means, "to be strong, to prevail, act insolently, to rise up in arrogance against God." It is the same root word used when describing Nimrod, the "mighty hunter" in Genesis 10:9. That word in Genesis is *gibbor* and comes from *gabar*, and means, "arrogant, tyrant, powerful." It's no coincidence that Nimrod is a type of antichrist or that secret

Destination Hell

societies are looking for his return/resurrection so he can finish the work he began at the Tower of Babel. But here, Daniel 9:27 hints that the antichrist also acts in arrogance.

This covenant is with the nation of Israel. Many Bible scholars believe it is not only a peace treaty but allows Israel to build her third Temple. Isaiah 28:15-18 talks about this last-days covenant and calls it a *"covenant with death and hell."* Israel enters this agreement knowing it is evil. And they do it because they believe that *"when the overflowing scourge shall pass through, it shall not come unto us."* A lot is happening. An *"overflowing scourge"* covers planet earth, and apparently Israel's leaders see this covenant as a way of escaping it.

What is this *"overflowing scourge"*? Bill Salus talks about the end times in his many books, including *The Next Prophecies*. Using Scripture, he lays out the various conflicts he believes will happen prior to the rapture, immediately after it, and during the Tribulation. These are prophetic events that have yet to occur. Citing Jeremiah 49:34-39, Salus believes either Israel will attack Iran's nuclear Bushehr facility or there will be a mighty earthquake in that area which already has a history of seismic activity. The result will be a Chernobyl-like catastrophe forcing people to relocate.

If this comes by Israel's hand, it will cause a domino effect and lead to the war of Psalm 83, an Arab-Israeli conflict involving the ten nations or people groups sharing common borders with Israel. Their purpose in invading Israel is to take the land, probably to create a Palestinian state. But, according to Ezekiel 25:14, Israel's military is divinely empowered and wins. Though Israel will suffer heavy causalities, according to Obadiah v 18 and Jeremiah 49:10, their enemies are decimated, especially the Palestinians.

As a result, the Israeli army becomes feared and known as the "exceeding great army," (Ezekiel 37:10). In addition, Israel will expand her territory. And somewhere along the line, Damascus becomes a ruinous heap (Isaiah 17:1). *"Behold, Damascus is taken away (will cease) from being a city, and it will be a ruinous heap."* This has never happened. Damascus has been continuously inhibited for nearly 5000 years. But it's interesting to note that many terror groups have their headquarters in Damascus.

Along with more territory, Israel will also acquire great spoils, making her wealthier. This sets her up for the second Arab-Israeli conflict, the War of Gog and Magog as described in Ezekiel 38-39. This war is not for land but for "spoils." Ezekiel 38:10-12 says, regarding Russia, *"thou shalt think an evil*

Destination Hell

thought And thou shalt say, I (Russia) *will go up to the land of unwalled villages; I will go to them that are at rest, that dwell safely, all of them dwelling without walls, and having neither bars nor gates, To* **take a spoil, and to take a prey.**"

It is a Russian-Iranian led coalition against Israel with nine different nations or people groups involved. These are what Salus calls the "outer ring," those nations not bordering Israel. This time, God Himself will supernaturally destroy the invaders in order to make His holy name known amid His people Israel (Ezekiel 39:7).

Scripture tells us that in the last days the whole world will be against Israel. Anti-Semitism is already on the rise. Even the so-called "church" is against them. A case in point: in June 2011, the World Council of Churches met in Bolos, Greece to discuss the growing number of Christians murdered at the hands of Muslims. And what was their conclusion? *Israel was responsible!* Furthermore, they declared the Jewish state a "sin"! If that weren't enough, they went on to say that Christians had the responsibility to resist this "offensive" Jewish existence.

More recently (November 9, 2021), the U.N., in a vote of 160-1, passed an unlimited "right of return" for Palestinian refugees to Israel. Sadly, America abstained, retreating from Trump's pro-Israel policies in favor of Palestinians.[328] What this U.N. resolution suggests is that Palestinians have the right to overwhelm Israel's population with their own, making it essentially a Palestinian state. Since Israel will never allow this, it means more tension in the area.

Then on November 11, 2021, marchers in Kalisz, Poland chanted, "Death to the Jews, Jews out of Poland," and demanded they be expelled from the country.[329] Though it was immediately condemned by Polish officials, expect to see anti-Semitism rising throughout Europe.

By December 2021, Israelis felt certain they were on the brink of war with Iran and began planning to attack that nation, as well as internally strengthening themselves for retaliatory missile strikes. At the same time, Iranian proxies prepared by hiding their assets among the civilian population. All signs pointed to a full-blown confrontation which could occur by the release of this book. Is this the prelude to the Ezekiel 38 Gog and Magog war? Possibly.[330]

Satan hates the Jews and has always worked against them. Why? Remember, it was the Seed from their bloodline that sealed his doom. And it will be to their capital, Jerusalem, where that Seed,

Destination Hell

Jesus, will oust Satan's men, the antichrist and false prophet, and chain Satan for a thousand years while Jesus goes on to rule and reign.

Does worldwide hatred of Jews and warfare prior to the Tribulation make Israel ripe for the antichrist and create their willingness to enter into a *"covenant of death and hell"*? If so, they must believe it is the only way to protect themselves and ensure peace for their nation. Whatever the reason, Israel will enter this evil covenant which is "confirmed" by the antichrist, thus starting the Tribulation clock.

The first half of the seven-year Tribulation:

The stage is set. The restrainer, via the church, has been removed. Scripture tells us that the Spirit of God will not strive with man forever (Genesis 6:3). There comes a time when God will leave man to his own evil devices and their consequences. And that time comes when Jesus takes the scroll. In the first half of the Tribulation, seven seals and seven trumpet judgments will be poured out on earth.

The first seal:

Revelation 6:1-2 says, *"and I saw when the Lamb opened one of the seals, and I heard as it were the noise of thunder, one of the four beasts saying, Come and see.*

And I saw, and behold a white horse: and he that sat on him had a bow; and a crown was given unto him: and he went forth conquering and to conquer." Here we see a rider on a white horse gallop out. But notice, the rider comes out only after Jesus opens the seal, indicating that Jesus is in total control.

Who is this rider? It is the antichrist.

God's first judgment on the world is to give it a false leader who promises a false peace and a false Utopia. A world that has rejected Jesus is now ready to embrace an imposter. The rapture has occurred, and the world is in chaos. Referring to the end times, Jesus spoke of this in Luke 21:8. The first thing He mentioned was deception. *"Take heed that ye be not **deceived**: for many shall come in my name, saying I am Christ."* Now, the granddaddy of all deceivers has come upon earth's stage!

As many as two billion people have disappeared. Confusion and lawlessness abound. Government agencies are strained and unable to meet all the demands for help. Police departments aren't big enough to quell the chaos, looting, or violence. Fear and terror permeate the world. And because the restrainer is no longer restraining, evil is out of control.

Destination Hell

If children killed other children for their sneakers while the restraining influence of the church was still here, and if people shot and killed others for cutting them off in their car, imagine what is going to happen after the church is removed!

Next, notice the horse. It's white. Biblically speaking, white is symbolic of purity and righteousness. In Revelation 19, Jesus returns on a white horse, confirming that the first rider is a usurper, one who is not only against Christ, but who puts himself in place of Christ, and audaciously tries to mimic Him.

Then note that the rider carries a bow but no arrows indicating he has not obtained his position through war. Perhaps a deal was made in some back-room or by a committee of elites. It also suggests dishonesty and subterfuge. He comes under the false colors of peace while planning conquest. Revelation 6:2 clearly tells us his motives, *"conquering and to conquer."* He will eventually conquer three kings or leaders to secure power. He will also bring about a world war. Jesus, on the other hand, carries a sword and His intentions are perfectly clear, rid the world of evil.

1 Thessalonians 5:3, referring to the end times, says, *"For when they shall say, Peace and safety; then sudden destruction cometh upon them, as travail upon*

a woman with child; and they shall not escape." This is a sobering warning. Instead of peace, destruction is coming. And once the first seal is opened, there will be no stopping it. There will be no escape.

The rider is given a crown (singular). It is a **stephanos**, a wreath. Perhaps it's his reward for confirming that *"covenant with many"* spoken about in Daniel. In contrast, when Jesus returns, He wears many crowns or **diadema,** which are kingly crowns. Not a wilting crown of leaves handed to him by man, but crowns of gold given to Him by God the Father for laying down His life for the world.

Also, a *stephanos* was the kind of wreath presented to a Roman general in honor of his military achievements. During the triumph, the general rode in a chariot. Beside him stood a slave holding a *stephanos* over the general's head and gently reminding him that though he was a god that day, it would not last. It's interesting to note the rider in the first seal will also try to make himself a "god" and demand to be worshipped, but that won't last, either.

Next, the antichrist rides alone while Jesus, when He returns, will be followed by the armies of heaven.

Destination Hell

The antichrist on the white horse in Revelation 6 and Jesus on the white horse in Revelation 19 are spiritual opposites. The first rider (antichrist) will usher in a time of terror so brutal that, by comparison, Hitler will look like a kindergarten teacher. On the other hand, Jesus Christ will usher in 1000 years of peace and blessing.

Sometime at the beginning of the Tribulation, God sends His two witnesses from heaven to Jerusalem. For three and a half years, they testify and prophesy, preparing Israel for Christ's return. They have the power to send plagues and kill those who try to stop or harm them. Most scholars believe they will either be Elijah and Moses, or Elijah and Enoch.

No doubt Elijah will be one of the witnesses. For centuries, Jews have anticipated his arrival and even set a place for him at every Passover meal. And Malachi 4:5 speaks about the coming of Elijah *"before the great and dreadful day of the LORD."*

Those who believe the second witness will be Moses say it's because many of the miracles and plagues done by this witness mirror those done by Moses in Egypt. In addition, Jesus, during His transfiguration, with its reference to *"after six days"* alluding to six thousand years or the end times when He will return as King of Kings, spoke to both Moses and Elijah (Matthew 17:1-4). This could point to the fact that they are the dynamic duo referred to in Revelation. A strong point, but personally I favor Elijah and Enoch because neither one died but were raptured. Hebrews 9:27 tells us that *"it is appointed unto men once to die, but after this the judgment."* But God can do anything He wants, so only time will reveal their identity.

These witnesses must come on the scene at the beginning of the Tribulation because they are allotted three and a half years to preach. Revelation 11: 3 says, *"I* (God) *will give power unto my two witnesses, and they shall prophesy a thousand two hundred and threescore days* (three and a half years) *in sackcloth."* Then they are killed by the antichrist during the middle of the Tribulation. *"And when they shall have finished their testimony* (at the end of three and a half years) *the beast* (antichrist*) that ascendeth out of the bottomless pit shall make war against them, and shall overcome them, and kill them,"* (Revelation 11:7).

In addition, there are 144,000 Jewish evangelists who faithfully share God's Word and will bring many to Christ. We learn more about them in Revelation 7.

Also, early in the first half of the Tribulation, the Jews begin building their Temple. It is interesting

Destination Hell

that currently many Jews believe building the Temple will bring about the coming of the Messiah. This Temple must be finished by the middle of the Tribulation since that is when the antichrist will desecrate it and proclaim himself god. Much to their dismay, the Jews will realize this is not the Messiah they were hoping for.

The second seal:

Revelation 6:3-4, *"When He* (the Lamb) *had opened the second seal, I* (John) *heard the second beast say, Come and see. And there went out another horse that was red: and* **power** *was given to him that sat thereon to take peace from the earth, and that they should* **kill** *one another: and there was given unto him* **a great sword.**"

This time the horse is red, signifying blood, sorrow, death, and destruction. The rider is given two things: power to take peace from the earth, and a great sword. Notice these are **given** to him, again indicating Jesus is in control.

The results are terrifying. You are talking global warfare and violence. People are killing and being killed. To add to this picture, the rider's **great sword** is a *megas machaira*. This implies butchery and slaughter. While the world has seen many wars and conflicts, they are nothing compared to what's going to happen during this second seal judgment.

The third seal:

Revelation 6:5-6, *"And when he had opened the third seal, I heard the third beast say, Come and see. And I beheld, and lo a black horse; and he that sat on him had a pair of balances in his hand. And I heard a voice in the midst of the four beasts say,* **A measure of wheat for a penny; and three measures of barley for a penny** *and see thou hurt not the oil and wine."* Here we see a black horse. The color black in Scripture is ominous, symbolizing judgment, darkness, and terror. It's a foreboding that something awful is coming.

This rider carries scales to measure the wheat and barley, the amount that can be purchased with a day's pay. In normal times, twenty-four measures of barely could be had for a day's wages. Now, people can only get three. Likewise, fifteen measures of wheat were the norm, not one. You're talking hyper-inflation and global shortages, especially of basic food supplies. These will not only be rationed but expensive, costing a day's wage to feed one adult with wheat and three adults with barley. These food shortages could be the result of the global war because shortages often follow war since people are displaced and cannot

Destination Hell

plant crops. Again, this is going to be **worldwide famine.** This is **starvation** on a massive scale.

When famines produce mass starvation, it devastates entire populations. To understand how horrible they can be, we just need to look at what's happened in the past. During World War II and immediately after, the world experienced famines. From the Warsaw Ghetto to Kiev to the Netherlands, millions died due to starvation.[331] And although not all the horrendous things mentioned below occurred in each locale, this composite shows that as things become more desperate, people become more desperate and more willing to do the unthinkable.

In past famines, streets were littered with dead bodies that looked like skeletons. Some began eating their pets. Others turned to cannibalism and began eating the bodies of the dead or even killing and eating their own babies. Some murdered others for food. Still others roved in small bands, breaking into the homes of those they believed were hiding provisions, then torturing them to reveal the hiding places. Those who couldn't bring themselves to do these things began eating toothpaste, glue, leather, sawdust, the bark of trees, grass, or anything else they could find. Others just closed themselves in their homes and waited for death. It's an ugly picture of the depth of human degradation such tragedies produce.

During the Tribulation, it will become necessary to move about in groups for it won't be safe to walk the streets alone due to marauding thugs. If caught alone, there will be no one to help. Even if others see your struggle, they won't care. Self presservation will be the rule.

Even now we are glimpsing this. Years ago, if someone witnessed an assault or robbery, he called the police or tried to help. No longer. Americans have become hardened toward crime and its victims. Recently, a woman riding a suburban Philadelphia train at night was raped while onlookers neither tried to stop it nor bothered to call the police. It's believed that some even recorded the incident on their phones.[332]

What a sad commentary on where we are as a nation. But imagine how much worse it will be when absolute evil is unleashed. The world will be filled with violence and cruelty. It will be every man for himself. No one will care what happens to his neighbor.

Going back to Revelation 6:5, it's interesting to note that the oil and wine are left unharmed, indicating this famine will be hard on the poor and

Destination Hell

those with limited incomes, while the rich are still able to obtain most of the things they want.

The fourth seal:

Revelation 6:7-8, *"And when he had opened the fourth seal, I heard the voice of the fourth beast say, Come and see. And I looked, and behold a pale horse: and his name that sat on him was Death, and Hell followed with him. And power was given unto them over the fourth part of the earth, to kill with sword, and with hunger, and with death, and with the beasts of the earth."*

When the Lamb opens this seal, Death, riding a pale horse, comes galloping out with Hell following closely behind. That word "pale" indicates a "yellowish green" color. Picture the color of a rotting corpse and you'll get the idea. Again, it is Jesus Who gives this rider power.

But notice, Jesus sets boundaries. Death and Hell can only take one-fourth of the world's population. How many people is that? In 2021, the world's population was 7.9 billion. And in 2019, Pew claimed there were 2.5 billion Christians worldwide. Assuming two billion are raptured that leaves 5.9 billion. One-fourth of that means nearly 1.5 billion people are doing to die as a result of the culmination of what these four horsemen unleash.

That's seven times more deaths than those which occurred in all the wars of the last century!

The earth will be covered with pale, decaying corpses. So many people will die that Hell is at Death's heels scooping them up. The fact that Hell is doing the collecting indicates those dying are unsaved.

How is all this death accomplished? We are told in Revelation 6:8 that it will be with *"sword, and with hunger, and with death, and with the beasts of the earth."* We've already seen that sword and famine have killed people. Now "death," which the Amplified Bible calls "plague" instead, and "beasts" are added to the list. I don't think it unreasonable to assume that all the dead bodies lying around, along with the mass starvation, trigger plagues and problems with animals.

Plagues are common during and after a war. They can decimate a population with incredible speed. Perhaps biological weapons have also been used. If so, it's going to be something never seen before and incredibly horrible because even ordinary plagues have wiped out huge sections of the population in the past.

And then there are the wild beasts. If there is a food shortage and animals can't find anything to eat, it's

Destination Hell

not unrealistic to believe they will soon start hunting man. But these plagues could also involve rats, snakes, killer bees, etcetera, that carry diseases or torment man. Amos 5:18-20 hints at this: *"Woe unto you that desire the day of the LORD* (the Tribulation)! *to what end is it for you? The day of the LORD is darkness and not light. As if a man did flee from a lion, and a bear met him; or went into the house and leaned his hand on the wall, and a serpent bit him."*

In the face of such death, destruction and tragedy, no government agency in the world will be able to cope with it all. There won't be enough hospital beds, medicine, or first responders. The world will be dark, dangerous, and spiraling out of control. The globe will look like a giant third-world nation with many necessities no longer available. If there is limited electricity, no garbage collection, the sewers backing up (which will only invite more rats and other animals) it will no longer look like the world we know.

The fifth seal:

Revelation 6:9-11 says, *"And when he* (the Lamb) *had opened the fifth seal, I saw under the altar the souls of them that were slain for the word of God, and for the testimony which they held: And they cried out with a loud voice, saying, How long, O Lord, holy and true, does thou not judge and avenge our blood on them that dwell on the earth. And white robes were given unto every one of them; and it was said unto them, that they should rest yet for a little season, until their fellow servants also and their brethren, that should be killed as they were, should be fulfilled"*

This is global martyrdom, the mass murder of believers. The two witnesses and 144,000 have been busy. A great world-wide revival has taken place, showing God's tremendous mercy and love for all mankind. But this mass murder also implies it's government orchestrated. Those heading the New World Order and One World Religion are not only condoning these actions but implementing them. Depraved men are now butchering those who have turned to God.

These martyrs cry out asking God to avenge them. They say, *"How long, O Lord, holy and true, does thou not judge and* **avenge our blood** *on them that dwell on the earth."* Jesus, the Son of man, our Kinsman Redeemer, will now become the blood avenger. The evil world has seen nothing yet!

Though God does indeed plan to avenge them, He tells them to *"wait a little longer until the number of their fellow servants and brothers who were to be killed as they had been was completed."* That means there will be more martyrs, more bloodshed. Revelation 17:6 confirms this gross slaughter by saying, *"the*

Destination Hell

woman was drunken with the blood of the saints, and with the blood of the martyrs of Jesus." The woman is Mystery Babylon which is the harlot One World Religion supported by the One World Government. This blood bath will be another inquisition but far worse than any before it.

It was Nimrod who successfully instituted the false religious system, Mystery Babylon, which encompassed forbidden occult knowledge as well as the worship of himself and his family (ancestor worship). They then went on to became "gods" in various cultures. Nimrod also introduced the worship of the twelve constellations. And all the above will be part of the One World Religion, which even now is being cobbled together by the U.N. and various secret organizations.

In September 2021, the U.N. came out with its globalist Common Agenda, a plan to get the whole world on the same page. Originally planned as the 2030 Project, some now hope to push it up to 2023. The U.N. also continues to promote "religious pluralism," another word for a one world religion.

Remember that the apostate church has been left behind. It's from this group that the One World Religion will be formed. Certainly included among them will be some of the hierarchy of both the Catholic and Protestant churches, as well as leaders of other religions. But I believe it will be the Catholic contingency that heads it all. Apparently, others think so, too, for many have called Pope Francis, "Vicar of the New World Order."[333] Interestingly, in 2013, *Time Magazine* put him on their cover and named him, "Person of the Year," honoring him for his socialist and globalist views. Truly, no one seems more eager to collect all religions under one umbrella than Pope Francis.

Steeped in paganism and tradition, the Catholic Church has played a large role in creating an apostate faith. In 1948, the Vatican opposed the formation of the Jewish state while in 1962 their *Nostra Aetate* declared that the god of Islam and the God of Christianity were one and the same. Vatican II (1962-1965) went on to open its door for a One World Religion with its ecumenicalism. In 1982, Pope John Paul II had a prayer meeting in Assisi, Italy which included pagans and voodoo priests, and where he claimed that voodoo possessed *"truth and good, seeds of the Word.*[334]

Renowned Catholic Bishop Fulton Sheen even predicted that the false prophet of Revelation would come from one of their own (a Catholic cardinal). But this was not a new fear. Martin Luther and Calvin believed it. So did John Knox, John Wesley, Charles Spurgeon, George Whitefield, and Jonathan Edwards. Dr. Henry Edward

Destination Hell

Cardinal Manning in 1861 also predicted a crisis and apostasy in the Catholic Church.[335]

Since then, many others have come forward and sounded the same alarm, including Father E. Sylvester Berry in his book, *The Apocalypse of Saint John*, Father Herman Bernard Kramer in his, *"The Book of Destiny,"* Father John F. O'Connor, Father Alfred Kunz, and Father Malachi Martin.[336]

Before he died, Father O'Connor preached a sermon in which he claimed that a "Masonic Conspirator" would control the pope and assist the false prophet in "deceiving the world's faithful into worshipping Antichrist."[337]

Then a March 11, 2010, ABC News article quoted Pope Benedict XVI's exorcist, Rev. Amorth, as saying, "The devil resides in the Vatican" and that "The consequences of the devil's work are evident: Cardinals who don't believe in Jesus, bishops who are linked with the devil."

There is even a Catholic prophecy connecting the final pope and the antichrist. Tom Horn in his book, *Petrus Romanus, the Final Pope is Here*, covers this extensively. The "Prophecy of the Popes" is a 12th Century prophecy by an Irish Archbishop named Malachy O'Morgair, Papal Legate of Ireland and later called Saint Malachy. In the prophecy, O'Morgair claims there would only be 112 more popes from his time forward until Jesus returned. Pope Francis is number 112.

O'Morgair said of this pope, *"In the extreme persecution of the Holy Roman Church, there will sit Peter the Roman, who will nourish the sheep in many tribulations; when they are finished, the City of Seven Hills will be destroyed, and the terrible and fearsome Judge will judge his people."*[338]

The prophecy indicates that this pope will be the end-times pope, the one who oversees the apostate church during the seven-year Tribulation. He will also see Rome destroyed and the return of the *"fearsome Judge"* (Jesus).

Over the years, several Jesuits have worked hard to debunk the prophecy as a forgery. But despite the push-back, renowned Jesuit, Rene Thibaut, published his claim that this prophecy was true. So did Jesuit Malachi Martin who was disturbed by the corruption in the church and wrote startling exposés of both the Jesuits and the Vatican hierarchy.[339]

Martin died under "suspicious" circumstances in 1999 while working on another book connecting the Catholic Church with the New World Order.[340]

Destination Hell

Is Pope Francis the end-time pope? I don't know. There are rumors he is ill and may not live past 2022. Perhaps he is the forerunner since he has made many unscriptural and even blasphemous statements. Here are a few:

- Christians and Muslims worship the same God.[341]
- He called "dangerous" and "harmful" the belief that one "can maintain a personal relationship with Jesus without the communion and mediation of the church." Yes, we as a body need each other, but his statement contradicts Scripture that says any true relationship with our Lord Jesus Christ must be personal.
- Even atheists can go to heaven.[342] Scripture clearly states that anyone not listed in the Lamb's Book of Life will be cast into the lake of fire (Revelation 3:5, Revelation 17:8, Revelation 20:15, Revelation 21:27). And how does one get into this book? Only by accepting Jesus as Savior. Jesus himself said in John 14:6, *"I am the way, the truth, the life: no man cometh unto the Father, but by me."* Does that mean Pope Francis is calling Jesus a liar?
- He said, "proselytism is solemn nonsense, it makes no sense,[343]" even though

Jesus' command us to, *"Go ye therefore, and teach all nations* (the gospel) *baptizing them in the name of the Father, and of the Son, and of the Holy Ghost,"* (Matthew 28:19, Mark 16:15).

- He doesn't believe people will go to hell for all eternity. "No one can be condemned forever, because that is not the logic of the Gospel!"[344] Yet, Jesus spoke of hell and eternal damnation many times (Mark 9:43-48, Matthew 10:28, Mark 3:29, Luke 12:5, Hebrews 6:2, Jude 7, Revelation 1:18).
- He called Italian abortion advocate, Emma Bonino, a "forgotten great," the woman who also championed the decriminalization of recreational drugs, homosexual marriage, euthanasia, and graphic sex education.[345]

Pope Francis' desire for globalism and a one world religion is obvious. On September 23, 2015, he met with President Obama. Their topics of discussion were chilling to say the least. Topping the list was "a global constitution, a world court, and world government." The pope then went to the U.N. two days later and broached these same subjects.[346]

In February 2019, Pope Francis and Muslim Sheikh, Ahmed al-Tayeb, signed an agreement to

Destination Hell

merge their religions for the sake of world peace. The goal of their "Higher Committee of Human Fraternity" is to coalesce backgrounds, nationalities, and religions. To achieve this, they plan to build a complex called the "Abrahamic Family House" which will include a mosque, synagogue, and church. But not all in the Catholic Church are happy. "Archbishop Carlo Maria Vigano compared the Abrahamic Family House to the Tower of Babel and called it 'Pope Francis' initiative to convert the Catholic Church into a global New Age religion.'" Even so, this "House" is expected to open sometime in 2022.[347]

Also, President Biden met with Pope Frances the end of October 2021 to promote a global tax. Biden hopes to force a tax rate of 15% on all countries, in the name of human dignity, climate change, and the poor.[348]

That same month, the pope urged U.S. tech companies to censor, "fake news" and "conspiracy theories," among other things.[349]

Again, Archbishop Carlo Maria Vigano refused to be silent, and in November 2021, called for "the creation of an anti-globalist alliance to defeat the evil elites who wish to enslave free men and women and promote a 'Religion of Humanity' that cancels Faith in Christ."[350]

But even before all this, the Vatican in 2011, under Pope Benedict XVI, had already shown its true colors and made its objectives clear when it published, *Toward Reforming the International Financial and Monetary Systems in the context of a* **Global Public Authority**. It espoused the same goals as those of the New World Order, declaring the need for individuals and nations to surrender their rights and authority in order to achieve "global civil and economic security." And how was this to be accomplished? Their answer: "At the cost of a gradual balance transfer of a part of each nation's powers to a world authority and to regional authorities."[351]

Remember, Jesus said you will know them by their fruits.

The sixth seal:

Revelation 6:12-17 says, *"And I beheld when he had opened the sixth seal, and lo, there was a* **great earthquake;** *and the sun became black as sackcloth of hair, and the moon became as blood; And the stars of heaven fell unto the earth, even as a fig tree casts her untimely figs, when she is shaken of a mighty wind. And the heaven departed as a scroll when it is rolled together, and every mountain and island were moved out of their places. And the kings of the earth, and the great men, and the rich men, and the chief captains, and*

Destination Hell

the mighty men, and every bondman, and every free man, hid themselves in the dens and in the rocks of the mountains, And said to the mountains and rocks, Fall on us, and hide us from the face of him that sitteth on the throne, and from **the wrath of the Lamb:** *For the great day of his wrath is come, and who shall be able to stand?"*

Now, the very elements of heaven and earth turn against man. God uses them in His role of blood avenger to punish man for murdering His people, as well as for their many other sins. And the thing is, the people know it. Notice, they understand that what is happening is due to *"the wrath of the Lamb,"* yet they refuse to repent. Instead, they hide in fear. One must wonder what it will take to bring these people around. So much devastation has occurred it's hard to believe they aren't falling on their faces before God and begging His forgiveness.

It's probably the **great earthquake** that triggers most of the other calamities in this seal. Those words "great earthquake" are *megas seismos*. This is a block buster. It's off the scale. It's massive. In addition, earthquakes trigger other disasters like mudslides, tsunamis, and volcanic eruptions. These in turn cause other problems. Tsunamis flood entire towns, while mudslides bury towns, and volcanoes burn them down. Volcanoes also fill the air with ash, debris, and toxic gases, which in turn can create a solar winter by darkening the sun. The darkening of the sun can, in turn, cause crop failure. Volcanic eruptions can also change the color of the moon and affect the planet's temperature. When this great earthquake hits, millions will die. And forget FEMA, they won't be able to help.

What about the falling stars? That word "stars" in Greek is *aster* from which we get our word, asteroid. Many scholars believe this could be a meteor shower. And it's serious because they are going to be dropping like figs from a tree shaken *"by a mighty wind."* As they fall, they can produce shock waves in the air or explosions when they land. They can also create tsunamis, change the temperature of land, air, sea, and wipe out every structure in a wide radius. And if the shower falls on a major city, it could turn it into rubble. All this translates into more death and destruction.

What about the heaven departing as a scroll? That word "departed" literally means, "to rend apart, to separate." Some Bible scholars believe the sky will split open and for a brief moment people on earth will be able to see into another dimension, that of God's throne, and realize who is behind all this destruction. It could also mean that this earthquake is so powerful it creates a shift in the earth's axis causing the constellations to no longer line up to their former settings.

The sealing of the 144,000:

After the sixth seal, God is ready to further damage the earth via the four winds. But before He does, He pauses. Revelation 7:1-4 says, *"And after these things* (the opening of the first six seals) *I* (John) *saw four angels standing on the four corners of the earth, holding the four winds of the earth, that the wind should not blow on the earth, nor on the sea, nor on any tree. And I saw another angel ascending from the east, having the seal of the living God: and he cried with a loud voice to the four angels, to whom it was given to hurt the earth and the sea, Saying, Hurt not the earth, neither the sea, nor the trees, till we have* **sealed** *the servants of our God in their foreheads. And I heard the number of them which were sealed: and there were sealed an hundred and forty and four thousand of all the tribes of the children of Israel."*

I believe these 144,000 were already commissioned at the beginning of the Tribulation along with the two witnesses, but now God seals them. Why? That word "seal" is *sphragizo* and means, "to stamp for security or preservation." Because what comes next will kill so many people, God needs to keep them safe until their work is finished. This is His great mercy and love on display. He wants as many as possible to hear from these 144,000 and repent and come to Him.

Revelation 7:5-8 goes on to give us more information about the 144,000. They are 12,000 from every tribe of Israel except Dan's. His tribe is replaced by the tribe of Manasseh (Joseph's son). And these 144,000 Jews will bring in a great harvest. Millions will come to Christ. And the fruits of it are revealed in verse 9. *"After this* (after the sealing of the 144,000) *I* (John) *beheld, and lo, a* **great multitude***, which no man could number, of all nations, and kindreds, and people, and tongues, stood before the throne, and before the Lamb, clothed with white robes, and palms in their hands."*

These people accepted Christ before dying during the Tribulation. Their robes are clean, and they are worshipping in heaven. Just to make sure there is no question of who these people are, verse 14 says, *"These are they which came out of* **great tribulation***, and have washed their robes, and made them white in the blood of the Lamb."*

We know they have suffered greatly because verse 17 says that Jesus *"shall feed them, and shall lead them unto living fountains of waters: and God shall wipe away all tears from their eyes."* This indicates they experienced great hunger and thirst. But Jesus Himself will care for them now. He will also

Destination Hell

console them, wipe away their tears, and heal their trauma as they cry in His arms.

What a wonderful God we serve! He is so tender, kind and loving. He rewards those who come to Him and wants no one to perish!

The seventh seal:

Revelation 8:1-2 says, *"And when he had opened the seventh seal, there was silence in heaven about the space of half an hour. And I saw the seven angels which stood before God; and to them were given seven trumpets."*

Again, it is the Lamb Who opens this seal which begins the seven trumpet judgments. Since we are told about the silence in heaven it must be significant. What does it mean? Is this the eye of the storm? Is it a chance for mankind to repent? Is it the prelude for something so terrible it makes those in heaven remain with their mouths open, unable to speak?

Whatever it is, mankind doesn't repent. Perhaps they thought the worst was over and now the One World Government could get on with creating Utopia. But their worst nightmare is just beginning. There are still fourteen judgments left. But here is an interesting point. In verse 3, an angel holds a golden censer, and the smoke of it, along with the **prayers of the saints**, ascends before God. This triggers the first of seven angels to sound his trumpet. God is not only unleashing His wrath, but He is now answering the prayers of the saints and their request that their blood be avenged.

The first trumpet:

The result of this first trumpet sounding is the falling of hail, fire, and blood upon the earth, burning one-third of all the trees along with all the grass. Picture an out-of-control fire sweeping through acres and acres of land, destroying everything in its path while additional hail, fire, and blood continue raining down on everyone's head. This could be a supernatural event or the result of nuclear war. Either way, it's devastating.

The second trumpet:

The world hardly has time to draw breath when the second trumpet sounds, sending a *"great mountain burning with fire"* into the sea. Many scholars believe this could be an asteroid. Even now, NASA is monitoring hundreds of asteroids[352] and have issued warnings of possible collisions in the future.[353] It could also be referring to an erupting volcano spilling burning lava into the sea. Or, again, it could indicate nuclear warfare and the type of destruction that comes with it.

Destination Hell

Whatever it is, it results in one-third of the sea turning to blood, the killing of one-third of all sea creatures, and the destruction of one-third of the ships.

The third trumpet:

Following that, the third trumpet causes a burning star, called Wormwood, to fall into earth's rivers making the water bitter, and killing many.

The fourth trumpet:

Then the fourth trumpet sounds, smiting one-third of the sun, moon, and stars, causing daylight to be decreased by one-third. It appears that the first to fourth trumpets sound in rapid fire. People will reel from the devastation as one disaster after the other hits them. And if things couldn't get any worse, this is followed by an angel who flies over the earth shouting, *"Woe, woe, woe, to the inhabiters of the earth by reason of the other voices of the trumpet of the three angels which are yet to sound!"* (Revelation 8:13)

His three woes are dire warnings that something even worse is coming. Daniel 12:1 calls these times *"a time of trouble, such as never was since there was a nation* (Israel),*"* while Isaiah 13:9 says, *"Behold, the day of the LORD cometh, cruel both with wrath and fierce anger, to lay the land desolate: and he shall destroy the sinners thereof out of it."* Though this is a forewarning of more disaster, it also reflects God's mercy. He is telling people to wake up and repent before it's too late; to come to Him, because in this next round the chances are good they won't survive, and they'll be lost forever.

The fifth trumpet:

Immediately after the angel's warning, the fifth trumpet sounds and *"a star falls from heaven unto the earth: and to **him** was given the key of the bottomless pit,"* (Revelation 9:1). Although the word for "star" here is also *aster*, it cannot mean an asteroid or meteor because of the pronoun "him." This is not an object but a living being. Thus, we can assume it is an angel. That word "fall" is *pipto* and means, "alighting, light on, to fly." So, this is an angel who flies from heaven and lands on earth. This angel opens the bottomless pit. When he does, *"the smoke of a great furnace"* comes pouring out. This is the putrid smoke from the pit of hell itself. It is so dense it darkens the sun and moon.

But that's not the worst of it. The Bible says that a horde of locusts come rushing out. These are not insects, but demonic beings who are given power to torment those not marked by God. In other words, those not sealed like the 144,000 Jews are fair game. The only thing these demonic locusts can't do is kill. During this time, people will want to die but can't. Revelation 9:6 says, *"And in those days shall men seek death, and shall not find it; and shall desire to die, and death shall flee from them."*

Scripture gives a macabre picture of what these locusts look like: horses with faces of men, having wings and stinging tails. It says their king is Apollyon, which is another name for Satan.

The sixth trumpet:

The six trumpet looses the four angels *"bound in the great river Euphrates"* to slay one-third of those remaining on earth. The sounding of the fourth and fifth trumpets have already caused mass casualties. Now, the sixth trumpet looses a two-million-man army. Some scholars believe this is a demonic army. They ride horses with lion heads. Their breastplates are of fire and brimstone and their mouths spew fire and brimstone. Other scholars believe they are tanks or helicopters or some other modern implements of war. I believe it could be either, though I favor the demonic version.

Whatever they are, the horror they unleash is obvious. But the sad part is that no one repents. Revelation 9:20-21 says, *"And the rest of the men which were not killed by these plagues* (trumpets four to six) *yet repented not of the works of their hands, that they should not worship devils, and idols of gold, and silver, and brass, and stone, and of wood: which neither can see, nor hear, nor walk: Neither repented they of their murders, nor of their sorceries* (that word is *pharmakeia* meaning, 'medication, magic, drug use, pharmacy'), *nor of their fornication, nor of their thefts."*

Notice the five sins emphasized in this Scripture: idolatry, murder, occult activities and drug use, fornication, and thefts. They are hardly the only sins. But this tells us that evil will be rampant and demonstrates the utter depravity of man. It shows the depths to which man can sink and still justify himself when the restraining power of the Holy Spirit is removed. Every village, town and city will be affected. There will be no escape. And those who come to the Lord and try to live righteously will be hunted down and killed.

The midpoint between the first half and second half of the Tribulation:

Chapters six to nine describe the first half of the Tribulation while chapters sixteen to eighteen describe the second half. At the midpoint, between the two, several important things occur.

Destination Hell

In Revelation chapter ten, an angel gives John a book that he is told to eat. Then the angel swears *"that there shall be time no longer,"* indicating no more delays. Soon, the fullness of God's wrath will be complete.

Then John is given a measuring rod to measure the third Jewish Temple, the one built during the first half of the Tribulation. We are also given insight into the two witnesses who have been prophesying for three and a half years, and who the antichrist is finally able to kill. Their bodies lie in a Jerusalem street for three and a half days. Revelation 11:8 says, *"And their dead bodies shall lie in the street of the great city, which spiritually is called Sodom and Egypt, where also our Lord was crucified."*

The world will celebrate their deaths by sending each other gifts. At last they are rid of their tormentors who spoke of God and pronounced judgments. Now, life can get back to normal, and once again they can live the way they want without consequences. But their joy won't last because suddenly, a loud voice from heaven issues the command to *"Come up hither,"* and the dead witnesses come to life, then are taken to heaven. An earthquake follows, destroying one-tenth of Jerusalem and killing 7000 people, (Revelation 11:13).

Revelation chapter 12 talks about Israel, the birth of Jesus, Satan's rebellion and how he first tried to destroy the Seed (Jesus), then the nation of Israel. There is also a war in heaven between Satan and Michael the archangel, and Satan is cast down to earth. That's when he becomes really vicious. Revelation 12:13 says, *"And when the dragon* (Satan) *saw that he was cast unto the earth, he persecuted the woman* (Israel) *which brought forth the man child,* (Jesus).*"*

Revelation chapter 13 gives us additional insight into the antichrist and false prophet. It is at this midpoint that the antichrist will violate the covenant with Israel and declare himself god. 2 Thessalonians 2:4 tells us this happens in Jerusalem's Temple. The antichrist, *"Who opposeth and exalteth himself above all that is called God, or that is worshipped: so that he as God, sitteth in the temple of God, shewing himself that he is God,"* thus, desecrating the Temple and stopping all Temple sacrifices, (Daniel 9:27).

The Jews are horrified. They can't believe it. This is the "abomination of desolation" spoken about by both Daniel and Jesus. And it is intolerable, because for a Jew there can be no God but Yahweh. They offend the antichrist by refusing to accept him as god, causing him to initiate a massive extermination campaign against them. According

Destination Hell

to Zechariah 13:8, two-thirds of the Jewish people will be killed. During this time, the antichrist will also make war against the believers in Jesus.

But God will protect a remnant of Jews by bringing them into a desert city and feeding them for the remainder of the Tribulation or 1,260 days. Many believe this refuge will be Petra, a city carved into the mountains of Jordan.

This is the Jewish remnant who realize Jesus is their Messiah and cry out for His return. Hosea 5:15 speaks about this: *"I (the Messiah Jesus) will go and return to my place, till they (the Jewish people) acknowledge their offence, and seek my face: in their affliction (the Tribulation) they will seek me early."* Zechariah 12:10 adds to this: *"And I (Jesus) will pour upon the house of David, and upon the inhabitants of Jerusalem, the spirit of grace and of supplications: and they shall look upon me whom they have pierced, and they shall mourn for him, as one mourneth for his only son, and shall be in bitterness for him, as one that is in bitterness for his firstborn."*

During this time, the false prophet creates the image and mark of the beast. He also performs demonic miracles. In Revelation 13:11, he is described as having *"two horns like a lamb."* Because Jesus was also pictured as a lamb, this suggests the false prophet will be a religious leader. Indeed, he is the one who commands everyone to worship the image of the beast and take his mark or be executed. *"And he* (the false prophet) *had power to give life unto the image of the beast, that the image of the beast should both speak, and cause that as many as would not worship the image of the beast should be killed. And he causeth all, both small and great, rich and poor, free and bond, to receive a mark in their right hand, or in their foreheads: And that no man might buy or sell, save he that had the mark, or the name of the beast, or the number of his name. Here is wisdom. Let him that hath understanding count the number of the beast: for it is the number of a man; and his number is Six hundred threescore and six* (666)," (Revelation 13:15-18).

If a talking image that can kill people sounds far-fetched, then consider the technology already here. "The Giant" was created by a company in Dublin, Ireland. It's a ten-story tall statue that talks and sings and can even take on the image of any person.[354] Imagine what a thing like this can do in the hands of the antichrist!

But what about a mark capable of monitoring every purchase a person makes? This means a global digital economy, which the World Economic Forum is already trying to implement. And the technology to do it is here. Also, remember Bill Gates is funding those working on a vaccine ID

Destination Hell

which contains Luciferase. As mentioned in the last chapter, Luciferase is an enzyme which makes an "implantable quantum dot microneedle vaccine delivery system work."[355]

You are talking about a vaccine/tattoo that is computer-like and can track not only every person's movement, but their buying, selling, their bank accounts, their health history, and even their moods. You are also talking about a mark that can possibly alter human DNA making them "other," or human 2.0, something detestable to God. And as previously noted, scientists already have that ability.

We have all the technology the beast needs to implement his One World Order. Current technology can track every human on earth; can enable the world to view the dead bodies of the two witnesses via satellite television; can control people's ability to buy or sell; can enable a statue to move and talk. All the antichrist has to do is flip the switch.

By Revelation 14, we see the results of this evil duo. Their killing spree is swift because the 144,000 are with the Lamb singing a new song. They brought many to Christ during the first half of the Tribulation, and now are rejoicing in heaven, indicating they have been martyred sometime after the antichrist declared war on the Jews. They are called, *"the first fruits unto God and to the Lamb."* But this isn't the end of God's mercy because He sends another angel to fly over the earth to proclaim, *"the everlasting gospel,"* to *"them that dwell on the earth, and to **every** nation, and kindred, and tongue, and people,"* (Revelation 14:6).

Bear in mind, the antichrist and his henchmen have been killing Jews and every believer in Jesus they can find. Yet, amid this bloodbath, God still desires *"whosoever will"* to come to Him! Even now, He is concerned about the people who are still alive. After all the evil they have done, and all the hatred and contempt they have shown Him, God still desires that none should go to hell. What an amazing God! Who can understand His great love? It defies human logic. Considering how great His love is and considering the many opportunities He has given all the people during this time to come into His waiting and outstretched arms, it's hard to believe there are those who still reject it. But when it's over and they stand before the Great White Throne they will be without excuse. They will be unable to say they weren't warned or given every opportunity.

The One World Religion doesn't fare too well, either. For three and a half years the antichrist has put up with this apostate religion, allowing its leaders to persecute and kill true believers. Now,

Destination Hell

its usefulness is over. What need has he of any other religion when **he** is god? It's time to get rid of all those other gods and have the world just worship him, alone.

So, Revelation 14: 8-11 tells us that this harlot Babylonian religion has fallen. But it also includes a warning for those who take the mark of the beast. *"Babylon is fallen, is fallen, that great city, because she made all nations drink of the wine of the wrath of her fornication* (spiritual fornication). *And the third angel followed them, saying with a loud voice, If any man worship the beast and his image, and receive his mark in his forehead, or in his hand, The same shall drink of the wine of the wrath of God, which is poured out without mixture* (not diluted, it's full strength!) *into the cup of his indignation; and he shall be tormented with fire and brimstone in the presence of the holy angels, and in the presence of the Lamb: And the smoke of their torment ascendeth up* **for ever and ever**: *and they have no rest day nor night, who worship the beast and his image, and whosoever receiveth the mark of his name."*

Praise God, there will be many who refuse to take this mark because Revelation 14:13 says, *"blessed are the dead which die in the Lord from henceforth."* And Revelation 15:2 mentions them in heaven. *"And I saw as it were a sea of glass mingled with fire: and them that had gotten the victory over the beast, and over his image, and over his mark, and over the number of his name, stand on the sea of glass, having the harps of God."* What a glorious day that will be! All their pain and suffering will be forgotten as they worship the Lord.

But for those who take the mark, God's sickle is about to reap them and cast them in the *"great winepress of the wrath of God."* It's a winepress so full that *"blood came out of the winepress even unto the horse bridles, by the space of a* **thousand and six hundred furlongs,"** (Revelation 14:20). A furlong is 220 yards or one-eighth of a mile. That means this is an area of 200 miles. Imagine blood splashed on the bridle of warhorses (or modern counterparts) scattered over a two-hundred-mile battlefield.

The stage is set. The final seven plagues or vials are about to be poured upon earth. And according to Revelation 15:8, *"no man was able to enter into the temple, till the seven plagues of the seven angels were fulfilled."* Why was man kept out? The Bible doesn't say. But as I thought about it, I came up with the following. (Please note they are simply my opinions.) I think God refuses entrance into His temple because first, He is unwilling to hear any petitions to stay His wrath since He is determined to end it. And secondly, I believe this is breaking God's heart. He loves those who are dying on earth. He desires that they come to Him. He also loves the world He created. Now, because His

Destination Hell

justice must be satisfied, He is destroying both, and this grieves Him.

I even imagine He is weeping. I say this because Ezekiel reveals God's heart. *"Have I any pleasure at all that the wicked should die? Saith the Lord GOD: and not that he should return from his ways, and live?"* (Ezekiel 18:23). And Ezekiel 33:11 says, *"As I live, saith the Lord GOD, I have **no pleasure** in the death of the wicked: but that the wicked turn from his way and live: turn ye, turn ye from your evil ways; for why will ye died, O house of Israel?"*

It is evident that God **wants** to forgive everyone's sins. But there are only two ways He can deal with sin: through grace—forgiveness obtained through the shed blood of Jesus, or wrath—judgment and eternal damnation.

The last three and a half years of the Tribulation:

Now it's really going to get rough! As we've seen, Satan has been kicked out of heaven and knows his time is short. And he's furious. Through the antichrist, who he indwells, he will ruthlessly pursue his dream of being worshipped and will destroy anyone who refuses to do so.

The antichrist has already shown his true colors. Revelation chapter 13 describes him as a "beast."

Other Scriptures call him: the insolent and willful king, a vile person, the son of destruction, and the man of lawlessness. Empowered by Satan, he will be vile, vicious, treacherous, and the embodiment of evil. A hater of God, he will speak great blasphemes. And with an iron fist, he will establish his ruthless, anti-God kingdom.

The first through fifth vials:

These vials seem to come in rapid order, much like the first through fourth trumpets. The first vial is poured out in Revelation 16:2 causing all those who have taken the mark of the beast to develop *"a grievous sore."* That word "grievous" is *poneros* and means, "pain, hurtful, anguish," while "sore" means "ulcer." This is a painful ulcer or ulceration of some kind. Perhaps it covers their whole body or just where they have the mark. In any case, it is no ordinary sore.

The second vial turns the sea into blood, killing every living creature in it. No more fishing, or crabbing, or using lobster traps. Nothing in the sea is edible anymore. This will add to the food shortages. Not only will grain products be a day's wages, now people living near coastlines can't even supplement their rations by catching food themselves. Life continues to become increasingly difficult.

Destination Hell

The third vial turns the rivers and *"fountains of waters"* into blood, meaning much of the water in rivers, aquifers, and underground streams become polluted and undrinkable. People can go weeks without food, but only three to seven days without water. And certainly, there will be no water for bathing or brushing teeth. This lack of personal hygiene will only add to everyone's poor health.

The fourth vial affects the sun, causing a heatwave and men to be "scorched."

The fifth vial produces darkness. During this blackness, Revelation 16:10-11 says, *"and they gnawed their tongues for pain, And blasphemed the God of heaven because of their pains and their sores, and repented not of their deeds."*

Imagine there is little food or water. People are covered with painful ulcers. The rivers and streams stink because everything in it is dead and decaying. You can't go outside because of the violent roving gangs. You can't call the police or EMT for help. There are no assistance programs left. They have all gone bankrupt. Many of the people you know are dead. And now it's pitch-black outside. It's also sweltering. Temperatures are off the charts. But because of the rolling blackouts you have no electricity or air conditioning. You are hot, hungry, thirsty, and frightened, and probably alone, and all you can do is sit in the dark and hope no one breaks into your house looking for food or valuables.

But if you have not taken the mark of the beast your fate will be even worse. Remember, you can't buy or sell so where do you get food? Maybe from the black market if you have anything left to barter, or perhaps you find some rotten, moldy scraps in a trashcan.

Your bank account has been frozen. You've lost your job because you're not marked. You can't go home because the antichrist's Gestapo-like police have staked out your house and will arrest you, then take you to the extermination camp for non-compliance. So now, you're alone and on the street, homeless and subject to the elements as well as easy prey for the roving thugs who seem to be everywhere. And even though you have nothing worth stealing, they could, just for sport, rough you up, or rape you, or even kill you. And if they don't get you, chances are the police patrols, who have an APB out for your arrest, will. There is no repose day or night because you must stay one step ahead of them all. It's just a matter of time before you die of starvation or are murdered.

There will be so much death that by the end of the Tribulation a man will be as scarce and rare as gold. Isaiah 13:9-13 sums it up this way: *"Behold, the day of the LORD cometh, cruel both with wrath and fierce anger, to lay the land desolate: and he shall destroy the sinners thereof out of it. For the stars of heaven and the constellations thereof shall not give their light: the sun shall be darkened in his going forth, and the moon shall not cause her light to shine. And I will punish the world for their evil, and the wicked for their iniquity; and I will cause the arrogancy of the proud to cease, and will lay low the haughtiness of the terrible.* **I will make a man more precious** (rare) **than fine gold, even a man** (scarcer) **than the golden wedge of Ophir.** *Therefore, I will shake the heavens, and the earth shall remove out of her place, in the wrath of the LORD of hosts, and in the day of his fierce anger."*

God has been warning the inhabitants of earth for centuries. Can people say He is cruel when after all His warnings and pleadings they don't listen, and He must, because He is holy and righteous, send judgment?

I think not.

The sixth vial:

The opening of the sixth vial sees the drying up of the Euphrates River and the amassing of a great army. The beast and false prophet have sent demonic spirits to the leaders of the world *"to *gather them to the battle of the great day of God Almighty,"* (Revelation 16:14). *"And he gathered them together into a place called in the Hebrew tongue Armageddon,"* (Revelation 16:16). This army plans to battle God.

The seventh vial:

The seventh and final vial sees a *"great earthquake such as was not since men were upon the earth, so mighty an earthquake, and so great,"* (Revelation 16:18). There has never been an earthquake like this one. *"And the great city was divided into three parts, and the cities of the nations fell: . . . And every island fled away, and the mountains were not found,"* (Revelation 16:20). It destroys every island and every mountain. Next, picture the cities of the world collapsing. All those high risers and skyscrapers will be rubble. Homes will also crumble. Towns, communities, all will be gone. This earthquake will level the planet.

On top of that, sixty-to-seventy-five-pound hailstones will come raining out of the sky crushing everything that isn't already flattened. *"And there fell upon man a great hail out of heaven, every stone about the weight of a talent,"* (Revelation 16:21).

What the earthquake doesn't destroy, the hailstones will. And that means crops, if there are any

Destination Hell

left, as well as trees, plants, animals, weakened remaining structures, and those people who cannot find shelter. And what will man's reaction be? *"and men blasphemed God because of the plague of the hail; for the plague thereof was exceeding great,"* (Revelation 16:21).

Though words cannot accurately describe the horror of these seven years, Zephaniah 1:14-18 comes close: *"The great day of the LORD* (the seven-year Tribulation) *is near, it is near, and hasteth greatly, even the voice of the day of the LORD: the mighty man shall cry there bitterly. That day is a day of wrath, a day of trouble and distress, a day of wasteness and desolation, a day of darkness and gloominess, a day of clouds and thick darkness. A day of the trumpet and alarm against the fenced cities, and against the high towers. And I* (God) *will bring distress upon men, that they shall walk like blind men, because they have sinned against the LORD: and their blood shall be poured out as dust, and their flesh as the dung. Neither their silver nor their gold shall be able to deliver them in the day of the LORD'S wrath; but the whole land shall be devoured by the fire of his jealousy: for he shall make even a speedy riddance of all them that dwell in the land."*

Revelation 17 and 18 talk about the fall of Mystery Babylon, the Mother of Harlots—the antichrist's One World Religious System. Remember, when declaring himself god, the antichrist destroyed the One World Religion of the apostate church and created his own One World Religion, featuring himself as its head. Also destroyed is Babylon the Great—the antichrist's One World Government and economic system. The wrath of God in now complete.

Revelation 19 sees the return of Jesus on a white horse with His bride following. No longer the Lamb, He comes as King of King and Lord of Lords. And He is fearsome to behold. *"His eyes were as a flame of fire, and on his head were many crowns; and he had a name written, that no man knew, but he himself. And he was clothed with a vesture dipped in blood: and his name is called the Word of God,"* (Revelation 19:12-13). What a marvelous sight that will be!

The antichrist and false prophet, along with the armies of the world, are waiting for Him. It's laughable to think they, as created beings, actually believe they can overcome the Creator Himself! It shows how deceived they are, and how badly Satan has deceived himself. He still believes he can prevail.

Romans 1:21-32 describes these types of rebels. *"when they knew God, they glorified him not as God, neither were thankful; but became vain in their*

Destination Hell

imaginations, and their foolish heart was darkened. Professing themselves to be wise, they became fools, And changed the glory of the uncorruptible God into an image made like to corruptible man, and to birds, and four footed beasts, and creeping things. Wherefore God also gave them up to uncleanness through the lusts of their own hearts, to dishonour their own bodies between themselves: Who changed the truth of God into a lie, and worshipped and served the creature more than the Creator, who is blessed for ever. Amen. For this cause God gave them up unto vile affections: for even their women did change the natural use into that which is against nature: And likewise also the men, leaving the natural use of the woman, burned in their lust one toward another: men with men working that which is unseemly, and receiving in themselves that recompence of their error which was meet. And even as they did not like to retain God in their knowledge, God gave them over to a reprobate mind, to do those things which are not convenient; Being filled with all unrighteousness, fornications, wickedness, covetousness, maliciousness; full of envy, murder, debate, deceit, malignity; whisperers, Backbiters, haters of God, despiteful, proud, boasters, inventors of evil things, disobedient to parents, Without understanding, covenant breakers, without natural affections, implacable, unmerciful: Who knowing the judgment of God, that they which commit such things are worthy of death, not only do the same, but have pleasure in them that do them."

These people not only despise God but want to continue their evil lifestyle and encourage others to live evil lives as well.

But Jesus is about to put an end to it all. He opens His mouth and releases a sword, vanquishing the rebels in an instant. Following that, the beast and false prophet are cast into the lake of fire, while Satan is chained and thrown into the bottomless pit.

There is an interesting point worth mentioning. Since I have already covered the issue of the Nephilim in my book, *The Coming Deception*, I won't spend much time on it now. But briefly, fallen angels cohabitated with human women to create hybrids called Nephilim and Rephaim. They did this to corrupt the human genome. Many in the Satanic Illuminati claim to be their descendants. This attempt to corrupt human DNA, to make man "other," is still going on today.

Daniel 2:42-43 describes the ten toes of Nebuchadnezzar's statue. *"And as the toes of the feet were part of iron, and part of clay, so the kingdom shall be partly strong, and partly broken. And whereas thou sawest iron mixed with miry clay, they shall mingle themselves with the seed of men: but they shall not cleave one to another, even as iron is not mixed with clay."*

Destination Hell

Nebuchadnezzar is a type of antichrist, and the ten toes represent the final worldly kingdom, the revived Roman Empire, which will be the antichrist's kingdom. It will not be as strong as the original Roman Empire. But as often is the case in Scripture, there is a double meaning here.

In this revived empire someone or something will mingle themselves with the seed of men and not cleave one to another. That word mingle is *arab* and means, "commingle, mix to braid, to traffic as if by barter, become surety, a pledge, a guarantee, a kind of exchange, occupy." Seed means a physical seed. Cleave (*debeq/dabaq*) means, "to cling or join to." It's the same word used in Genesis 2:24. *"Therefore shall a man leave his father and his mother, and shall **cleave** unto his wife: and they shall be one flesh."*

This seems to imply that these men are hybrids, those whose seed has been corrupted by fallen angels and this time not because of "cleaving" sexually to their wives but by DNA manipulation. DNA manipulation and transhumanism (the remaking of human 2.0) were also discussed in my book.

Was this commingling the result of a Satanic bargain by which these rulers gave up their status as true "men" for the pledge, the guarantee of global dominance, and the power to rule the world?

Whoever "they" are, the mix isn't good. It is weak because this kingdom will be *"partly strong and partly broken."* A quick look at the meaning of these words gives a fuller picture. Strong (*taqqip*) means "overpower." Broken (*tebar*) means "break in pieces, judgmental punitive activity." While partly (*qesat*) means "the end, the last of a thing; cut off."

This word study suggests that because both entities are only "partly" it means their end. They are the last of a thing and will be cut off. It also implies that the partly strong will overpower the other which will break in pieces as a punitive judgment against this kingdom. Neither will last but be destroyed by Jesus before He sets up His kingdom.

Scripture also tells us that these Nephilim hybrids are an abomination to God and will be damned forever. Since both the antichrist and false prophet are thrown into the lake of fire without a trial, which will be afforded every human being on earth, it suggests that they were not fully human, but hybrids.

Conclusion:

We have seen that the entire seven-year Tribulation is contained in Jesus' scroll; first the seven seals, which in turn contains the seven-trumpet judgments, which in turn contains the seven vial judgments. And it is all unleashed by Jesus' hand. During the entire seven years of Tribulation, Jesus is in total control. Daniel 2: 21 clearly states that it is God Who sets up kings and removes them. He is the One who controls world events. And Isaiah 14:24 and 46:9-10 assure us that whatever God has planned will come to pass. Not maybe, but **will**. It's set in stone.

And yes, for a season, Satan and his crowd will have their way. But God always gets the last laugh.

"Why do the heathen rage, and the people imagine a vain thing? The kings of the earth set themselves, and the rulers take counsel together, against the LORD, and against his anointed, saying, Let us break their bands asunder, and cast away their cords from us. He that sitteth in the heavens shall laugh: the LORD shall have them in derision," Psalms 2:1-4.

Proverbs 29:1 makes it clear. Those repeatedly corrected and warned by God but who harden their hearts will be destroyed. There will be no remedy. Only God's wrath awaits, (Romans 2:5).

2 Thessalonians 1:6-10 says, *"Seeing it is a righteous thing with God to recompense tribulation to them that trouble you* (the saints, believers in Jesus); *And to you who are troubled rest with us, when the Lord Jesus shall be revealed from heaven with his mighty angels, 10In flaming fire taking vengeance on them that know not God, and that obey not the gospel of our Lord Jesus Christ. Who shall be punished with everlasting destruction from the presence of the Lord, and from the glory of his power; When he shall come to be glorified in his saints, and to be admired in all them that believe (because our testimony among you was believed) in that day."*

This is where the earth and unsaved mankind are headed. But like in the days of Noah and Lot, people are going about their business, eating, partying, marrying; not paying attention to the signs of the times nor concerned with the things of God, unaware of the horrors ahead.

Revelation concludes by telling us that after the chaining of Satan there will be another seventy-five days of mopping up operations when the Gentile sheep and goats are separated, the earth restructured, and the resurrection of Old Testament and Tribulation saints. Then Jesus begins His one-thousand-year reign in Jerusalem during which time He, as the Jewish Messiah, keeps His

Destination Hell

promise to Israel by setting up a Davidic Messianic Kingdom of Peace.

All this time, the globalists have strived to create a one world government, but it will be Jesus who creates the global one world government and rules it. He is the stone from heaven that will pulverize all empires at the end of the age. Daniel 2:34-35 says, *"Thou sawest till that a stone* (Jesus) *was cut out without hands, which smote the image* (of the antichrist kingdom) *upon his feet that were of iron and clay, and brake them to pieces. Then was the iron, the clay, the brass, the silver, and the gold* (all the kingdoms of the world) *broken to pieces together, and became like the chaff of the summer threshing floors; and the wind carried them away, that no place was found for them: and the stone that smote the image became a great mountain, and filled the whole earth."* All too late the elites will understand Jesus' caution when He said, *"For what shall it profit a man, if he shall gain the whole world, and lose his own soul?"* (Mark 8:36).

Praise our great God! For believers, these are exciting times because our King is coming! Soon, Jesus will rule and reign! And when He does, all weapons will be beaten into plow shares (Isaiah 2:4 and Micah 4:3). And peace and justice will prevail.

Even so, come quickly Lord Jesus!

Hell of the Underworld

Years ago, Dr. Lester Sumrall, pastor and evangelist for sixty-five years, had a disturbing revelation which he described in his book, *Run with the Vision*. His words paint a horrifying picture: "God lifted me up until I was looking down upon that uncountable multitude of humankind. He took me far down the highway until I saw the end of the road. It ended abruptly at a precipice towering above a bottomless inferno. When the tremendous unending procession of people came to the end of the highway, I could see them falling off into eternity. As they neared the pit and saw the fate that awaited them, I could see their desperate but vain struggle to push back against the unrelenting pressure of those to the rear. The great surging river of humanity swept them ever forward. God opened my ears to hear the screams of damned souls sinking into hell . . .. I could see their faces distorted with terror. Their hands flailed wildly, clawing at the air."[356]

While the above is unsettling, some will ask, "Is hell even real?" I believe it is. Let's look at what I call myth and reality.

Sylvia Bambola

The myth:

There is no hell. A loving God would never send anyone to such a horrible place. Those who say this emphasize God's great love. Yes, God is love itself, but what these people fail to consider is that God is also a just judge Who cannot tolerate sin. When people readily believe in one aspect of God while completely rejecting another aspect clearly defined in Scripture, they are creating a god after their own wishful thinking.

Others say hell will be one big, wild party. They joke and laugh how all their friends will be there. They envision a place where vices are indulged, meaning plenty of drugs, alcohol, sex, or whatever else they deem fun and games. On the other hand, these same people say heaven will be boring, with people floating on clouds and strumming lyres for all eternity. So, which is it? Is hell the Playboy Mansion of the underworld?

Those who claim they have been there have never described it that way. Rather, they've talked about the horrible smell, the suffocating heat, and people screaming in agony. No one, to my knowledge, has ever described it as a happy or fun place.

Destination Hell

Perhaps it doesn't matter that hell isn't pleasant. After all, one can live it up here, and there's still Purgatory, then a chance for heaven. Right?

No. Purgatory doesn't exist. There is no temporary holding pen for people to hang out and suffer a little before eventually being allowed through the pearly gates. Nowhere does the Bible mention Purgatory or any place resembling it. Rather, the Bible is clear. Our eternal destination is either heaven or hell.

So, where and how did the idea of Purgatory originate?

It's a pagan concept. Heraclides Ponticus, Plato, and other pagan authors wrote about it. Called "celestial Hades," it was a place for the departed to land before being either reincarnated or escorted to a higher plain of existence. It eventually found its way into Jewish philosophy, especially during the time of the Maccabees when people began praying for the dead. Eventually, Christians adopted this practice, believing they could change the outcome of their dearly departed's future. The idea was that the dead who didn't make it into heaven could be purified in flames. When they were sufficiently cleansed, they could enter their celestial home. By the late 11th Century, it was an official teaching of the Catholic Church and described as the place where the dead "underwent purification as preparation for the happiness of heaven."[357]

The reality:

The truth is due to our sin nature we are already on the road to hell, and if we don't accept Jesus, the remedy, we will continue on it until we reach the precipice where there is no path left but down.

From time immemorial, cultures around the world have had an innate understanding of their sin nature and their need to appease God. Ingrained in every human being, no matter how deeply buried, is the knowledge there is a God Who he often offends, and that there is an afterlife, one of indescribable joy and wonderment, and one of indescribable terror and torment. Thus, they established elaborate rituals to achieve holiness and oneness with God, but their emphasis was always on *works*.

Most people secretly fear the concept of hell, and rightly so. It's a prison of the worst kind. Some who claim to have been there have written about their experiences. Bill Wiese is one of them. He is a Christian, and his book, *23 Minutes in Hell*, details the horrors of what he saw and felt. He claims that when he returned, he found himself on his living

Destination Hell

room floor screaming in terror and curled in a fetal position. Only his wife's prayers calmed him down.

I've never been to hell. And rather than recounting Wiese's or anyone else's experiences, I will use Scripture to describe it.

First, it is important to understand that hell was created for the devil and his rebel angels, not for man (Matthew 25:41b). In Isaiah 14:12-14, Satan boastfully listed his five "I wills" saying how he was going to be like God. In verse 15, God responded by telling him, *"Yet thou shalt be brought down to **hell**, to the sides of the **pit**."* And 2 Peter 2:4 talks about how God didn't spare the angels who sinned but cast them into hell where they are currently chained. At present, not all fallen angels are in hell. According to Jude 6, those in hell are the ones who left their first estate. *"And the angels which kept not their first estate but left their own habitation, he hath reserved in everlasting chains under darkness unto the judgment of the great day."* These are the angels who *"saw the daughters of men that they were fair; and they took them wives of all which they chose,"* (Genesis 6:2). They are the very angels who fathered the giants of old, and who fill the pages of Greek mythology.

But after the Fall, hell also became our default destination. Psalm 9:17 says, *"The wicked shall be turned into **hell**, and all the nations that forget God."* Though God is merciful, He is also holy. And both need to be satisfied. Thus, He sent Jesus. *"For God so loved the world, that he gave his only begotten Son, that whosoever believeth in him should not perish, but have everlasting life,"* (John 3:16).

God doesn't want anyone to go to hell. And He gave His all, His best, to keep that from happening. He shed His blood. *What more can He do?* It must break His heart that so many reject His sacrifice, and by failing to appropriate His sin remedy, consign themselves to a horrendous eternity.

When Jesus took His disciples to Caesarea Philippi, where the entrance to hell was believed to be located, He asked them who they thought He was. Peter answered, *"Thou art the Christ, the Son of the living God,"* (Matthew 16:13, Mark 8:27). It will be our answer to this very question that will either relegate us to hell or save us from it.

So, we see that hell is for Satan and the fallen angels, as well as fallen, unrepentant man. It's not a place where anyone should want to go. In Luke 12:5, Jesus said, *"But I will forewarn you whom ye shall fear: Fear him which after he hath killed hath power to cast into **hell**; yea, I say unto you, Fear him."* In

Destination Hell

Matthew 10:28, He said something similar. *"And fear not them which kill the body, but are not able to kill the soul: but rather fear him* (God) *which is able to **destroy both soul and body in hell.**"*

This tells us people in hell will have both a soul and body which will undergo destruction. The body is our flesh, the physical part of us. Scripture tells us that raptured believers are given glorified bodies (Philippians 3:20-21). But what kind of bodies do people have in hell? The Bible doesn't say. But obviously it is one that feels pain, as well as suffers decay and destruction.

And what about the soul? It is *psuche* in Greek from which we get psyche and psychology. It is our mind, will, our personality. And that word "destroy" (*apollumi*) means, "to destroy fully, **grind to powder.**" Grind to powder? What an awful image! What suffering there must be in hell as both mind and body are destroyed!

The Bible's description of hell:

Hell is mentioned fifty-three times in the Bible. Additional Scriptures refer to it as the pit, Gehenna, the abyss, lowest part of earth, hades, Shoal, and eternal or everlasting punishment. With so many references, it's obvious God wants us to know about it.

Isaiah 24:21-22 tells us it is a prison. *"And it shall come to pass in that day* (the end times) *that the LORD shall punish the host of the high ones that are on high* (fallen angels*), and the kings of the earth upon the earth. And they shall be gathered together, as **prisoners** are gathered in the **pit**, and shall be shut up in the **prison**, and after many days shall they be visited,"* (for judgment).

Job 17:16 and Jonah 2:6 tell us this prison has bars. And we've already seen in Jude 6 that it also has chains.

This prison is described as a pit. Numbers 16:32-33 recounts Korah's judgment. Because he fomented a rebellion against Moses and Aaron, he and those rebelling with him were swallowed alive by the earth. *"And the earth opened her mouth, and swallowed them up, and their houses, and all the men that appertained unto Korah, and all their goods. They, and all that appertained to them, went down alive into the **pit**, and the earth closed upon them: and they perished from among the congregation."*

And Ezekiel 32:23, when talking about the fall of Egypt, says, *"Whose* (the Egyptians) *graves are set in the sides of the **pit**, and her company is round about her grave: all of them slain, fallen by the sword, which caused terror in the land of the living."*

Destination Hell

In Psalm 30:3, King David praised God for delivering him from his enemies. *"O LORD, thou hast brought up my soul from the grave: thou hast kept me alive, that I should not go down to the **pit**."*

Scripture also indicates that this pit is deep beneath the earth. Ephesians 4:9 talks about Jesus, and how after His death, He descended *"into the **lower parts of the earth**."*

When God judged Tyrus, He said in Ezekiel 26:20, *"When I* (God) *shall bring thee* (Tyrus) *down with them that descend into the **pit**, with the people of old time, and shall set thee in **the low parts of the earth**, in places desolate of old, with them that go down to the **pit**, that thou be not inhabited; and I shall set glory in the land of the living."*

Psalm 88:6, written for the sons of Korah (the one previously mentioned who rebelled against Moses and Aaron) says, *"Thou hast laid me in the **lowest pit**, in darkness, in the deeps."*

Deuteronomy 32:22 says, *"For a fire is kindled in mine* (God's) *anger, and shall burn unto the **lowest hell**."*

And finally, Revelation 9:2, 11:7, and 20:1-3 call hell the *"**bottomless pit**."* That word "bottomless" is *abussos* in Greek and means, "depthless, deep," indicating it is beyond measuring. It just goes on and on.

So, we see that this maximum-security prison is underground. Scripture also suggests this prison or pit has levels. When we read lowest pit/hell in Psalm 88:6, Deuteronomy 32:22, and elsewhere, it suggests there must be higher ones. 2 Peter 2:4 talks about the angels who are chained in hell, the ones who left their first estate. That word there for hell is *Tartaroo* from *Tartaros* and means, "the deepest abyss of Hades," again indicating hell has levels.

But if the above signifies there are different levels in hell, could there also be different degrees of punishment? Could someone like Hitler experience a harsher hellish existence than say, Aunt Matilda, who lived a decent life but continually rejected Jesus even though her town had a church on every corner, copiously stocked Christian bookstores, and Christian T.V. and radio programs that continuously shared the gospel? And in light of that, could her fate be worse than someone who lived in a remote area and only heard the gospel once via a passing missionary, and rejected it? Perhaps.

Scripture tells us to whom much is given, much is required. While no level of hell will be pleasant, it's

Destination Hell

possible that those who have been given hundreds of opportunities to come to Christ verses those who have had few, will experience a more severe level of hell.

In Matthew 10:14-15, Jesus implied this very thing. He commissioned His disciples to preach throughout Israel that the kingdom of heaven was at hand, as well as heal the sick and cast out demons. Then He added this: *"And whosoever shall not receive you, nor hear your words, when ye depart out of that house or city, shake off the dust of your feet. Verily I say unto you,* **It shall be more tolerable for the land of Sodom and Gomorrha in the day of judgment, than for that city.**"

Jesus again suggested this in Matthew 23:14. *"Woe unto you, scribes and Pharisees, hypocrites! for ye devour widows' houses, and for a pretence make long prayer: therefore* **ye shall receive the greater damnation.**"

Paul also indicated this in Hebrews 10:28-29 when he talked about how those who *"despised Moses' law died without mercy under two or three witnesses,"* but how those who reject Jesus will incur **"much sorer punishment."**

And finally, Revelation 20:13 speaks of the Great White Throne Judgment of those not written in the

Lamb's Book of Life, meaning they are all destined for hell. Even so, it says these people will be judged by their "works," possibly to determine their level of hell.

So, what is this deep, escape-proof pit like? It's a fire pit. Jesus described it in Mark 9:43-48. He talked of a *"fire that never shall be quenched; Where their **worm** dieth not."* Between verses 43-48, He mentioned the unquenchable fire four different times, leaving no room for doubt that it will never go out but will burn for all eternity.

King David, when praising God's justice in Psalm 11:6, talked about what God will do to the wicked: *"Upon the wicked he* (God) *shall rain snares, **fire** and brimstone, and an horrible tempest: this shall be the portion of their cup."*

Again, in Isaiah 66:24, God described the fate of the wicked. *"And they* (those living during the millennial reign) *shall go forth, and look upon the carcases of the men that have transgressed against me: for their **worm** shall not die, neither shall their **fire** be quenched; and they shall be an abhorring unto all flesh."* Revelation 9:2 and 14:10-11 also speak of the fires of hell.

And where there is fire there is smoke. Imagine hot blazing flames filling the air with strangulating,

Destination Hell

thick smoke. Because people will still have the ability to feel, the scorching heat will be unbearable. In addition, smoke will sting their eyes and clog their nostrils, making it difficult to breathe. Eventually, their lungs will ache and their mouths will feel like sandpaper.

Jesus highlighted this when He spoke about Lazarus, who was in Paradise, and the rich man in hell. The rich man begged Abraham to let Lazarus dip his finger in water and give it to him. The reason is found in Luke 16: 24, *"to cool my tongue; for I am **tormented** in this flame."* Abraham responded by saying it was impossible because between the hell of torment and Paradise there was a great gulf no one could cross.

And according to Psalm 49:19, 2 Peter 2:4, 2 Peter 2:17, and others, the only light will be from the fires. It will be mostly dark, making it impossible to see the worms mentioned in Isaiah 66:24 and by Jesus in Mark 9:43-48, crawling on them. But they will feel them. Job 24:20 also talks about these worms when describing the fate of sinners. *"The womb shall forget him* (the sinner); *the **worm shall feed sweetly on him**; he shall be no more remembered; and wickedness shall be broken as a tree."* This conjures up a macabre picture of flesh-eating worms which, in turn, brings up the question of smell. What must this place smell like? I imagine something so disgusting and foul it is beyond our comprehension.

Now, repeating Isaiah 66:24, notice the parentheses and words in bold. *"And they* (those living during the millennial reign) *shall go forth, and look upon the carcases of the men that have transgressed against me: for their **worm** shall not die, neither shall their **fire** be quenched; and they shall be an abhorring unto all flesh."* Here, it clearly states that people living during Jesus' earthly reign will see those in hell and the torments they endure. Why?

The survivors of the Tribulation, those who did not worship the beast or take his mark, will enter Jesus' millennial reign with mortal bodies. Their lifespan will be lengthy, and they will have children, who, in turn, have children with long lifespans, who, in turn, have children, etcetera. During this time, each person must come into his own saving knowledge of Jesus. Though Jesus' rule will be an incredible time of peace and joy, these people will still have a sin nature. Perhaps that's why God lets them see the fate of the wicked, to help them make the right decision. The sad part is that after Satan's release from the pit, he will convince many to rebel.

We've seen what happens to a body, the physical part of a person, in hell. Now, what about the soul?

Destination Hell

What about the mental aspect, the *psuche*? Remember, Jesus said both body and soul will be destroyed.

I imagine that people will feel incredible sorrow for having missed their opportunity for eternal happiness. In addition, I believe they will also feel incredible terror that this hell hole is now their destiny. Certainly a torrent of emotions will flood their minds as they try to grasp their new, permanent, and horrifying reality.

And according to Isaiah 5:14-15, they will also experience humiliation. *"Therefore hell hath enlarged herself, and opened her mouth without measure: and their* (the wicked) *glory, and their multitude, and their pomp, and he that rejoiceth, shall descend into it.* **And the mean man shall be brought down, and the mighty man shall be humbled, and the eyes of the lofty shall be humbled."**

All striving and conniving to achieve a worldly prize has come to worse than nothing. Instead of a lasting reward it has brought these people to hell and to humiliation and shame. Here, all pretenses are stripped away. There will be no boasting or posturing. No one will brag about that great job he had, that big house or impressive bank account.

Ezekiel 32:24 talks about the fate of Elam, the wicked enemy of Israel, but it could just as well be describing the fate of all the wicked, *"yet have they* (the wicked) *borne their **shame** with them that go down to the pit."*

So, sorrow, humiliation, shame will be felt in hell. And because this is an eternal state, it will never get better. Jesus, in Matthew 25:46, said the wicked *"shall go away into **everlasting punishment**: but the righteous into life eternal."* Jesus again indicated that hell was everlasting in Matthew 18:8 and Mark 9:43-45. Other Scriptures, such as Jude 13, Daniel 12:2 and Psalm 49:19, also indicate that once in hell, it is forever.

2 Thessalonians 1:7-9 also says this fate will be everlasting. *"And to you who are troubled rest with us, when the Lord Jesus shall be revealed from heaven with his mighty angels. In flaming fire taking vengeance on them that know not God, and that obey not the gospel of our Lord Jesus Christ: Who shall be punished with **everlasting destruction** from the presence of the Lord, and from the glory of his power."*

The poignancy of this horrible everlasting state is reflected in Alighieri's, *Dante's Inferno,* where he describes hell and writes that above its gate is the inscription: ***Abandon Hope All Who Enter Here***. Think of what that does to a person, mentally?

Destination Hell

Once in hell, his fate is sealed. There is no hope for a pardon or parole. There is no escape. The situation is hopeless. And in the absence of hope comes despair along with depression and fear. Job 8:13 says, *"So are the paths of all that forget God; and the hypocrite's* **hope shall perish***."* Proverbs 11:7 says the same thing, *"When a wicked man dieth, his expectation shall perish: and* **the hope of unjust men perisheth.***"*

On top of that, there will be no meaningful or satisfying work to occupy the time. Just endless emptiness and suffering. Every part of a person will be in torment. He will be alone and in darkness, without purpose, and confined to an eternity of deterioration. No companion or friend will comfort him or speak kind or encouraging words. If there is a pit for each individual, then everyone will be isolated and left to suffer alone. If it is a corporate pit, the only sounds will be shrieks of pain.

The Bible tells us that every good gift is from above. That means all good things come from God. In hell, people are separated from Him, indicating there is nothing good there. No light, no peace, no joy, no love, no fulfillment, no companionship. They will never see another sunrise or blue sky or flowers. They will never feel a gentle breeze on their face or see a person smile. They will never again hear the sweet singing of a canary or nightingale or lark. Or hear music or laughter. Instead, loneliness, hopelessness, and torment will fill their days. It will be a place of endless misery and suffering.

And the pain in hell will be unrelenting. There will be no release or escape. Three times Luke 16 mentions that the rich man was "tormented" or "in torments." When something is mentioned that many times it means, "pay attention." Revelation 14:11 is even more graphic. It talks about the fate of those who take the mark of the beast. *"And the smoke of their **torment ascendeth up for ever and ever: and they have no rest day or night**, who worship the beast and his image, and whosoever receiveth the mark of his name."*

I think it safe to say that our worst day on earth is better than the best day in hell.

In Mark 9, Jesus said if our hand, foot, or eye causes us to sin it's better to cut them off (hand-foot) or pluck it out (eye). He didn't mean it literally. Rather, He was stressing the point that hell is so terrible we should avoid it at all costs. This is repeated in both Matthew 5:29-30 and Matthew 18:8-9.

Destination Hell

Hell is the fate of all those on the broad way who don't accept Jesus before they die. But can Christians go there? I have covered this in my book, *12 Questions New Christians Frequently Ask*, but will repeat it here.

Can Christians go to hell?

Before going further, that word "Christian" must be defined. If the question is being asked about **cultural** Christians, those who say they are Christian because their parents were or because they attend church on Easter and Christmas, then yes, hell is in their future. Why? Because they are Christians in name only. I understand them since I was one of them.

And if the question is asked about **carnal** Christians, those who mouthed the sinner's prayer, giving it lip service but not coming from the heart, and who still live like those in the world, then, yes, hell is their destination as well.

And just because someone has been baptized into a church or attends services or tries to follow their church's rules and regulations doesn't make him a genuine Christian, either. A true Christian is one who has acknowledged he is a sinner, has accepted Jesus as Savior, has acknowledged that it's only

Jesus' blood sacrifice that restores him to God the Father and therefore has a relationship with Him.

Jesus gave a stern warning in Matthew 7:21-23. *"Not every one that saith unto me, Lord, Lord, shall enter into the kingdom of heaven; but* **he that doeth the will of my Father** *which is in heaven. Many will say to me in that day* (the day of judgment) *Lord, Lord, have we not prophesied in thy name? and in thy name have cast out devils? and in thy name done many wonderful works? And then will I profess unto them, I never knew you; depart from me, ye that work iniquity."* Jesus looks at the heart. Our good deeds don't fool Him. He knows who's genuine and who's not.

In Revelation 3:5, Jesus said, *"He that overcometh, the same shall be clothed in white raiment; and I will not blot out his name out of the book of life."* And Revelation 20:15 says, *"Whosoever was not found written in the book of life was cast into the lake of fire."*

So, anyone NOT written in the book of life will go to hell. The Bible can't be any clearer.

However, if we are taking about a genuine born-again Christian, regardless of denomination, one who has surrendered and made Jesus his Lord and Savior, then that question becomes more difficult to answer. And exploring it feels a bit like wading into quicksand.

Destination Hell
How can a genuine Christian be blotted out?

I want to tread carefully here. God's grace is so incredible. His blood pays for all our sins: past, present, and future. And there is no sin too great God can't or won't forgive if we confess it and repent. But I fear that the current teaching of "hyper grace" can lead believers astray. Grace does not give us license to live any way we want. God is holy and we are called to live holy lives, too, submitted and obedient to Him.

Galatians 6:7 says, *"Be not deceived; God is not mocked: for whatsoever a man soweth, that shall he also reap."* There is no fooling God. Our fruits will always give us away.

But can a genuine Christian, one who isn't prefect but who loves God and tries to live a holy life, go to hell? I believe the one thing that can derail a genuine Christian is unforgiveness, and perhaps even keep him from heaven. Why? Because Jesus Himself said, *"For **if ye forgive** men their trespasses, your heavenly Father will also forgive you; But **if ye forgive not** men their trespasses, neither will your Father forgive your trespasses,"* (Matthew 6:14-15).

The whole reason we, as born-again believers, have assurance of heaven is that we are forgiven, and our sins are covered by the blood of Jesus. But here, Jesus is saying that our sins are **NOT** forgiven if we don't forgive others.

In Mark 11:25-26, Jesus said, *"And when ye stand praying, **forgive**, if ye have ought against any: that your Father also which is in heaven may **forgive** you your trespasses. But if ye do not **forgive**, neither will your Father which is in heaven **forgive** your trespasses."* If our sins are not forgiven by God then we are considered sinners, and no sinner will enter the kingdom of heaven.

Jesus continued this theme in Luke 6:37. *"Judge not, and ye shall not be judged: condemn not, and ye shall not be condemned: **forgive**, and ye shall be **forgiven**."*

When Jesus taught His disciples the Lord's prayer, He said in Luke 11:4, *"And **forgive us** our sins; **for we also forgive every one** that is indebted to us."* Again, God's forgiving us is tied to us forgiving others. No forgiveness for others, then no forgiveness for us.

Remember Revelation 3:5? Jesus said, *"He that overcometh, the same shall be clothed in white raiment; and I will not **blot out** his name out of the book of life."* Here, Jesus indicates it's possible to be blotted out of the book of life. What then? *"Whosoever was not found written in the book of life was cast into the lake of*

Destination Hell

fire." Let that not happen to us because of unforgiveness.

We have no right to keep grudges or maintain a heart of unforgiveness. Jesus has forgiven us everything. Therefore, we must also forgive others. It's up to God to settle accounts. Romans 12:19b says, *"Vengeance is mine; I will repay, saith the Lord."* So, let's leave it to Him.

While I was struggling with this issue, I happened to see a Christian program where an African pastor was relaying an amazing story. It was a story documented and certified by both his wife and community. He had had an argument with his wife and rejected her numerous apologies, refusing to forgive her as well as punishing her with the silent treatment for nearly a week. At the end of it, he had a terrible car accident resulting in a death experience and found himself in hell. He described the horror of it and how he cried out to God that this had to be a mistake. He was a pastor and a true lover of Jesus. An angel appeared to him and told him if God were to leave him in this state, hell would be his eternal home. Because he refused to forgive his wife, God could not forgive him. The pastor immediately repented and found himself on a slab in the morgue.

We don't have to accept every Christian's supernatural experience as fact, so believe or not as you will. But it does provide food for thought as well as give the above Scriptures a startling and horrifying sense of realism.

Even so, it's not our job to scrutinize people in our church to determine who does and doesn't go to heaven. Only God knows the heart. Only He knows who is genuine and who isn't. So, we must leave judgment to Him.

But I can't say this enough: God doesn't want anyone to go to hell. He is saying to each person, *"I call heaven and earth to record this day against you, that I have set before you life and death, blessing and cursing: therefore choose life, that both thou and thy seed may live,"* (Deuteronomy 30:19).

And for those who choose life, Jesus says, *"and him that cometh to me I will in no wise cast out,"* (John 6:37).

Oh, how wonderful and gracious God is!

Hell in the Lake of Fire

The convict, Satan, has been released from prison. And despite Jesus' one-thousand-year rule of unprecedented peace and joy, this con artist is able to deceive mankind once again. Revelation 20:8 tells us these rebels will be *"as the sand of the sea,"* implying large numbers will buy Satan's lies.

Does Satan promise them what he promised Adam and Eve, what he promised the transhumanists, that they would become *"as god"*? Whatever the promise, multitudes join Satan in an offensive against Jesus. Revelation 20:9 says they, *"compassed the camp of the saints about, and the beloved city* (Jerusalem)."

It's hard to imagine that Satan and these people, all created beings, believe they can defeat the Creator Himself. Obviously, Satan learns nothing while in prison. His end, and the end of those with him, is swift. *"And fire came down from God out of heaven, and devoured them* (all the rebels). *And the devil that deceived them was cast into the* **lake of fire** *and brimstone, where the beast and the false prophet are, and shall be tormented day and night for ever and ever,"* (Revelation 20:9-10).

Satan, the age-old enemy of mankind, finally comes to his end. His various names in Scripture depict his evil nature: serpent, dragon, evil one, murderer, liar, father of lies, deceiver, lawless one, the accuser of the brethren, and (counterfeit) angel of light. How wonderful that the world is finally and forever rid of him! Also, this ends the ancient cosmic battle between God and Satan which began when Satan polluted heaven with his pride. It's been a long war with many casualties. But oh, the patience of God! His longsuffering allowed Satan to fully expose himself; to show himself to be utterly unredeemable. Had God disposed of him immediately after his first rebellion, there would forever be a question in heaven, "Did those angels who remained faithful do so out of love or fear?" The answer, "love" was now indisputable.

After the dispatching of Satan comes the great White Throne Judgment, a day of sorrow for all who stand before it. Jesus, the great Judge, has already judged the raptured believers at the Bema Judgment, then those believers who died during the Tribulation without worshipping the beast or taking his mark (Revelation 20:4). He also judged the earth throughout the seven-year Tribulation, followed by His judgment of nations and kings for how they treated Israel and for dividing her land (Isaiah 24:21, Joel 3:2). Now, Jesus will judge unbelievers. I've already discussed this in my book,

Destination Hell

Encountering Jesus Throughout the Bible, but will repeat a portion here.

The judgment of unbelievers:

This is the last of the judgments, and the one that makes me weep because it doesn't have to be since God made a remedy. After Satan is cast into the lake of fire, Revelation 20:11-12 says, *"And I (John) saw a **great white throne**, and him that sat on it, from whose face the earth and the heaven fled away; and there was found no place for them. And I saw the dead, small and great, stand before God; and the **books** were opened: and another **book** was opened, which is the **book of life**: and the dead were judged out of those things which were written in the **books**, according to their works."*

Did you know God has written a book about you? About each of us? It's filled with His desires and plans for us, which are only for good and not evil (Jeremiah 29:11). And they never included hell. He wants only the best for us.

The books mentioned in Scripture are:
- The book of tears in Psalm 56:8 which records all those times we have wept. Our tears are even collected in a bottle.
- The book of the living in Psalm 69:28 and Revelation 20:12 which contains God's plan

for every person who ever lived, as well as how their life actually turned out.
- The book of remembrance in Malachi 3:16, written for those who fear the Lord and how they honored His name.
- And the Lamb's book of life in Revelation 21:27, containing the name of everyone who accepted Jesus as Lord and Savior.

At the White Throne Judgment these books will be opened and examined. Every human being will be judged. No one will escape. The great as well as the lowly will have their day in court when, according to Revelation 20:13, the dead will be summoned. *"And the sea gave up the dead which were in it; and death and hell delivered up the dead which were in them; and they were judged every man according to his works."*

We must understand that every deed, every thought, every word of every person has been recorded, and those records have been kept in heaven. And when each person comes before the Great Judge, he must give an account. Ecclesiastes 12:14 says, *"For God shall bring every work into judgment, with every secret thing, whether it be good, or whether it be evil."* All things will be exposed. True justice will be served. And those found guilty will be cast into the lake of fire for all eternity.

Destination Hell

But found guilty of what? Revelation 20:15 tells us; *"whosoever was not found written in the book of life was cast into the **lake of fire**."* And that's the thing that sends them into eternal torment—*not being found written in the* (Lamb's) *book of life*. This book is also mentioned in Revelation 21:27.

We already know that only believers in Jesus are listed in that book. Philippians 4:3 talks about the followers of Christ and His gospel and *"whose names are in the **book of life**."* And Jesus, in Luke 10:20, told His disciples to *"rejoice not, that the spirits are subject unto you; but rather rejoice, **because your names are written in heaven** (the Lamb's book of life)."* At the White Throne Judgment, it will be too late for anyone to change his mind about accepting Jesus.

Not only are the unrepentant cast into the lake of fire, but also death and hell. That means all the horrors of hell are included in the lake of fire. Thus, the lake of fire becomes the eternal place of torment. Revelation 21:8 describes the people who go there. *"But the fearful, and unbelieving, and the abominable, and murderers, and whoremongers, and sorcerers, and idolaters, and all liars, shall have their part in **the lake which burneth with fire and brimstone**: which is the second death."*

These are the only Scriptures mentioning the lake of fire. But rest assured they are not symbolic. They mean exactly what they say. Consider the words, lake and fire. Lake is *limne* in Greek and means, "a pond, a harbor, lake." While fire is *pur* and means, "fire, fiery, lightening." So, we can conclude that this will be an actual lake made up of actual fire.

Those who think they will have more than one life and therefore more than one chance to get into heaven should pay heed to Hebrews 9:27, *"it is appointed unto men once to die, but after this the judgment."* We will not be reincarnated thousands of times until we get it right and become spiritually evolved. We only have one shot at it, one life. Then judgement. And the lot of those who reject Jesus is eternal damnation. It's the law of reciprocity, the law of sowing and reaping. What these people have sown throughout their life they will now reap (Galatians 6:7).

The difference between them and believers is not that believers have never sinned. It's that believers have accepted Jesus as their Savior, and His blood covers their sins. And because Jesus paid for these sins, believers don't have to. But because non-believers have rejected Jesus, the payment for their sins is still due. Therefore, they must pay for them on their own.

Destination Hell

In Revelation 1:17, when John was in heaven, he saw Jesus in all His glory. *"And when I (John) saw him (Jesus), I fell at his feet as dead. And he laid his right hand upon me, saying unto me, Fear not: I am the first and the last."* What a picture! The sight of Jesus glorified was so overpowering that John collapsed. And oh, how sweet Jesus was! He immediately told John not to fear. Why? Because John was one of His. Those who belong to Jesus will have nothing to fear when coming face to face with Him.

And that's the tragedy. It's the easiest thing in the world to avoid the White Throne Judgment. God made it so simple according to Acts 16:31, *"Believe on the Lord Jesus Christ, and thou shalt be saved."* And the alternative? Hebrews 10:31 says it well, *"It is a fearful thing to fall into the hands of the living God."*

It's sad to think many, when facing God, will believe their good deeds will balance out their bad ones. But good works won't cut it. Ephesians 2:8-9 is clear. *"For by grace are ye saved through faith; and that not of yourselves: it is the gift of God:* **Not of works***, lest any man should boast."* No matter how wonderful, good deeds won't get anyone listed in the book of life.

The alternative:

I'd like to end by talking about the alternative: an eternity in heaven. Like hell, heaven is a tangible place. Paul, in 2 Corinthians 12:2, tells us he went to the third heaven. In verse four, he says he *"heard unspeakable words, which it is not lawful for a man to utter."*

In recent times, many who claim to have gone there say their words can't do it justice. But I think all we need do is look at the beauty of our world to get a small glimpse of what heaven will be like. Though we live in a fallen world, it is still incredibly beautiful. Now, imagine a perfect place void of sin and filled with the presence of God. Imagine a place with no pain, suffering, or strife. Imagine a place where no one and nothing wears out, decays, or dies. Imagine a place where children pet lions, tigers, and bears. This is the future of all believers. And after the rapture, we, too, will have glorified bodies that never wear out, decay, or die (Philippians 3:21). It will be a perfect body suitable for a perfect dwelling place.

What the Bible says:

As mentioned, according to Paul there are three heavens. The first heaven is the air above us, our atmosphere. The second heaven contains the

Destination Hell

planets and stars. The third heaven is God's abode. Several places in the Bible (Deuteronomy 10:14, 1 Kings 8:27, 2 Chronicles 2:6, 6:18, Psalm 68:33) mention the "heaven of heavens," which I believe refers to the third heaven. Recently, the idea of there being seven heavens has resurfaced, but this is an old pagan concept.

There are many references to heaven in Scripture. It's mentioned almost six-hundred times, while "heavens" is mentioned over one-hundred times and "heavenly," twenty-three times.

First, we need to understand that, according to Deuteronomy 26:15, God's habitation (*maown*), His tabernacle, is **holy**. Psalm 20:6 also says heaven is "holy." And that word "holy" (*qodesh*) means, "a sacred place, sanctity, consecrated, clean." 2 Chronicles 30:27 calls it His *"holy dwelling place (maown),* while 1 Kings 8:30, 39, 43, and 49 refer to heaven simply as God's *"dwelling place (hashab)."* Notice *hashab* is used in 1 Kings instead of *maown*. It means, "to sit down as judge, to settle, to marry, habitation," and gives us a fuller picture. In addition to heaven being God's holy abode, this also indicates it is a seat of judgment, and portrays Him as a bridegroom.

According to Psalm 11:4, God does indeed sit on a heavenly throne in His *"holy temple."* God Himself confirmed this in Isaiah 66:1, *"Thus saith the LORD, The heaven is my **throne**, and the earth is my footstool."* And Psalm 103:19 says, *"The LORD hath prepared his **throne** in the heavens: and his **kingdom** ruleth over all."*

So, we see that God is a King who sits on a throne and rules over a Kingdom. In Daniel 4:37, Nebuchadnezzar, after recovering from seven years of insanity, acknowledged God as the "King of heaven." The New Testament is full of references to the "Kingdom of Heaven." Matthew, especially, speaks of this, while Mark, Luke and John constantly refer to the "Kingdom of God."

And as a King with a Kingdom, God also has an army (Daniel 4:35). In addition, His word is *"settled in heaven,"* (Psalm 119:89), meaning His Word is established law and makes up the very foundation and pillars by which heaven is governed. Job 26:11 mentions heaven's pillars (*ammuwd*). That word means, "a column, stand, established." God is in total control. And because God is holy and just, His laws are holy and just, thus heaven is also holy and just.

As mentioned, God has an army as befitting the ruler of a Kingdom. 1 Kings 22:19 tells us that God sits on a throne surrounded by the host of heaven (angels). It doesn't take much imagination to

Destination Hell

envision them standing by, eager to carry out His every command. Revelation 19:14 says, *"And the **armies** which were in heaven followed him* (Jesus) *upon white horses, clothed in fine linen, white and clean."* It's an army of powerful angels but also includes believers who, the Bible says, return with Him after the Tribulation.

Numerous Scriptures talk about the Captain of the heavenly host. The "Captain" is Jesus. In Joshua 5:13-15, Moses has died, and Joshua leads Israel. Preparing to enter the Promised Land and take Jericho, Joshua encounters the Captain of the heavenly host and worships Him. Remember, Jews understood that only God was to be worshiped. *"And Joshua fell on his face to the earth, and did **worship**, and said unto him, What saith my lord unto his servant? And the **captain of the LORD'S host** said unto Joshua, Loose thy shoe from off thy foot; for the place whereon thou standest is holy, and Joshua did so."* Like the Great I Am Who Moses encountered and Who asked him to take off his sandals because the ground was holy, so, too, Jesus, the same Great I Am, told Joshua to remove his, as well.

In Luke 2:13, we see the angel of the Lord announcing the birth of Jesus to the Bethlehem shepherds. *"And suddenly there was with the angel* (who announced this momentous event) *a* *multitude of **the heavenly host** praising God."* A multitude implies a vast number. This tells us there is a great angelic population in heaven. Some are warring angels. Others are ministering spirits, assigned to help and protect us during our time on earth. Imagine finally meeting them!

According to 2 Kings 17:16, 21:3, 5, the host of heaven can also refer to the stars and planetary bodies. And 2 Kings 23:5 says, *"And he* (Hilkiah, the high priest under orders from King Josiah) *put down the idolatrous priests, whom the kings of Judah had ordained to burn incense in the high places in the cities of Judah, and in the places round about Jerusalem; them also that burned incense unto Baal,* **to the sun, and to the moon, and to the planets, and to all the host of heaven,***"* Psalm 19:1 tells us that *"the heavens declare the glory of God."* And Psalm 148 and Romans 1:20 tell us that all creation declares God's glory, revealing His greatness. Because His creation clearly reveals God's glory, Romans 1:20 says that those who reject Him are *"without excuse."*

Interestingly, there are windows in heaven (2 Kings 7:2, 19); windows or portals that can be shut according to 1 Kings 8:35 and Luke 4:25, or opened, according to Malachi 3:10 and Luke 3:21. When opened, they provide a means of God's blessings to be poured upon earth, demonstrating His love and goodness. When closed, they are a means of

Destination Hell

rendering judgement in order to bring sinners back to Him.

And according to Psalm 78:24 and 105:40, there is also food in heaven. It speaks of the angels' food, heavenly manna, and corn. That shouldn't surprise us. Jesus promised believers a wedding feast. Imagine the menu! Because God is so creative, it will surely be unique and delicious. And since we will have glorified bodies, I'm counting on this feast to come without calories and weight gain!

Matthew 16:19 says that heaven has keys. Heaven also contains "mysteries," (Matthew 13:11). And both Deuteronomy 33:13 and Matthew 19:21 say there are precious gifts and treasures in heaven, while Luke 6:23 refers to "rewards."

Jesus also said there are mansions or dwelling places for every believer. Mansions in Greek is *mone* and means, "a residence, our own." That means we will have our very own place in heaven, tailor-made for us. And since Jesus, the Creator of the Universe, has crafted them Himself, they will be incredibly beautiful. Can God be any more gracious?

Heaven will be amazing. Our wonderful, just, and kind King oversees everything. And He will protect us and care for us for all eternity. And since every good and perfect gift comes from above (James 1:17) that means heaven is full of good and perfect gifts. But the best gift will be hearing God say, "Well done thou good and faithful servant," then being in His presence for all eternity, wherein is fullness of joy (Psalm 16:11).

Think of it! We will tangibly see God and communicate with Him. All eternity will not be enough to praise Him, thank Him, love Him, and discover the many wonderful facets of His nature. Also, I imagine we will get to explore His universe and do interesting and satisfying work.

The above just scratches the surface. For those who want to know more about heaven, read Randy Alcorn's book, *Heaven*. It's comprehensive and Scripturally based.

But we can know this: *"Eye hath not seen, nor ear heard, neither have entered into the heart of man, the things which God hath prepared for them that love him,"* (1 Corinthians 2:9).

The new heaven and earth:

Revelation 20:11 talks about how *"the earth and the heaven fled away; and there was found no place for them."* This was predicted in Isaiah 34:4, 51:6, and 2 Peter 3:10, which describe how the heavens will

Destination Hell

be rolled together like a scroll, vanish like smoke, and be dissolved.

But to what purpose? To make way for a new heaven and earth! Isaiah 66:22 mentions the new heaven and new earth. And God, in Isaiah 65:17, said this, *"For behold, I create new heavens and a new earth: and the former shall not be remembered, nor come into mind."* And Hebrews 12:22 even mentions a new heavenly Jerusalem.

Revelation 21:1-4 adds to all this. *"And I saw a **new heaven and a new earth**: for the first heaven and the first earth were passed away; and there was no more sea. And I John saw the holy city, new Jerusalem, coming down from God out of heaven, prepared as a bride adorned for her husband. And I heard a great voice out of heaven saying, Behold the tabernacle of God is with men, and he will dwell with them, and they shall be his people, and God himself shall be with them, and be their God. And God shall wipe away all tears from their eyes: and there shall be no more death, neither sorrow, nor crying, neither shall there be any more pain: for the former things are passed away."* This is the wonderful new heaven and earth Jesus will create after His millennial reign.

Revelation 21:10-14 goes on to describe the beautiful New Jerusalem. After an angel takes John to a high mountain, he sees, *"the holy*

Jerusalem, descending out of heaven from God. Having the glory of God: and her light was like unto a stone most precious, even like a jasper stone, clear as crystal; And had a wall great and high, and had twelve gates, and at the gates twelve angels, and names written thereon, which are the names of the twelve tribes of the children of Israel: On the east three gates; on the north three gates; on the south three gates; and on the west three gates. And the wall of the city had twelve foundations, and in them the names of the twelve apostles of the Lamb."

Then the angel measures the city, which is in the form of a cube, made of pure gold and covered with precious gems. The streets are also gold. And the gates are twelve large pearls (Revelation 21:15-21). *"And I (John) saw no temple therein: for the Lord God Almighty and the Lamb are the temple of it. And the city had no need of the sun, neither of the moon, to shine in it: for the glory of God did lighten it, and the Lamb is the light thereof,"* (Revelation 21:22-23).

Revelation chapter 22 describes the river proceeding from the throne of God and how the trees of lifeline both sides. These trees produce twelve different fruits, one kind each month. And the leaves heal the nations. This is a place of indescribable beauty, a place where we will be able to interface with God and serve Him.

Destination Hell

This will be our eternal home.

Something to think about:

God loves you more than you can imagine. Oh, how rich, how deep, how wide is His love! It passes all understanding (Ephesians 3:19). And He wants you to spend all eternity with Him.

To those who say, "I don't believe in God or the Bible," I say this: As a former cultural Christian who didn't believe in Scripture or Jesus as Savior, I understand. But that didn't discourage God. Even when I was far from Him, He was there, protecting me in my folly, and orchestrating things in a way that could only be described as miraculous. Then when my heart softened, I finally prayed, "God **IF** you are real and **IF** Jesus is real, then I want to know you." And oh, how wonderfully He answered. God is no respecter of persons. What He does for one, He will do for others. And God is not offended by your questions. It means you are seeking, and that pleases Him. If you ask with a sincere heart, He will answer in a way meaningful to you.

Or, if you are one who has walked on the wild side and think you are too far gone and that God could never love someone like you, then rest assured, if you are sincere, He will not turn you away. He knows your name. He even knows the number of hairs on your head (Matthew 10:30, Luke 12:7). Remember, He has a book in heaven about you, which includes details of your life, His wonderful hopes, plans and dreams for you. He's pulling for you and wants you to succeed. And He loves you no matter what you've done. In fact, no one could love you more!

But as we've already seen, works won't cut it. They never have. So, it's not a matter of cleaning up your act before you can come to Him. Remember, all our good deeds/works are like filthy rags compared to His holiness and righteousness. Only innocent blood can remove sin and make us righteous. So, praise God for Jesus! He paid the ultimate price. The problem is that while Jesus' sin payment is for everyone, it can only be appropriated by those who believe it and receive it, which means one must personally accept Jesus and what He did.

If you are still hesitant, then consider the rest of the material in this book and ask yourself, "Do I really want to stay on that clogged superhighway heading for disaster? If the answer is "no" why waste more time? Come to Jesus now. Come to the One Who loves you most and knows you best. He is calling your name. If you want to answer, then pray this prayer and mean it:

Destination Hell

Father God, I come before you in the name of Jesus. I acknowledge that I am a sinner and can't save myself. Forgive me for my sins and for trying to live a life without Jesus. I accept Him now as my Savior. I believe He is Your only begotten Son, that He came to earth in the form of man and died for my sins, that He was buried and rose from the dead on the third day, that He ascended into heaven where He now sits at the right hand of God, and that He will come again to rule as King and Judge over the earth. I also want to make Jesus Lord over my life and to serve him all my days. Amen.

If you have prayed this prayer, angels are rejoicing in heaven! The next step is to get a Bible, read it, and connect with a solid Bible-believing church.

Love and Blessings,
Sylvia Bambola
sylviabambola45@gmail.com

Sylvia Bambola

Destination Hell

Notes:

1. *CBS News*, The most terrifying cults in history, Elisha Fieldstadt, Jessica Learish, June 30, 2021, https://www.cbsnews.com/pictures/cults-dangerous-deadly-history/4/
2. Aldous Huxley, https://www.britannica.com/biography/Aldous-Huxley
3. Ron Rhodes, *End-Times Super Trends* (Harvest House Publishers, Eugene, Oregon, 2017) 109.
4. Ibid., 109.
5. Wikipedia, Isaiah Scroll, Isaiah Scroll - Wikipedia
6. (Bible Manuscripts (allaboutthejourney.org)
7. Stephen M. Bauer, *The Math of Christ* (Defender Publishing, Grand, MO 2010) 95-96.
8. The Expository Files, How We Got the New Testament (bible.ca)
9. Perry Stone, *American's Apocalyptic Reset* (Voice of Evangelism Ministries, Cleveland, TN 37320, 2021) 68.
10. *How Did Christianity Become the Dominant Religion of the Later Roman Empire?* Alanna Speer, editorial-vol-3-no-1.pdf (wordpress.com), 93.
11. Ibid., 95-96.
12. Amazing Discoveries, Paganism and Catholicism, Professor Walter J. Veith, PhD, February 17, 2009, Paganism and Catholicism | Catholic Church Practices (amazingdiscoveries.org)

13. When Did Latin Die, Blake Adams, https://ancientlanguage.com/when-did-latin-die/
14. Dark Ages (historiography) - Wikipedia
15. The Dark Ages (allabouthistory.org)
16. Wikipedia, Martin Luther, https://en.wikipedia.org/wiki/Martin_Luther
17. Britannica, William Tyndale, https://www.britannica.com/biography/William-Tyndale
18. Roberts Liardon, *God's Generals* (Albury Publishing, Tulsa, OK, 1996) 46, 78, 196, 270, 310.
19. *The Zondervan Pictorial Encyclopedia of the Bible* (Regency Reference Library, Grand Rapids, Michigan, 1976) Volume 1, Asia, 363.
20. *The Zondervan Pictorial Encyclopedia of the Bible* (Regency Reference Library, Grand Rapids, Michigan, 1976) Volume 2, Ephesus, 324-330.
21. *The Zondervan Pictorial Encyclopedia of the Bible* (Regency Reference Library, Grand Rapids, Michigan, 1976) Volume 5, Smyrna, 462-464.
22. *The Zondervan Pictorial Encyclopedia of the Bible* (Regency Reference Library, Grand Rapids, Michigan, 1976) Volume 4, Pergamum, 701-704.
23. *The Zondervan Pictorial Encyclopedia of the Bible* (Regency Reference Library, Grand Rapids, Michigan, 1976) Volume 5, Thyatira, 743-744.
24. Ibid., Sardis, 278.
25. *The Zondervan Pictorial Encyclopedia of the Bible* (Regency Reference Library, Grand Rapids, Michigan, 1976) Volume 4, Philadelphia, 753.
26. *The Zondervan Pictorial Encyclopedia of the Bible* (Regency Reference Library, Grand Rapids, Michigan, 1976) Volume 3, Laodicea, 877-879.
27. Gateway Pundit, Cassandra Fairbanks, September 7, 2021, Christian University Commissions Murals of Trans Flag and Failed

Destination Hell

Dem Gubernatorial Candidate Stacey Abrams (thegatewaypundit.com)
28. David Fiorazo, Veritas? No Surprise Harvard Hires Atheist 'Chaplain', September 1, 2021, Veritas? No Surprise Harvard Hires Atheist 'Chaplain' | David Fiorazo
29. *Prophecy Watcher*, October 2017, "The Last Days Apostasy of the Church" Part One, Andy Woods, 37.
30. Harbingers Daily, October 29, 2021, Ken Ham Rebukes Liberal 'Pastor's' Claim That Christians Have 'Made The Bible An Idol' | Harbingers Daily
31. Dr. Stanley Monteith, *Brotherhood of Darkness* (Oklahoma City, OK: Hearthstone Publishing, 2000), 49-51.
32. Ron Rhodes, *End-Times Super Trends* (Harvest House Publishers, Eugene, Oregon, 2017) 62.
33. Olive Tree Ministries, "When Your Church Awakens to Wokeness," Jan Markell and Pastor Brandon Holthaus, July 23, 2021, Complete Archives Archive | Page 2 of 47 | Olive Tree Ministries (olivetreeviews.org)
34. Christianity Today, "Solar light of the World: Evangelicals Launch Global Clean Energy Campaign," Griffin Paul Jackson, December 11, 2019, Solar Light of the World: Evangelicals Launch Global Clean...... | News & Reporting | Christianity Today
35. Billy Crone, *Prophecy in the News Magazine*, March 2015, pp. 11-14.
36. Social Gospel - Wikipedia
37. Ibid.
38. Christians Together : Kingdom Now teaching: beware!; **The Deception Of Dominion Theology:**

Sylvia Bambola

Basic Principles Of Dominionism (dominion-theology.blogspot.com)

39. Terry James, Editor, *Deceivers* (New Leaf Press, 2018) "Middle East Misdirection", Phillip Goodman, 151.
40. Ibid., 152.
41. https://smartfaith.net/2018/05/17/pop-gospel-viii-the-seeker-sensitive-movement/#:~:text=The%20seeker-friendly%20or%20seeker-sensitive%20church%20movement%2C%20epitomised%20by,non-threatening%2C%20entertaining%20and%20relevant%20to%20their%20perceived%20needs;
42. Terry James, Editor, *Deceivers* (New Leaf Press, 2018) "Religionist Deceivers Rampant", Jan Markell, 21.
43. Ron Rhodes, *End-Times Super Trends* (Harvest House Publishers, Eugene, Oregon, 2017) 29.
44. What is the emerging church? Is it biblical or not? | carm.org; What is the Emergent Church? What Do They Believe? (whatchristianswanttoknow.com)
45. Was Jesus a Palestinian? Scholars Debate (themonastery.org); Was Jesus a Palestinian? (christiandoctrine.com)
46. Ron Rhodes, *End-Times Super Trends* (Harvest House Publishers, Eugene, Oregon, 2017) 27.
47. FAQ: Is it okay for Christians to practice Yoga? - Rapture Ready; Yoga is New Age – Ambassadors for Jesus Christ (flavyanson.com)
48. 22 Important Bible Verses About Psychics And Fortune Tellers (biblereasons.com)
49. Apostate Churches Promoting Sin - Berean Research; Apostasy in the Church 2021 Updates

Destination Hell

| Amos37; Today's Apostasy - Decision Magazine
50. Vatican Admits the Catholic Church is based on TRADITION not the Bible. (amredeemed.com)Paganism and Catholicism | Catholic Church Practices (amazingdiscoveries.org); Paganism in Catholic Church | Roman Catholicism;
51. Cris Putnam & Thomas Horn, *Exo-Vaticana* (Crane, MO: Defender, 2013), 38.
52. Ibid., 307-308.
53. Thomas Horn & Cris Putnam, *Petrus Romanus* (Crane, MO: Defender, 2012), 90-93.
54. Ibid., 51.
55. Ibid., 90.
56. Ibid., 466.
57. http://liberationtheology.org/library/liberation_theology_article_marian_hillar.htm
58. Terry James, Editor, *Deceivers* (New Leaf Press, 2018) "The Israel Revilers", Jim Fletcher, 275.
59. Bill Salus, *The Final Prophecies* (Prophecy Depot Publishing, La Quinta, CA, 2020) 55.
60. The Welsh Revival of 1904-1905 - Truth in History
61. Ron Rhodes, *End-Times Super Trends* (Harvest House Publishers, Eugene, Oregon, 2017) 7.
62. Barna: State of the Church, Signs of Decline & Hope Among Key Metrics of Faith - Barna Group
63. End Time Headlines, Americans Who hold to a Biblical World View Declines Yet Again. September 30, 2020; Americans Who Hold To A Biblical Worldview Declines Yet Again (endtimeheadlines.org)
64. Ron Rhodes, *End-Times Super Trends* (Harvest House Publishers, Eugene, Oregon, 2017) 22-23.

Sylvia Bambola

65. My Christian Daily, Biblical Beliefs Nosedive as 60% of Christians Under 40 Say Jesus Not Only Way to Salvation, Kevin Simingon, August 24, 2021; Biblical beliefs nosedive as 60% of Christians Under 40 Say Jesus not only way to salvation | My Christian Daily
66. Ron Rhodes, *End-Times Super Trends* (Harvest House Publishers, Eugene, Oregon, 2017) 25.
67. James K. Walker, *Today's Religions and Spirituality* (Harvest House Publishers, Eugene, Oregon, 2007) 7.
68. Grace Ambassadors, Half of Pastors Don't believe the Bible, Justin Johnson, August 19, 2008, Modified, July 16, 2016; Half of Pastors Don't Believe the Bible (graceambassadors.com)
69. 25 Church Statistics You Need To Know For 2021 - REACHRIGHT (reachrightstudios.com)
70. Ron Rhodes, *End-Times Super Trends* (Harvest House Publishers, Eugene, Oregon, 2017) 37.
71. Ibid.
72. James K. Walker, *Today's Religions and Spirituality* (Harvest House Publishers, Eugene, Oregon, 2007) 8.
73. Ron Rhodes, *End-Times Super Trends* (Harvest House Publishers, Eugene, Oregon, 2017) 36.
74. James K. Walker, *Today's Religions and Spirituality* (Harvest House Publishers, Eugene, Oregon, 2007) 8.
75. Barna: State of the Church, Signs of Decline & Hope Among Key Metrics of Faith - Barna Group
76. The Hive Law, 2021 Divorce Rate in America, How Many Marriages End in Divorce Statistics, Shawn, May 1, 2021, (2021 Divorce Rate In America) How Many Marriages End In Divorce Statistics - The Hive Law

Destination Hell

77. Got Questions, April 26, 2021, Is the divorce rate among Christians truly the same as among non-Christians? | GotQuestions.org
78. The Christian Post, 70% of Women Who Get Abortions Identify as Christians, Survey Finds, by Samuel Smith, November 25, 2015, 70% of Women Who Get Abortions Identify as Christians, Survey Finds | U.S. News | The Christian Post
79. Religious Tolerance, U.S. abortions date, The religion of women who have an abortion, The religious affiliation of women who have abortions in the U.S. (religioustolerance.org)
80. Human Life International, What is the Christian Consensus on Abortion, Brian Clowes, PhD, July 22, 2020, The Consensus of Christians on Abortion (hli.org)
81. President Clinton's Record on Abortion, Douglas Johnson, President Clinton's Record on Abortion | EWTN President Clinton's Record on Abortion | EWTN President Clinton's Record on Abortion | EWTN
82. Church Militant, U.S. Defunding Abortion Worldwide, Rodney Pelletier, April 4, 2017, U.S. Defunding Abortion Worldwide (churchmilitant.com)
83. LiveAction, Biden announces U.S. will again fund abortions overseas, Nancy Flanders, January 28, 2021, Biden announces U.S. will again fund abortions overseas (liveaction.org) Biden announces U.S. will again fund abortions overseas (liveaction.org)
84. Pew Research Center, Key Findings on marriage and cohabitation in the U.S., Nikki Graf, November 6, 2019, Key findings on marriage

and cohabitation in the U.S. | Pew Research Center
85. Majority of Americans Now Believe in Cohabitation - Barna Group
86. Ibid.
87. Christians and Cohabitation: What You Need to Know, Hope Bolinger, May 6, 2021, Christians and Cohabitation: What You Need to Know - Christian Marriage Help and Advice (crosswalk.com)
88. American Addiction Centers, June 28, 2021, Addiction Statistics | Drug & Substance Abuse Statistics (americanaddictioncenters.org)
89. National Center for Drug Abuse Statistics, Drug Abuse Statistics, NCDAS: Substance Abuse and Addiction Statistics [2021] (drugabusestatistics.org)
90. National Center for Drug Abuse Statistics, Drug Abuse Statistics, NCDAS: Substance Abuse and Addiction Statistics [2021] (drugabusestatistics.org)
91. Pastors Unlikely, Christians and Alcohol,-- Shocking Drinking Statistics, Christians and Alcohol - Shocking Drinking Statistics | Pastor Unlikely
92. Pastoral Care Inc. Statistics on Addictions, 2020, Statistics on Addictions (pastoralcareinc.com)
93. Pastoral Care Inc., Pastoral Addictions, Statistics for Pastors (pastoralcareinc.com)
94. Mission Frontiers, 15 Mind-Blowing Statistics About Pornography and The Church, Taken from Nov-Dec 2020 Issue: Human Trafficking: The Church Should Stop Supporting it!, Kingdom Works Studios, November 01, 2020, Mission Frontiers - 15 Mind-Blowing Statistics About Pornography And The Church

Destination Hell

95. Religion News Service, Pornography: A Christian crisis or overblown issue? Jonathan Merritt, January 20, 2016, Pornography: A Christian crisis or overblown issue? (religionnews.com)
96. Mission Frontiers, 15 Mind-Blowing Statistics About Pornography and The Church, Taken from Nov-Dec 2020 Issue: Human Trafficking: The Church Should Stop Supporting it!, Kingdom Works Studios, November 01, 2020, Mission Frontiers - 15 Mind-Blowing Statistics About Pornography And The Church
97. Pastoral Care Inc., Pastoral Addictions, Can a pastor Wrestle with an Addiction? Pastoral Addictions (pastoralcareinc.com)
98. journeyonline.Com, Pornography in the Church a New Epidemic, Mike McCormick, Pornography in the Church A New Epidemic - JourneyOnline
99. Catholic Church sex abuse cases in the United States - Wikipedia
100. Lawyers.com, How Many Catholic Priests Have Been Accused? Roy D. Oppenheim, August 27, 2021, How many Catholic priests have been accused? - Class Actions Legal Blogs Posted by Roy D. Oppenheim | Lawyers.com
101. Report: Protestant Church Insurers Handle 260 Sex Abuse Cases a Year (insurancejournal.com)
102. Protestant Churches Guilty of Hiding Sexual Abuse | O'Hara Law Firm (oharaattorney.com)
103. Mission Frontiers, 15 Mind-Blowing Statistics About Pornography and The Church, Taken from Nov-Dec 2020 Issue: Human Trafficking: The Church Should Stop Supporting it!, Kingdom Works Studios, November 01, 2020,

Sylvia Bambola

Mission Frontiers - 15 Mind-Blowing Statistics About Pornography And The Church
104. Enough Is Enough: Pornography
105. NIH News in Health, Ten Suicide, Understanding the Risk and Getting Help, September 2019, Teen Suicide | NIH News in Health
106. American SPCC, Teenage Suicide, Teenage Suicide: Statistics & Risk Factors | American SPCC - Prevention & Signs
107. Terry James, Editor, *Deceivers* (New Leaf Press, 2018) "Religionist Deceivers Rampant", Jan Markell, 20-22.
108. Got Questions, What is the New Apostolic Reformation? What is the New Apostolic Reformation? | GotQuestions.org
109. Berean Research, New Apostolic Reformation (NAR) - Berean Research
110. Ibid.
111. *The Prophecy Watcher*, September 2021, The Symmetry of Biblical History, Gary Stearman, 4-19.
112. Wikipedia, Georgia Guidestones, Georgia Guidestones - Wikipedia
113. Luis Vega, April 26, 2020, GEORGIA GUIDESTONES - Lucifer's 10 Commandments for the New World Order (fivedoves.com)
114. *Prophecy in the News*, August 2014, "Gaia Worship is Thriving," Gary Stearman, 3-5.
115. Terry James, Editor, *Deceivers* (New Leaf Press, 2018) "Media Manipulators, Todd Strandberg, 226.
116. News Punch, Oxford University: Satanism 'Fastest Growing Religion' in America, Baxter Dmitry, January 15, 2018, Oxford University:

Destination Hell

Satanism 'Fastest Growing Religion' In America (newspunch.com)

117. Carl Teichrib, "Report from the Toronto Parliament of the World's Religions," *Prophecy Watcher Magazine,* June 2019, pp. 26-37.
118. Terry James, Editor, *Deceivers* (New Leaf Press, 2018) "Demon-Conjuring Con Men", Dr. Billy Crone, 244-245.
119. Roanoke Colony, https://en.wikipedia.org/wiki/Roanoke_Colony
120. Paul McGuire & Troy Anderson, *The Babylon Code* (NY, NY: *Faith Words*, Hachette Book Group, 2015), 205.
121. Thomas Horn, *Apollyon Rising 2012* (Crane, MO: Defender, 2009), 71.
122. "The Mastery of Life" http://www.rosicrucian.org/about/master/master.pdf pg. 31
123. Thomas Horn, *Apollyon Rising 2012* (Crane, MO: Defender, 2009), 324.
124. Ibid., 16-17.
125. Stanley Monteith, *Brotherhood of Darkness* (Oklahoma City, OK: Hearthstone Publishing, 2000), 74.
126. Thomas Horn, *Apollyon Rising 2012* (Crane, MO: Defender, 2009), 19.
127. Warren Weston, *Father of Lies* (London: cir. 1930), 29.
128. Stephen Quayle, *Angel Wars* (Bozeman, MT: End Time Thunder Publishers, 2011), 221.
129. Manly P. Hall, *The Secret Destiny of America,* (The Philosophical Research Society, Inc., Los Angeles, CA, 1944), 126.
130. Dr. Stanley Monteith, *Brotherhood of Darkness* (Oklahoma City, OK: Hearthstone Publishing, 2000), 73.

Sylvia Bambola

131. Thomas Horn, *Apollyon Rising 2012* (Crane, MO: Defender, 2009), 110.
132. Ibid., 123.
133. Paul McGuire & Troy Anderson, *The Babylon Code* (NY, NY: *Faith Words*, Hachette Book Group, 2015), 40.
134. *Charisma News*, Michael Snyder, February 17, 2017, The 'Arch of Baal' Was on Display for the Third Time In Honor of the 'World Government Summit' — Charisma News
135. Paul McGuire & Troy Anderson, *The Babylon Code* (NY, NY: *Faith Words*, Hachette Book Group, 2015), 170.
136. Dr. Michael Lake, *The Shinar Directive* (Crane, MO: Defender, 2014), 239.
137. Dr. Stanley Monteith, *Brotherhood of Darkness* (Oklahoma City, OK: Hearthstone Publishing, 2000), 56.
138. Dr. Michael Lake, *The Shinar Directive* (Crane, MO: Defender, 2014), 184-185.
139. National Legion of Decency - Wikipedia
140. Terry James, Editor, *Deceivers* (New Leaf Press, 2018) Demon-Conjuring Con Men, Dr. Billy Crone, 239.
141. PNW, Jonathon Van Maren, July 21, 2021, Not Just Social Media - The Woke Mob Wants To Censor The Book Industry (prophecynewswatch.com)
142. Sexual revolution in 1960s United States - Wikipedia
143. Palm Partners Recovery Center, History of Drug Abuse: The 60's (palmpartners.com)
144. All About History, School Prayer (allabouthistory.org)

Destination Hell

145. Dr. Stanley Monteith, *Brotherhood of Darkness* (Oklahoma City, OK: Hearthstone Publishing, 2000), 73-74.
146. Roe v. Wade | Summary, Origins, & Influence | Britannica
147. Christian Life Resources, Total Abortions Since 1973, U.S. Abortion Statistics By Year (1973-Current) - Christian Life Resources
148. Wikipedia, Same-sex marriage legislation in the United States - Wikipedia
149. Gateway Pundit, Jim Hoft, July 9, 2021, Leftist Group Drapes "God Bless Abortions" Over 65 Foot Christ of Ozarks Statue - Plan on Selling T-Shirts with Same Message (thegatewaypundit.com)
150. *The Washington Free Beacon*, Patrick Hauf, November 17, 2021, Progressive Cities Give Paid Leave to Employees Who Get Abortions (freebeacon.com)
151. Gateway Pundit, Jim Hoft, September 6, 2021, Satanists Admit They Are Making Child Sacrifice Through Abortion an Official Ritual by the Satanic Temple (thegatewaypundit.com)
152. Gateway Pundit, Cristina Laila, September 5, 2021. Portland to Ban Texas Travel and Trade to Protest New "Heartbeat" Abortion Law (thegatewaypundit.com)
153. Gateway Pundit, Cassandra Fairbanks, September 5, 2021, Satanic Temple Attacks Texas Abortion Law, Argues That it Violates Their 'Religious Freedom' to 'Abortion Rituals' (thegatewaypundit.com)
154. Gateway Pundit, Jim Hoft, September 25, 2021, Pelosi Cheers as Dems Pass Radical Abortion Without Limits Bill - Legalizes Partial Birth

Abortion, Dismembering Babies, Lifts All Restrictions (thegatewaypundit.com)
155. Terry James, Editor, *Deceivers* (New Leaf Press, 2018) Introduction, Terry James, 10.
156. Terry James, Editor, *Deceivers* (New Leaf Press, 2018) Tracking Truth in Deceptive Times, J. Michael Hile, 83.
157. Ibid.
158. Ibid., 90.
159. PM, Libby Emmons, November 26, 2021, California's new educational guidelines say math is racist | The Post Millennial
160. The Epoch Times, Isabel van Brugen, December 7, 2021, Hundreds of Mathematicians, Scientists, Sign Open Letter Against Social Justice-Based Curriculum (theepochtimes.com)
161. *Issues & Insights*, Terry Hones, July 2021, I&I/TIPP Poll: Just 36% of Young People Are Proud To Be American – Issues & Insights (issuesinsights.com)
162. Gallup, Frank Newport, April 8, 2016, Sanders, the Oldest Candidate, Looks Best to Young Americans (gallup.com)
163. PBS News Hour, Courtney Vinopal, March 11, 2020, Sanders banked on young voters. Here's how the numbers have played out | PBS NewsHour
164. *Townhall*, Spencer Brown, September 16, 2021, 'Inclusion': History Teacher Hangs 'F*** the Police' Poster, Palestinian Flag in Classroom (townhall.com)
165. Rantz: School bans pro-police flag, but allows BLM and LGBT messages (mynorthwest.com)
166. Gateway Pundit, Julian Conradson, September 25, 2021, UNHINGED: Florida Teacher Has a Meltdown, Berates Students For Supporting

Destination Hell

Classmate Who Brought In a Trump Flag; "Trump Brings Out Racism in Trashy People" - (Video) (thegatewaypundit.com)

167. The Dailywire, Megan Basham, August 30, 2021, 'Christian Evangelicals Are America's Taliban': Actors, Journalists Equate American Christians To The Taliban | The Daily Wire
168. Gateway Pundit, Jim Hoft, October 27, 2021, AG Merrick Garland Sent HELICOPTER and the Feds to Intimidate Parents at Fairfax County School Board Meeting (thegatewaypundit.com); Blaze Media, Leon Wolf, October 9, 2021, A Wyoming high school student refused to wear a mask, so police locked down the entire school and arrested her - TheBlaze
169. Gateway Pundit, Julian Conradson, October 2, 2021, National School Boards Association Begs Biden To Label Outraged Parents "Domestic Terrorists" and Use The Patriot Act Against Them (thegatewaypundit.com)
170. Gateway Pundit, Joe Hoft, October 6, 2021, AG Garland Threatens Parents Who Criticize Critical Race Theory (CRT) - His Son-In-Law Sells CRT Books to Schools (thegatewaypundit.com)
171. Gateway Pundit, Joe Hoft, October 9, 2021, AG Garland's Son-In-Law's Company 'Panorama' Also Pushes CRT in Texas and Georgia, and a Deceitful Article Equating MAGA to the KKK (thegatewaypundit.com)
172. WN.com News, November 16, 2021, AG Garland Ripped After Whistleblower Exposes Tactics Against Parents (breitbart.com)
173. LeoHohmann.com, November 18, 2021, It Begins: FBI raids house, terrorizes family of mom who protested local school board, elections – LeoHohmann.com

Sylvia Bambola

174. Fox News, Tyler Olson, November 9, 2121, American Medical Association pushes pro-critical race theory materials in 'Health Equity' guide | Fox News
175. Gateway Pundit, Julian Conradson, October 9, 2021, California Becomes the First State that Requires High School Students to Pass a CRT-Based "Ethnic Studies" Course in Order to Graduate; New Law will Also Apply to Charter Schools (thegatewaypundit.com)
176. Gateway Pundit, Cristina Laila, September 29, 2021, VA Dem Gov. Candidate Terry McAuliffe: "I Don't Think Parents Should be Telling Schools What They Should Teach" (VIDEO) (thegatewaypundit.com)
177. Gateway Pundit, Cristina Laila, September 30, 2021, Biden's Radical Education Secretary Miguel Cardona Says Parents Should Not Be the "Primary Stakeholder" in Their Kids' Education (VIDEO) (thegatewaypundit.com)
178. Townhall, Spencer Brown, December 3, 2021, House Democrats Block GOP Effort to Codify Parents' Bill of Rights (townhall.com)
179. Gateway Pundit, Jim Hoft, December 7, 2021, Report: Rockwood School District Admits to Calling the FBI on Parents (thegatewaypundit.com)
180. WND, Bob Unruh, July 8, 2021, Gay chorus threatens: 'We're coming for your children' (wnd.com)
181. The Epoch Times, Brad Jones, November 20, 2021, Leaked Audio Reveals How California Teachers Recruit Kids Into LGBTQ Clubs (theepochtimes.com)

Destination Hell

182. Harbingers Daily, David Fiorazo, November 22, 2021, Next Stage of Rebellion: Normalizing Pedophilia | Harbingers Daily
183. Gateway Pundit, Jim Hoft, October 28, 2021, Florida School Board Member Chaperones Little Children on Gay Bar Field Trip (thegatewaypundit.com)
184. Gateway Pundit, Julian Conradson, October 13, 2021, SICKENING: Loudoun County Schools Covered Up Rape of a 14-Year-Old Girl and Prosecuted Her Father To Protect Male Transgender Student Who Was Permitted to Use Ladies Bathrooms (thegatewaypundit.com)
185. Gateway Pundit, Jacob Engels, October 27, 2021, VIDEO: Journalist Reads Filthy Porn Book from School's Library at FL School Board Meeting - Board Members Call Police to Have Him Forcefully Removed for Reading Obscene Content Aloud (thegatewaypundit.com)
186. Gateway Pundit, Cristina Laila, September 15, 2021, Ohio Mayor Puts School Board on Notice: 'Resign or Face Criminal Charges For Distributing Child Pornography' (VIDEO) (thegatewaypundit.com)
187. Harbingers Daily, September 28, 2021, Parents Outraged After Sex Ed Program Asks Students to Role Play Gay, Trans Sex Scenarios | Harbingers Daily
188. Gateway Pundit, Jordan Conradson, December 8, 2021, EXCLUSIVE: North Carolina Parents Identify Over 100 Book Titles Containing Obscene Content, File CRIMINAL Charges Against Wake County School Board (PHOTOS) (thegatewaypundit.com)

189. WND, Bob Unruh, July 8, 2021, Gay chorus threatens: 'We're coming for your children' (wnd.com)
190. Forbes, Ralph Benko, February 24, 2014, What Facebook's 58 Genders Mean For Politics (forbes.com)
191. IAmAWatchman.com, from *Harbingers Daily*, Joseph Kerr, They're Coming for your Children – Welcome to I Am a Watchman!
192. *Washington*, *Examiner*, Asher Notheis, November 8, 2021, Nearly a third of millennials identify as LGBT, study finds | Washington Examiner
193. WND News Services, Mary Margaret Olohan, July 21, 2021, Tom Cotton rips 'liberals' for blocking ban on 'life-altering' trans procedures for kids (wnd.com)
194. Midlands Directory, November 22, 2019, Celine Dion Starts Weird Demonic Clothing Line For Kids (midlandscbd.com)
195. Gateway Pundit, Cristina Laila, October 11, 2021, 'Journey of Self-Discovery' - Superman Comes Out as Bisexual in DC Comics (thegatewaypundit.com)
196. Rapture Ready, Children As Battlefields, Bill Wilson, August 3, 2021, Children As Battlefields :: By Bill Wilson - Rapture Ready
197. Gateway Pundit, Julian Conradson, December 1, 2021, BREAKING: 15-Year-Old Michigan High School Shooter Identified - Prosecutors Announce That Teen Will be Tried as Adult and is Charged With Terrorism and Murder (VIDEO) (thegatewaypundit.com)
198. Fox News, Audrey Conklin, July 30, 2021, Murders rise 16% in 2021 across major US cities: report | Fox News

Destination Hell

199. The Epoch Times, Jack Phillips, September 27, 2021, FBI: US Murders Increased by 29.4 Percent in 2020 (theepochtimes.com)
200. The Brownshirts: The Role of the Sturmabteilung (SA) in Nazi Germany | History Hit
201. Preserving a Constitution Designed for a Moral and Religious People - Robertson Center for Constitutional Law (regent.edu) Preserving a Constitution Designed for a Moral and Religious People - Robertson Center for Constitutional Law (regent.edu)
202. WND, Andrew Powell, August 8, 2021, What the devil? U.S. turns to dark side as Americans make Satan mainstream (wnd.com)
203. Ibid.
204. Ron Rhodes, *End-Times Super Trends* (Harvest House Publishers, Eugene, Oregon, 2017) 81.
205. Ibid., 89.
206. Gospel News Network, Randolph Jason, July 20, 2021, Hunted by Police Helicopter, Thrown in a 'Small Cage', Canadian Pastor Found Himself Ministering to Fellow Inmates - Gospel News Network
207. The Epoch Times, Jocelyn Neo, September 13, 2021, CCP Is Sinicizing Christianity, Other Faiths to 'Align' Them to Its Ideology: Chinese American Pastor (theepochtimes.com)
208. Dr. Michael Lake, *The Shinar Directive* (Crane, MO: Defender, 2014), 335-336.
209. PNW, *White House Flagging Facebook Posts!*, Matt Agorist, July 17, 2021, The Road To Fascism? White House And Facebook Merge To Censor Problematic Posts (prophecynewswatch.com)
210. Financial Survival Network, End of the American Dream, Michael Snyder, August 17, 2021, They Have Come Up with Some Ominous

Sylvia Bambola

New Definitions for What Constitutes "Domestic Terrorism" | Financial Survival Network

211. LeoHohmann.com, LeoHohmann.com, DHS issues terror alert equating Americans who oppose government Covid restrictions with 9/11 terrorists – LeoHohmann.com
212. The Epoch Times, Ken Silva, September 22, 2021, DHS Touts Counter-Domestic Extremism Plan; Rights Groups Cite Threats to Civil Liberties (theepochtimes.com)
213. Ibid.
214. LeoHohmann.com, Digital health passports: The snare that will lure many into the one-world cashless system – LeoHohmann.com
215. Breitbart, Allum Bokhari, July 26, 2021, Big Tech 'Counterterrorism' Org Shifts Focus from Islamic Extremism to 'Far Right' (breitbart.com)
216. The Epoch Times, Jack Phillips, September 29, 2021, YouTube Bans All 'Harmful Vaccine Content' From Its Platform (theepochtimes.com)
217. Gateway Pundit, Richard Abelson, August 6, 2021, Apple Reveals Plans to Spy on Everyone's iPhones - Here's How to Check for Spy Software (thegatewaypundit.com)
218. PNW, July 18, 2021, Big Tech Censorship Sets The Stage For The Rise Of The Antichrist (prophecynewswatch.com)
219. The Gateway Pundit, Mike LaChance, July 23, 2021, Liberal Media Types Want Trump Supporters To Be 'Deprogrammed' (VIDEO) (thegatewaypundit.com)
220. *New York Post*, Jesse O'Neill, July 28, 2021, NYT reporter Katie Benner deletes tweets berating Trump supporters (nypost.com)

Destination Hell

221. Gateway Pundit, Joe Hoft, September 26, 2021, Liberal George Soros Connected Group Sends Letter to FCC Calling to "Shoot Republicans" - Stillness in the Storm
222. Breitbart, Wendell Husebo, August 4, 2021, Former Obama Official Demands 'a No-Fly List for Unvaccinated Adults' (breitbart.com)
223. Gateway Pundit, Jim Hoft, July 29, 2021, It Begins... Illinois Superintendent Will Hand Out Yellow ID Badges Based on Vaccination Status (thegatewaypundit.com) It Begins... Illinois Superintendent Will Hand Out Yellow ID Badges Based on Vaccination Status (thegatewaypundit.com)
224. The Epoch Times, Jack Phillips, July 26, 2021, California City: Vaccinated Employees Should Wear Stickers If They Want to Work Without Masks (theepochtimes.com)
225. PNW, Jeff Thompson, August 23, 2021, Why Is The National Guard Hiring Internment/Resettlement Specialists? (prophecynewswatch.com)
226. LeoHohmann.com, LeoHohmann.com, DHS issues terror alert equating Americans who oppose government Covid restrictions with 9/11 terrorists – LeoHohmann.com
227. Townhall, Julio Rosas, February 9, 2021, Biden's America: COVID Restrictions for Americans, But Not Illegal Immigrants (townhall.com)
228. Gateway Pundit, Cristina Laila, November 23, 2021, https://www.thegatewaypundit.com/2021/11/biden-will-require-essential-travelers-crossing-us-land-borders-truck-drivers-fully-vaccinated-amid-supply-chain-crisis/

229. Gateway Pundit, The Scoop, September 29, 2021, Democrats Vote AGAINST COVID Tests for Illegal Immigrants Entering U.S. (thegatewaypundit.com)
230. Lifesite News, Peter A. McCullough, MD, MPH, August 26, 2021, Study: Fully vaccinated healthcare workers carry 251 times viral load, pose threat to unvaccinated patients, co-workers - LifeSite (lifesitenews.com)
231. Ibid.
232. Stephen Quayle, *Terminated* (Bozeman, MT: End Time Thunder Publishers, 2018), 17.
233. Ibid., 16.
234. Gateway Pundit, Jim Hoft, December 6, 2021, Report Shows Nearly 300 Athletes Worldwide Collapsed or Suffered Cardiac Arrests after Taking COVID Vaccine This Year - Many Died (thegatewaypundit.com)
235. Christianity Daily, Olivia Cavallaro, July 23, 2021, CDC Caught Deleting 6,000 COVID Vaccine Deaths From VAERS Website, Report Says : US : Christianity Daily
236. Gateway Pundit, Jim Hoft, November 18, 2021, EXCLUSIVE: European Medicines Agency Data Shows 1,163,356 Adverse Drug Reactions and 30,551 Fatalities by COVID-19 Vaccinations (thegatewaypundit.com)
237. Gateway Pundit, Joe Hoft, December 9, 2021, In the UK 300,000 Are Suddenly Facing Heart Problems Which Two 'Doctors' Claim Is Due to Pandemic Stress (No Mention of the Vaccine) (thegatewaypundit.com)
238. USSA News, December 9, 2021, FDA Says It Now Needs 75 Years to Fully Release Pfizer COVID-19 Vaccine Data | The Food and Drug Administration (FDA) says it now needs 75

Destination Hell

years to fully release Pfizer COVID-19 vaccine data to the public – twenty years more than it originally agreed on November 15. The request to increase the time limit is to comply with demands for basic transparency and accountability over the FDA decision in […] (ussanews.com)

239. The Epoch Times, Zachary Stieber, December 8, 2021, FDA Says It Now Needs 75 Years to Fully Release Pfizer COVID-19 Vaccine Data (theepochtimes.com)
240. PMC, US National Library of Medicine, Deaths following vaccination: What does the evidence show? (nih.gov)
241. Gateway Pundit, Jim Hoft, October 4, 2021, Pennsylvania House Democrat Introduces Forced Sterilization - Three-Child Limit Legislation (thegatewaypundit.com)
242. Perry Stone, *American's Apocalyptic Reset* (Voice of Evangelism Ministries, Cleveland, TN 37320, 2021) 29.
243. Rense.com, Bill Gates On 'Vaccines To Reduce Population', William Engdahl, March 4, 2010, Bill Gates On 'Vaccines To Reduce Population' (rense.com)
244. Ibid.
245. Gospel News Network, Randolph Jason, August 20, 2021, SHOCK AS IT'S REVEALED AN ENZYME CALLED LUCIFERASE IS WHAT MAKES BILL GATES IMPLANTABLE QUANTUM DOT MICRONEEDLE VACCINE DELIVERY SYSTEM WORK - Gospel News Network
246. LeoHohmann.com, Digital health passports: The snare that will lure many into the one-world cashless system – LeoHohmann.com

247. Gateway Pundit, Joe Hoft, August 30, 2021, As Inflation Skyrockets in the US, Russia and Saudi Arabia Sign Agreement Ending the 'Petrol Dollar', Putting the US Dollar and Economy at Even Higher Risk (thegatewaypundit.com)
248. Gateway Pundit, Cristina Laila, December 9, 2021, "I Think We Will Need a Fourth Dose" - Pfizer CEO Says 4th Covid Jab May Be Needed Sooner Than Expected (VIDEO) (thegatewaypundit.com)
249. Gateway Pundit, Cristina Laila, December 12, 2021, Dr. Fauci: Americans Will "Just Have to Deal with" Yearly Booster Shots if They Become Necessary (VIDEO) (thegatewaypundit.com)
250. Breitbart, Katherine Hamilton, August 3, 2021, They Have Come Up with Some Ominous New Definitions for What Constitutes "Domestic Terrorism" | Financial Survival Network
251. PNW, Peter Jacobson, The End Of Financial Privacy - Biden Wants To Monitor You Bank Account (prophecynewswatch.com)
252. Ronald Bailey, *Eco Scam, The False Prophets of Ecological Apocalypse* (NY, NY: St. Martin's Press, 1993) 1.
253. Dr. Michael Lake, *The Shinar Directive* (Crane, MO: Defender, 2014), 239.
254. What is the 2030 Agenda? - A Sustainable Agenda For All (ie.edu)
255. Gospel News Network, Randolph Jason, December 10, 2021, The UN Just Put Up A Giant Statue In New York That Resembles A "Beast" Described In The Book Of Revelation - Gospel News Network
256. Dr. Stanley Monteith, *Brotherhood of Darkness* (Oklahoma City, OK: Hearthstone Publishing, 2000), 71, 99.

Destination Hell

257. Thomas Horn, *Apollyon Rising 2012* (Crane, MO: Defender, 2009), 47-48.
258. Dr. Stanley Monteith, *Brotherhood of Darkness* (Oklahoma City, OK: Hearthstone Publishing, 2000), 39.
259. Paul McGuire & Troy Anderson, *The Babylon Code* (NY, NY: *Faith Words*, Hachette Book Group, 2015), 81.
260. Perry Stone, *American's Apocalyptic Reset* (Voice of Evangelism Ministries, Cleveland, TN 37320, 2021) 37.
261. ZeroHedge, Tyler Durden, August 1, 2021, Brandon Smith: Why Are Globalists And Governments So Desperate For 100% Vaccination Rates? | ZeroHedge
262. ClimateDepot, Marc Morano, September 13, 2021, Climate Lockdowns: New CO2 monitoring credit card enables tracking of 'carbon footprint on every purchase' – 'Monitors & cuts off spending when we hit our carbon max' – Mastercard & UN join forces | Climate Depot
263. Terry James, Editor, *Deceivers* (New Leaf Press, 2018) Conclusion, Terry James, 323.
264. The Epoch Times, Joseph Lord, September 25, 2021, Budget Bill Devotes Billions to New 'Civilian Climate Corps' (theepochtimes.com)
265. LeoHohmann.com, https://leohohmann.com/2021/08/04/digital-health-passports-the-snare-that-will-lure-many-into-the-one-world-cashless-system/
266. Armstrong Economics, Martin Armstrong, October 26, 2020, Klaus Schwab says – You will Own Nothing in 10 years | Armstrong Economics
267. Gateway Pundit, Joe Hoft, September 19, 2021, Data From Yelp Shows 60% of All Businesses

that Shut Down During COVID Are Now Permanently Closed (thegatewaypundit.com)
268. ZeroHedge, Tyler Durden, August 1, 2021, Brandon Smith: Why Are Globalists And Governments So Desperate For 100% Vaccination Rates? | ZeroHedge
269. Perry Stone, *American's Apocalyptic Reset* (Voice of Evangelism Ministries, Cleveland, TN 37320, 2021) 40-41.
270. Gateway Pundit, September 25, 2021, House Passes "Red Flag" Gun Confiscation Bill For Ex-Military Members -- And Lots Of Republicans Voted For It (thegatewaypundit.com)
271. PM., Hannah Nightingale, September 29, 2021, CDC implements gun violence study after naming it a 'public health threat' | The Post Millennial
272. *The Western Journal*, Grant Atkinson, July 30, 2021, It Looks Like People Are Facing Total Medical Tyranny as Military Rolls Into Major City to Enforce COVID Lockdowns (westernjournal.com)
273. The Daily Expose, August 17, 2021, Australia has fallen – Minister for Health tells parents 24,000 children will be herded into stadium like cattle to get the experimental Covid-19 vaccine – The Expose
274. Gateway Pundit, Julian Conradson, August 27, 2021, "Wellcamp: The Best Way To Keep You Safe" - Australian Health Officials Produce Creepy Dystopian Propaganda For New 'Mandatory Quarantine Camps' (Video) (thegatewaypundit.com)
275. Charlie Kirk, September 3, 2021, Australia State Uses Facial Recognition, Geolocation App to Force Quarantine | Charlie Kirk

Destination Hell

276. Harbingers Daily, September 9, 2021, Australian Officials Start Using 'New World Order' as a COVID Talking Point | Harbingers Daily
277. Rapture Ready, Daymond Duck, July 25, 2021, Warnings: By Daymond Duck - Rapture Ready
278. Harbingers Daily, September 9, 2021, Australian Officials Start Using 'New World Order' as a COVID Talking Point | Harbingers Daily
279. Gateway Pundit, Julian Conradson, September 22, 2021, This is What Tyranny Looks Like: Absolute Mayhem in Australia; Covid-Police Ambush Crowds and Shoot Protesters In the Back With 'Non-lethals' As They Run Away - (Video) (thegatewaypundit.com)
280. Gateway Pundit, Julian Conradson, September 25, 2021, More from Australia Where Police Are Engaging in Violent Acts to Mandate COVID Restrictions(Video) (thegatewaypundit.com)
281. LeoHohmann.com, CDC claims it has authority to use police to do everything you see going on in Australia; and Congress agrees – LeoHohmann.com
282. Gateway Pundit, Julian Conradson, October 2, 2021, CRAZY: Australian Authorities Show Up to Woman's Home and Harass Her Over Social Media Posts: "We Have Instructions Because You Have Been Posting Things" - (Video) (thegatewaypundit.com)
283. Gateway Pundit, Cristina Laila, September 29, 2021, New South Wales Premier Says Unvaccinated Sydney Residents Face Total Social Isolation *Indefinitely* When Covid Lockdown Ends (VIDEO) (thegatewaypundit.com)
284. Gateway Pundit, Jim Hoft, October 1, 2021, BREAKING: Tyrannical New South Wales

Sylvia Bambola

Premier Gladys Berejiklian RESIGNS in Disgrace Following Corruption Probe #LockHerUp (thegatewaypundit.com)

285. Gateway Pundit, Jim Hoft, September 30, 2021, Aussie Police Urge Government to Issue No-Fly Zones Over Melbourne So People Won't See How Massive the Anti-Government Protests Are (VIDEO) (thegatewaypundit.com)

286. Gateway Pundit, Jim Hoft, October 5, 2021, AUSTRALIA IS LOST: Government Launches Orwellian Selfie Check-In Program for Home Quarantine (VIDEO) (thegatewaypundit.com)

287. PNW, Tyler Durden, November 3, 2021, Australia Threatening Seizure Of Homes & Bank Accounts Over Covid Violations (prophecynewswatch.com)

288. Harbingers Daily, November 3, 2021, 'Unfettered Power': New Law Could See Australians Jailed For 2 Years For Breaking Covid Orders | Harbingers Daily

289. Gateway Pundit, Jim Hoft, November 22, 2021, DYSTOPIA DOWN UNDER: Australian Military Summoned to Relocate COVID-19 Positive and "Close Contacts" to Quarantine Camps (thegatewaypundit.com)

290. Breitbart, James Delingpole, December 5, 2021, Woman Held in Oz Covid Camp for Weeks Despite Negative Test: Claim (breitbart.com)

291. LeoHohmann.com, CDC claims it has authority to use police to do everything you see going on in Australia; and Congress agrees – LeoHohmann.com

292. LeoHohmann.com, John Whitehead and Nisha Whitehead, https://leohohmann.com/2021/10/01/covid-

Destination Hell

camps-are-government-round-ups-of-resistors-in-our-future/
293. Dr. Michael Lake, *The Shinar Directive* (Crane, MO: Defender, 2014), 340.
294. Stephen Quayle, *Angel Wars* (Bozeman, MT: End Time Thunder Publishers, 2011), 288.
295. Cris Putnam & Thomas Horn, *Exo-Vaticana* (Crane, MO: Defender, 2013), 120.
296. Ibid., 120-121.
297. *Pandemonium's Engine*, Thomas Horn, D.D., "Pandemonium and 'Her' Children," (Crane, MO: Defender, 2011) 31.
298. Stephen Quayle, *Terminated* (Bozeman, MT: End Time Thunder Publishers, 2018), 108.
299. Ibid., 159.
300. Ibid., 163.
301. Ibid., 214.
302. Ibid., 129.
303. Stephen Quayle, *Angel Wars* (Bozeman, MT: End Time Thunder Publishers, 2011), 233-234.
304. *Pandemonium's Engine*, Douglas Hamp, "Man Becoming His Own God?." (Crane, MO: Defender, 2011) 238.
305. *New York Post*, Natalie O'Neill, November 19, 2020, Scientists make bigger monkey brains using human genes (nypost.com)
306. Stephen Quayle, *Angel Wars* (Bozeman, MT: End Time Thunder Publishers, 2011), 270.
307. Stephen Quayle, *Terminated* (Bozeman, MT: End Time Thunder Publishers, 2018), 195.
308. Stephen Quayle, *Angel Wars* (Bozeman, MT: End Time Thunder Publishers, 2011), 272.
309. Stephen Quayle, *Terminated* (Bozeman, MT: End Time Thunder Publishers, 2018) 198.
310. Ibid., 232.
311. Ibid., 298-299.

Sylvia Bambola

312. Aftermath of the George Floyd protests in Minneapolis–Saint Paul - Wikipedia
313. Rapture Forums, Daniel Greenfield, September 29, 2021, Black Lives Matter Killed 2,000 Black People - Rapture Forums
314. Rapture Ready, Daymond Duck, September 12, 2021, The Plan: By Daymond Duck - Rapture Ready
315. Ibid.
316. Historical Records and Trends | National Centers for Environmental Information (NCEI) formerly known as National Climatic Data Center (NCDC) (noaa.gov)
317. Geophysical Fluid Dynamic Laboratory, Gabriel A. Vecchi and Thomas R. Knutson, Historical Atlantic Hurricane and Tropical Storm Records – Geophysical Fluid Dynamics Laboratory (noaa.gov)
318. EarthSky, Deanna Conners, March 4, 2021, Is the number of large earthquakes increasing? | Earth | EarthSky
319. Jamal S. Shrair, January 20, 2020, Extinct volcanoes are coming back to life (watchers.news)
320. Global Volcanism Program | Has volcanic activity been increasing?
321. NPR, Scott Neuman, December 22, 2017, Climate Change Likely To Increase Volcanic Eruptions, Scientists Say : The Two-Way : NPR
322. LiveScience, Ker Than, October 17, 2005, Scientists: Natural Disasters Becoming More Common | Live Science
323. World Economic Forum, *Natural disasters are increasing in frequency and ferocity. Here's how AI can come to the rescue,* How AI can improve disaster

Destination Hell

resilience and relief | World Economic Forum (weforum.org)
324. Harbingers Daily, September 23, 2021, UPDATE: Congress Passes Iron Dome Funding Bill After Severe Backlash Overrides Far-Left Anti-Semitism | Harbingers Daily
325. Gateway Pundit, Jim Hoft, September 26, 2021, Democrats Go After Christianity and Judaism's Holiest Sites: New Bill Turns Over Jerusalem's Jewish Quarter, Western Wall and Christian Holy Sites to Palestinians (thegatewaypundit.com)
326. Terry James, Editor, *Deceivers* (New Leaf Press, 2018) Demon-Conjuring Con Men, Dr. Billy Crone, 241-242.
327. Hayyim Schauss, *The Jewish Festivals* (Schocken Books, New York, 1938) 89.
328. PNW, Sean Savage/JNS.org, November 16, 2021, Israel Stands Alone - US Fails To Support In UN Vote (prophecynewswatch.com)
329. Harbingers Daily, TV7, November 15, 2021, 'Death To Jews:' Polish March Sees Calls For Zionist Expulsion, Burning Of Historic Book On Jewish Rights | Harbingers Daily
330. Amir Tsarfati, November 29, 2021, VIDEO: Is Israel on the Brink of War? - Olive Tree Ministries (olivetreeviews.org)
331. List of famines - Wikipedia
332. Gateway Pundit, Cristina Laila, October 16, 2021, HORROR: Woman Raped by Stranger on Train in Suburban Philadelphia as Bystanders Did Nothing (thegatewaypundit.com)
333. *NWO Report*, Kelen McBreen, March 15, 2021, Pope Francis Calls For "New World Order" As Fauci Pushes "Globalization" – Nwo Report

334. Thomas Horn & Cris Putnam, *Petrus Romanus* (Crane, MO: Defender, 2012), 449.
335. Cris Putnam & Thomas Horn, *Exo-Vaticana* (Crane, MO: Defender, 2013), 533.
336. Ibid., 535.
337. Thomas Horn, *Apollyon Rising 2012* (Crane, MO: Defender, 2009), 328.
338. Cris Putnam & Thomas Horn, *Exo-Vaticana* (Crane, MO: Defender, 2013), 533.
339. Thomas Horn & Cris Putnam, *Petrus Romanus* (Crane, MO: Defender, 2012), 91.
340. Ibid., 244.
341. Daily Beast, Jay Parini, December 7, 2014, updated April 14, 2017, https://www.thedailybeast.com/does-pope-francis-believe-christians-and-muslims-worship-the-same-god
342. Anthony Faiola, "8 of Pope Francis's most liberal statements," *The Washington Post*, September 7, 2015.
343. John-Henry Westen, *LifeSiteNews*, October 2013.
344. John-Henry Westen, *LifeSiteNews*, March 2015.
345. John-Henry Westen, *LifeSiteNews*, February 2016.
346. Rapture Ready, Daymond Duck, October 17, 2021, A New Era and a New Universal Agenda :: By Daymond Duck - Rapture Ready
347. Rapture Ready, Daymond Duck, October 10, 2021, God's Laughter Will Turn to Anger :: By Daymond Duck - Rapture Ready
348. Gateway Pundit, Jim Hoft, October 18, 2021, Joe Biden to Meet with Commie Pope in Rome and Push Globalist Minimum Tax (thegatewaypundit.com)
349. Gateway Pundit, Jim Hoft, October 22, 2021, Commie Pope Francis Invokes God to Urge Tech Giants to Crack Down on "Conspiracy Theories"

Destination Hell

and "Fake News" on their Platforms (thegatewaypundit.com)
350. Gateway Pundit, Joe Hoft, November 17, 2021, HUGE EXCLUSIVE: Archbishop Carlo Maria Viganò Calls on People of Faith to Unite in a Worldwide Anti-Globalist Alliance to Free Humanity from the Totalitarian Regime (VIDEO) (thegatewaypundit.com)
351. Cris Putnam & Thomas Horn, *Exo-Vaticana* (Crane, MO: Defender, 2013), 211-212; Thomas Horn & Cris Putnam, *Petrus Romanus* (Crane, MO: Defender, 2012), 471.
352. NASA, Overview | Asteroids – NASA Solar System Exploration
353. American Media Group, Medeea Greere, September 9, 2019, *NASA WARNING* | NASA Warns Giant Asteroid May Hit Earth in December 2019 - American Media Group (amg-news.com)
354. Azcentral, Elizabeth Montgomery, Arizona Republic, May 6, 2021, Meet 'The Giant.' a 10-story movable statue that could come to Phoenix (azcentral.com)
355. September 4, 2020, Bill Gates Vaccine Ingredient Says it All : An Enzyme Called LUCIFERASE is What Makes Bill Gates Implantable Vaccine Work - VACCINE ID - Stillness in the Storm
356. Lester Sumrall, *Run with the Vision* (South Bend, IN: Sumrall Publishing, 1986) 32-33.
357. History of purgatory - Wikipedia

www.ingramcontent.com/pod-product-compliance
Lightning Source LLC
LaVergne TN
LVHW051108080426
835510LV00018B/1951